Sexuality and Society

In this comprehensive introduction to the study of sexuality, Gargi Bhattacharyya guides readers through the key theoretical debates in the area, from the everyday understanding of sex, through Foucault's technologies of self, to Judith Butler on the performance of identity, and shows how these theoretical positions apply to sexuality as it is experienced in contemporary society. Key topics include:

- the ideology of heterosexuality
- sex and the state
- sex, 'race' and the 'exotic'
- age and sexuality
- sex education and pornography.

Throughout the book, Bhattacharyya argues that the study of sexuality is an essential part of broader debates on gender, 'race', citizenship and community. Topical and original, *Sexuality and Society* will provide students with a lucid map to the terrain and an exciting starting point for their own investigations.

Gargi Bhattacharyya is a lecturer in cultural studies and religion at the University of Birmingham.

Sexuality and Society

An introduction

Gargi Bhattacharyya

London and New York

First published 2002 by Routledge
11 New Fetter Lane, London EC4P 4EE

Simultaneously published in the USA and Canada
by Routledge
29 West 35th Street, New York, NY 10001

Routledge is an imprint of the Taylor & Francis Group

Typeset in Perpetua by
Prepress Projects Ltd, Perth, Scotland
Printed and bound by
Gutenberg Press Ltd, Malta

British Library Cataloguing in Publication Data
A catalogue record for this book is available from the British Library

Library of Congress Cataloging in Publication Data
A catalog record for this book has been requested

ISBN 0-415-22902-2 (hbk)
ISBN 0-415-22903-0 (pbk)

Contents

Acknowledgements

This book was written through some difficult and turbulent times. Its themes of intimacy and redemption probably reflect this lonely period.

Thanks are due, as always, to the students from the years of my sexualities course – most of what follows was tried out and thrashed out with you. Special thanks go to Dilip, Manju and Sonali for keeping me upright and to Stan who tries to make sure that I eat.

But in the end, and unexpectedly, this book is dedicated to David Triesman who, despite our many many disagreements, managed to persuade me that people don't have to be alike to get along.

Introduction

This work attempts to offer an introduction to recent debates in the study of sexuality. As a topic of academic discussion, sex seeps into a whole range of contemporary debates. From a position of relative marginality, now the study of sex has become quite respectable, part of the toolkit of any thoughtful understanding of modern life. This volume is a reflection of this rapid embourgeoisement – and the wide sweep of the work has been determined by the exponential growth of the field. However, rather than attempt a comprehensive survey, I have chosen to introduce key debates as part of a larger argument about the significance of all this varied sex talk. In this volume I argue that the particular and intensive concern about sex and intimacy that characterises our age is an indication of the everyday impact of economic restructuring and globalising forces. Learning to understand these various dilemmas offers both a means of comprehending the cultures of lived globalisation and a strategy for surviving this disruption. In the manner of so many other treatises on love, I present this as both an explanation and an injunction, a tale of what is and a promise of what might be. Throughout, I take the ancient and much maligned text of the *Kama Sutra* as a guiding lesson and organising framework. Most of all, what follows is an excursion into the West's long obsession with sexuality as a place apart – another country to be longed for, yet never known. And the book charts the strange developments of this obsession. The use of the *Kama Sutra* echoes the West's continued recourse to works of fiction and foreign conceptual frameworks when seeking to understand the rest of the world – the diversion through the *Kama Sutra* is a way of approaching the fictions and foreignness of sex from another viewpoint.

The *Kama Sutra* introduces sexual education and understanding as a central strand of general education. In its teachings, the techniques of physical pleasure and restraint are combined with meditations on the pursuit of a moral dutiful life. Understanding sex is part of understanding your place in the world. Although the work assembles a variety of strange material – from those famous positions to advice about the conduct of a spiritual life – it is, most of all, an education manual in a certain tradition. And that tradition, despite the salacious misreporting of generations of Western commentators and gossips, regards sexuality as another arena to be apprehended through dialogue and slow incremental stages of learning. The discipline of this scholarship augments and complements the discipline of other processes of study. The project is to apprehend the total life.

This work also begins with another hunch, not quite an assumption but at least a suspicion, an idea that learning is coming back around to the business of the spirit. Rather than focus on orthodox routes to faith and spiritual redemption, the suggestion is that people require a sense of well-being and place in a wider logic and system. So the book begins with the idea that sex matters because it is linked to matters of spirit and belief. To understand the particular heat and fear around sex in our cultural moment, we need to understand the reworking of faith cultures through globalisation and turbo-capitalism and the very significant impact these forces have on many people's sense of self.

In all the excessive and hyperbolic writing on globalisation, the catch-all term for social change in our time, very little has been said of the knock-on effect of economic changes on personal lives. Although the longer histories of those prime Western inventions, the individual, and private life, have been understood as components of much wider social changes, enabled by and enabling shifts that spread into many aspects of public and domestic existence, the present is a more opaque beast. In the manner of the *Kama Sutra*, perhaps we can begin to see sex as a highly socialised ritual, inextricably linked to those other social rituals of economic and political life.

My argument is that this special status of ongoing and irresolvable question – the hungry kernel at our heart – makes sex a particular kind of social issue and experience, that this longstanding quest for truth through sex is an indication of the strange overinvestment in splitting intimacy and physical closeness from other aspects of social life in later capitalism, and maybe always. This is one of those important links to faith – the ongoing belief that truth and essence reside somewhere, and are at least in part human, although beyond the control of humans.

As with so much else, the birth of sexuality comes with the formation of a Western subject grown by capital. The new economic possibilities of developing capitalism lead to new social possibilities, including the emergence of a demarcation between public and private spheres and a new privileging of some non-work activities as the space of the personal. Although bodies touched and groaned before this, and no doubt will long after, the special status of thing apart and separate sphere can come into being only with these other developments.

What is this thing called 'sexuality'?

Some quests have recurred through different moments of human history – the search for the secret of eternal life, the spell that will turn dirt to gold, the essence of love.

The question of how to make someone love you – or to understand why anyone loves and desires – appears in many times and cultures. No less than the search for untold riches, the alchemy that seeks to turn indifference into passion haunts many cultures. And despite our historically recent investment in romance, the alchemy of passion is as ruthlessly instrumental as any quest for gold from lead. The ability to shape human response – to, famously, make friends and influence people, or be irresistible to any woman or man – promises not only an immediate and personal reward in the form of love and sexual favours, but also the less dreamy gains of a route to influence. The mythology surrounding the alchemy of passion has always acknowledged that sex, money and power are close cousins. These connections have been forgotten only recently, through the development of sex as a separate sphere. So another suggestion of this book is that contemporary interest in the secrets held by sex retains an underlying belief in the wider significance of sexual knowledge. While no-one now suggests that sexual knowledge requires the attention and diligence of statecraft or financial training, the central tenet of the *Kama Sutra*, that sexual knowledge illuminates other realms of life, continues in more recent quests to know.

Although this work steers clear of proposing that there is some absolute human essence beyond all this cultural confusion, I do want to suggest that modern culture, in the widest sense, also makes the space for the secret. This suggestion is related to the belief that sexuality serves as the core of the human being – again, the search for the essence of humanity has been long and varied. Are we weak flesh animated by spirit or soul? Beyond the animality of our physicality, is there an essence to consciousness?

Of course, sex has been scrutinised and studied throughout the modern period. Although each new telling and depiction presents itself with the thrill of the new and only recently forbidden, in fact sex remains among the oldest stories in the book – pre-dating the book by some time. Sexuality, on the other hand, enters as a particular episode in the history of the West – part of the development of that hungry and expanding entity. Sexuality emerges as another instance of the quest for knowledge. Europe has come to rule the world through the development of a scientific understanding that has tried to explain nature and build an alternative nature created by humanity. This era has been marked by a will to map both globe and body – because the capacity to map and know has repositioned Euro-man at the centre of existence. This knowledge, which could unseat God, is the new magic, if ever magic there was. Yet even this new magic cannot master every aspect of life – however hard humanity tries. The long, and sometimes violent, quest for the meaning of sex exemplifies that wish for total mastery through knowledge that has characterised the modern era. Yet this particular endeavour to make knowledge total quickly comes up against the uncomfortable limit of rationality.

This is the point where scholarship folds into magic – a moment at the heart of the birth of science and enquiry. Those resistant areas that remain beyond the easy exploration or analysis, the arenas that take up the role of limit to reason, remain in the realm of the magical. At best, this retains the wonderment and mystery of the yet to be discovered – something like a check on the arrogance of learning, a reminder that, even without God, man is not omnipotent and knowledge is not perfect.

Sex has hovered in this in-between state since the formulation of reasoned enquiry – sometimes the wondrous key to human existence, sometimes the monstrous irrational to be tamed, or even destroyed. The effect has been to create an arena which is always in half-light – almost grasped but strangely changing in shape, something like an edge where knowledge seeps back into magic, where recognition is dream-like, where we understand but are not certain what we know. Sex remains in this still magical space – teasing scholarship, yet escaping into mystery, showing some part only to dissolve into darkness again. This is the mantle handed to sex – to stand in as limit and dream world, to be half-known and half-imagined, to circulate at the edge of public life as a contract of agreed secrecy. In modern existence, few arenas retain this smell of magic – and sex is hot, in part, because it does.

Because it is so difficult to remain open to the lessons of magic, I want to suggest that learning about sex involves a certain attitude of listening – because these are stories of exploration which bring your most familiar world back to you as foreign lands.

As the special secret elsewhere of modernity, sex can be magical. However, when modernity itself appears to be crumbling under its own weight, transmuting into something else despite itself, its magical underside also loses its lustre. If reason and progress turn out to be a sham, so then does the consolation of order, desire. Our incessant interest in sexuality is an indication of this deep disappointment, the realisation that the space of permitted magic cannot reimburse us for the failures of other arenas.

The study and conceptualisation of sexuality has undergone some significant developments across the twentieth century – some of these shifts changing both academic and popular thinking, some developing new ways of thinking about sex that echo the many changes in everyday sexual behaviour. For the purposes of this volume, there are three significant moments in the recent theorisation of sexuality – and each moment can be characterised by the work of a particular author. Although the works of each are formed by a more complex and extensive context, many of the key ideas that run through the following chapters rely on an understanding of the contribution of Sigmund Freud, writing from the late nineteenth century through the early decades of the twentieth century, and Michel Foucault, working in the 1960s and 1970s. In addition to this, recent decades have seen an expansion in academic discussions of sexuality, sexual identity and sexual diversity. These more recent debates can be introduced through the writings of Judith Butler, who began publishing her work in the last decade of the twentieth century. The discussion that follows introduces some key themes from each of these three formative moments.

A number of commentaries have outlined the sea-change in the conceptualisation of sexuality that was initiated by Freud's work. It was Freud who suggested that sexuality is central and formative to the social – this is the theorisation that views sexuality as the arena in which the subject is made. After Freud, sexuality can be conceived as the journey into social life, an unavoidable set of hurdles to be negotiated in the process of becoming human. Freud taught us that it is the raw material of drives and instincts that allows sociality, precisely through the organisation of drives, into sexuality. We will go on to consider this distinction.

Freud developed his theories of sexuality and identity formation from the experience of his therapeutic practice as a physician in Vienna. From this he proposed the analysis that neurosis arises from unresolved frictions in the process of attaining subjectivity. Freud was working at a time when neuroses of varying kinds presented an ongoing problem for those of a certain class:

> We started out from the aberrations of the sexual instinct in respect of its object and of its aim and we were faced by the question of whether these arise from an innate disposition or are acquired as a result of experiences in life. We arrived at an answer to this question from an understanding, derived from psycho-analytic investigation, of the workings of the sexual instincts in psychoneurotics, a numerous class of people and one not far removed from the healthy.
>
> (Freud 1962: 135)

Through this practice, Freud proposed a theory of infantile sexuality – and this is where he describes the central role of sexual organisation in the formation of subjectivity. Freud argues that the instinctual drives that flow across the body of the infant, showing us what will bring pleasure long before we learn any other more socialised interactions with others or with the world, lie at the heart of all human endeavour. Human culture is made from our convoluted attempts to contain and redirect the energies of sex:

> The fact that the onset of sexual development in human beings occurs in two phases, i.e. that the development is interrupted by the period of latency, seemed to call for particular notice. This appears to be one of the necessary conditions of the aptitude of men for developing a higher civilization, but also of their tendency to neurosis.
>
> (Freud 1962: 139)

Freud built his theoretical model around this idea that the entry into the social is a complicated process of redeploying and constraining the instinctual energies of human life. We come into the world as a mass of messy drives and physical sensations and our whole being is selfishly devoted to physical pleasure – as Freud writes – this means that the various infantile pleasures of eating and defecating become intertwined with the drive to obtain physical pleasure that becomes sexuality. Learning to be in the social world requires that the infant curbs this endless wish to self-pleasure, through any available means, and instead directs desire to socially sanctioned practices and objects. To achieve the niceties and creativity of civilisation, sexuality has to go under cover for a while. In the period of latency, when sexuality is submerged, we all learn to achieve satisfaction through other means. Yet it is precisely this disciplining of sexual impulses that creates the multiple and complex neuroses that mark human existence. One way or another, sexuality shapes the possibilities of what it is to be human.

There has been a long-running critique of the alleged heterocentric impetus in Freud's work – his accounts of cases describe the neurotic disturbance that is caused when patients have failed to accommodate themselves to the regimes of socially sanctioned heterosexual roles (see Freud and Breuer 1974). However, it is more interesting, for the purposes of this work, to consider Freud as enabling a conception of sexuality as always conflicted and pathological. Whatever the suggestions of ideal subject formation, that perfect story of a smooth if grudging alignment with the roles of the heterosexual family, Freud teaches us that subjectivity is never reached in a manner that erases the frictions of its emergence. Even for the apparently most normative of identities, sexuality remains a necessarily unresolved disruption at the heart of subjectivity.

Freud has had a significant effect on popular conceptions of sexuality (see Gay 1984) – and through this impact the everyday use of the idea of repression has emerged. Arguably, it is this concept that infects the understanding of sexual freedom or constraint – repression is what society does to our 'natural' urges. Freedom, apparently, is overcoming its painful grip. In academic debate, Michel Foucault overturns this investment in repression as the key issue and battle for sexual politics.

Foucault's work analyses the manner in which core institutions of modernity emerge as theatres of micro-power. His most famous works examine key processes in the formation of modern civil society – the techniques of surveillance that lie at the centre of the prison and the asylum and, by implication, of government itself; the internalisation of techniques of self-disciplining that give birth to the subject of modern humanism (see Foucault 1979a: 141). From Foucault we learn that discursive formations have the weight to elicit material outcomes – so the idea of madness can lead to incarceration for some, or the construction of the new figure of the homosexual can shift everyone's experience of sexual policing. Most particularly, in relation to the topic of sexuality, we learn that these most intimate techniques of the self, these culturally coded ways of being, are expressions and conduits of power. In *Discipline and Punish*, Foucault suggests that through the seventeenth and eighteenth centuries European culture developed a system of disciplines, a relation of docility–utility, and that while aspects of these systems had been in play through many times, in this period they became the general formulae of domination:

The historical moment of the disciplines was the moment when an art of the human body was born, which was directed not only at the growth of its skills, nor at the intensification of its subjection, but at the formation of a relation that in the mechanism itself makes it more obedient as it becomes more useful, and conversely.

(Foucault 1979a: 138)

Here Foucault is describing the manner in which individual subjects come to embody the exercise of power on and through their selves. A creative and practised attention to self comes to typify the route to all social goods – this is how the most rewarded styles of social being are made, the dutiful citizen, the obedient worker. It is also how the characters at the edge of the social contract are scrutinised – prisoners and the mentally ill inhabit their own disciplinary networks:

> Thus discipline produces subjected and practised bodies, 'docile' bodies. Discipline increases the forces of the body (in economic terms of utility) and diminishes these same forces (in political terms of obedience).

(Foucault 1979a: 138)

The emergence of docile bodies is a central theme through a range of Foucault's work. As part of this wider project, Foucault undertook to write a history of sexuality, a multivolume project that has never been completed. It is in this series of works that Foucault proposes some of his most well-known and influential ideas. Here Foucault suggests that the belief that modern societies have repressed sexuality is misplaced, most particularly in relation to our famously repressive forebears, the Victorians. Instead, Foucault argues that the relentless articulation of sexuality has represented another disciplining procedure:

> What is peculiar of modern societies, in fact, is not that they consigned sex to a shadow existence, but that they dedicated themselves to speaking of it *ad infinitum*, while exploiting it as *the* secret.

(Foucault 1979b: 35)

Far from working to silence sexuality, the modern society of the disciplines focuses an excessive energy on the speaking of sexuality – sex takes on an elevated status and comes to be seen as the kernel of the self:

> Sex, the explanation for everything.

(Foucault 1979b: 78)

Foucault describes his interest in the history of sexuality as part of the larger project of charting the emergence of the docile and disciplined subject of modernity. In the process, we learn that the subject of modernity itself emerges from a longer history of the realisation of a self-ordering individual. Foucault's examination of the histories of sexuality endeavours to unpack this development:

> [T]he problematization of sexual behaviour in antiquity could be regarded as a chapter – one of the first chapters – of that general history of the 'techniques of the self.'
>
> (Foucault 1986: 11)

Sexuality holds a special place in the conception of techniques of the self – because it is in this arena that the competing impulses of pleasure and constraint are balanced in the artwork of selfhood. Techniques of the self refer to the ways in which we learn to present ourselves as our own special creations, works of art that we make everyday. These creations both display the achievements of individual self-authorship and negotiate the limits of the social order. After an initial discussion of the Victorians, as near ancestors of the present, Foucault focuses his attention on the moral codes of antiquity. The titles of volumes 2 and 3 in the history of sexuality – *The Use of Pleasure* and *The Care of the Self* – reveal the key concerns of these works. Here Foucault explores the complex etiquette that develops in order to extract social use from the organisation of sexuality and the internalisation of sexual organisation that comes to typify one key aspect of the technique of self-care. These issues occupy the early volumes of the history of sexuality because Foucault argues that it is through an examination of this development of changing codes of intimacy that we will come to understand the mystery of the self:

> It is not the accentuation of the forms of prohibition that is behind these modifications in sexual ethics. It is the development of an art of existence that revolves around the questions of the self, of its dependence and independence, of its universal form and of the connection it can and should establish with others, of the procedures by which it exerts its control over itself, and of the way in which it can establish a complete supremacy over itself.
>
> (Foucault 1988: 238–9)

In this way, Foucault seeks to persuade us that the big questions of social existence, those at the very heart of social being, are exemplified in the careful techniques of sexual ethics. The study of sexuality is not a titillating aside – instead it is the project that promises to illuminate the secrets of modernity.

If Freud transforms the conception of subjecthood and its relation to subject formation, and Foucault introduces the idea that sexuality has become a special kind of discursive construct, the study of which can illuminate the complex project of finessing the self, then Judith Butler popularises ways of thinking that reveal the constrained flexibility of sexual identities.

With the publication of *Gender Trouble* in 1990, the debate about gender formation and sexual identity shifted and a new area of discussion emerged. Primarily, *Gender Trouble* addresses debates in feminist theory. By using the lessons of psychoanalysis and of Foucault, Butler re-examines the debate about the nature and formation of gender – because feminism appears to rely on the assumption that the category 'woman' is relatively untroubled. Unfortunately, as Butler argues through the insights of earlier proponents of the cultural construction of supposedly natural identities, gender is never such an untroubled category. Instead, Butler argues, gender is created in the process of its performance, and it is this dense and detailed performance that gives the appearance of some solid centre:

> [A]cts and gestures, articulated and enacted desires create the illusion of an interior and organizing gender core, an illusion discursively maintained for the purposes of the regulation of sexuality within the obligatory frame of reproductive heterosexuality.
>
> (Butler 1990: 136)

This forwarding of the importance of performance in the assumption of gender has a considerable impact on the study of gender and sexuality. Butler is building on debates about the non-biological basis of sex and the necessarily cultural construction of gender. By pursuing the implications of the constructionist argument, Butler suggests that gender cannot refer to the anchor of underlying biology, because there is no underlying anchor. The cultural performance is all there is:

> If the inner truth of gender is a fabrication and if a true gender is a fantasy instituted and inscribed on the surface of bodies, then it seems that genders can be neither true nor false, but are only produced as the truth effects of a discourse of primary and stable identity.
>
> (Butler 1990: 136)

Butler's subsequent work, including the much discussed volume *Bodies that Matter*, published in 1993, enlarges upon these themes and develops their implications for a politics of sexuality and of gender. In particular, Butler seeks to explore the possibilities offered through the space of negotiation. If gendering opens the opportunity for at least a little performative play, then this also represents a political possibility:

> [T]he imperative to be or get 'sexed' requires a differentiated production and regulation of masculine and feminine identification that does not fully hold and cannot be fully exhaustive. And further, this imperative, this injunction, requires

and institutes a 'constitutive outside' – the unspeakable, the unviable, the nonnarratizable that secures and, hence, fails to secure the very borders of materiality.

(Butler 1993: 187–8)

Butler is describing how difficult and incomplete the process of achieving gendering can be – as a result, the proper binary of masculine and feminine always suggests that there is something more, some ways of being that fall outside this tidy twosome. Much of the interest in Butler's work has been around this journey to the constitutive outside and the manner in which this unruly otherness becomes visible within the terms of normative cultures. With this insight, we see not only that the norm is not absolute and exhaustive, but also that the apparently unassailable powers of the norm are constantly on the brink of disarray. Even as we submit to the domination of the norm, the manner of our performative compliance holds the possibility of other ways of being:

> The practice by which gendering occurs, the embodying of norms, is a compulsory practice, a forcible production, but not for that reason fully determining. To the extent that gender is an assignment, it is an assignment which is never quite carried out according to expectation, whose addressee never quite inhabits the ideal s/he is compelled to approximate.
>
> (Butler 1993: 231)

Although there is a normative force here, the norm is never quite wholly enforceable. In a development of Freud's argument, Butler presents a view of gender as a never-completed project. Instead of an easy replication, gendering constantly flounders on the near misses of lived identities. This means that, despite the considerable power and impact of dominant cultures of gender and sexuality, the constitution of dominant identities is not so certain. There is always a gap between what is expected by the norm and what is actually played out in practice. It is this space of possibility that excites queer theory and all those who wish to imagine new ways of being gendered, sexed and constituted into any identity, because the space suggests that the powers that make us are not ultimately determining.

This work returns to that suggestion again and again. Sexuality is made through the networks of social power; sexual choices are constrained by economics, by social pressures from many directions, by habit, convention and expectation. Yet, despite these many pressures, sexuality retains this possibility of play and magic – a space where dreams can be negotiated, if not fully realised.

> If all science is founded more or less on a stratum of facts, there can be no harm in making known to mankind generally certain matters intimately connected with their private, domestic, and social life.

Alas! Complete ignorance of them has unfortunately wrecked many a man and many a woman, while a little knowledge of a subject generally ignored by the masses would have enabled numbers of people to have understood many things which they believed to be quite incomprehensible, or which were not thought worthy of their consideration.

(Burton and Arbuthnott 1993: 89)

This section outlines the model of learning that is suggested in the *Kama Sutra*. Some readers may prefer to skip this section and resume their reading at the next section break. However, for those who wish to consider the logic of the framing text, here is a brief discussion of the work's key themes.

The *Kama Sutra* begins with a consideration of worldly attainments, specified as *dharma*, *artha* and *kama*. Although Burton translates these as virtue, wealth and love, the translation is not so straightforward. Even in the specification of the chapter, the discussion shows the breadth of each term.

Dharma is the least understood of the translated terms. Burton stresses the importance of adhering to the 'Holy Writ of the Hindoos' by doing certain things and not doing others – as if the acquisition of peace, wisdom and virtue can be attained from unthinking obedience. This definition takes away from the active aspect of *dharma*, effacing the ongoing quest for knowledge. The rituals of sacrifice and abstinence are physical prompts to this greater contemplation – and the physical prompt is designed to help the body adapt to the contemplative mode – but in itself obedient adherence to ritual cannot attain *dharma*. For our purposes, let us think of *dharma* as spiritual wisdom. This is the highest form of worldly attainment.

The next level of attainment, *artha*, is 'the acquisition of arts, land, gold, cattle, wealth, equipages and friends. It is, further, the protection of what is acquired, and the increase of what is protected.' (Burton and Arbuthnott 1993: 102) Even the translated definition shows this to be far more than wealth alone. What is described is better understood as the attainment of worldly goods and skills – from the absolute property of land and livestock, to the trading benefits of cash, and including the less tangible goods of allies and arts. These are the attributes that bring comfort and security in the world – and learning *artha* is as much about learning to protect and maintain this security as it is about the accumulation of goods in themselves. There is a recognition here that material well-being occurs in a social context – and that wealth may bring its own social dangers. *Artha* is the ability to collect the attributes of material comfort and form the social relations that can maintain them. This is seen as an attainment below *dharma*, but above *kama*.

Kama, our central concern, is defined as 'the enjoyment of appropriate objects by the five senses of hearing, feeling, seeing, tasting and smelling, assisted by the mind, together with the soul. The ingredient in this is a peculiar contact between the organ of sense and its object, and the consciousness of pleasure which arises from that contact is called Kama' (Burton and Arbuthnott 1993: 102–3). Rather than being regarded as the lowest of worldly attainments, *kama* should be thought of as the third level of worldly attainment. Together the three levels of attainment make up the proper education and path to wisdom of the citizen. Although the mythology of the *Kama Sutra* fixates upon *kama* as a sexual education, the definition above shows that the project is closer to a sensual education. *Kama* is the sensual enjoyment felt at the interface between body and world – and the quality of this pleasure is enhanced by proper training.

These three aspects of worldly attainment together make up the total education of the public citizen, primarily coded as male. However, all aspects of this education are open to all – there is only a suggestion that the public woman may attend more closely to the practice of *kama* as her primary endeavour. For us, what is important is the suggestion that a person should practise *dharma*, *artha* and *kama* 'at different times and in such a manner that they may harmonize together and not clash in any way' (Burton and Arbuthnott 1993: 102) All three levels of attainment are necessary to the process of understanding – and the practice of each discipline requires a proper attention to the relationship between different aspects of life. The implication of this is that even *kama*, the third level of worldly attainment, has an irreplaceable role in the overall process of education. More than this, the practice of *kama* will itself illuminate the practice of the other disciplines. So in what follows, attention to the business of sex promises to illuminate other kinds of business. Private behaviour slips outwards into the world of public affairs and learning about one requires some education in the other.

This volume takes the example of sex in order to argue that an examination of everyday and local culture can illuminate our understanding of larger political agendas. More than this, I argue that this attention to the everyday has informed larger events throughout modernity.

The book begins with a discussion of the construction and changing nature of heterosexuality. Although heterosexuality has occupied a privileged status as nature's incentive to reproduce, the lived cultures of heterosexuality are undergoing rapid changes; not all of which are easy or pleasant. In fact, despite the status of this most privileged sexual choice, anxiety about the state of heterosexual living informs some of the core policy concerns of our time. The various types of new politics that litter the developed economies are made in response to shifts in the everyday cultures of things such as sex.

The chapter on history argues that this is no recent phenomenon. Sexuality emerges as the product of a particular historical conjuncture. Different attempts to write the history of sex and to explore the insights of such a project are reviewed. By examining the claims for a transhistorical sexual essence and the competing argument that there is no sexual meaning without context, a case for a historical understanding that addresses the changes of the present is put forward.

The chapter on economy and the state reviews the debates about the instrumentality of sexual relations. Is it possible that these most intimate of choices are determined by larger structures, the impersonal forces of economic imperatives or of state intervention? The suggestion that sexuality can be ordered to serve the requirements of economic or governmental organisation is revisited, and the chapter ends by taking the shifts of recent electoral politics in Britain as a case study to illuminate the place of sex in the economy and state.

The chapter on fragments of identities extends these previous discussions into the realm of more recent academic debate. By reviewing ideas about postmodernity and the fragmentation of all identity forms, it is argued that the emergence of 'queer' and subsequent anti-identity accounts of sexuality is itself a symptom of larger changes in our social framework. For this reason, the rhetoric of performing identity that has characterised much recent debate about sexual identity may offer a more general model for assuming subjectivity in uncertain times.

The chapter on exoticism extends the implications of this uncertainty to consider the changing self-conception of the West. While in previous times the more solid powers of Western ascendance could allow a pleasurable and objectifying sexualisation of the rest of the world, now global relations are not so certain. This opens previously privileged identities to the dangerous possibility of exotic status. Some possible outcomes of this are explored, and it is argued that structures of exoticism have reshaped to fit the new world order.

The chapter on representing sexuality reviews debates about the impact and role of sexual representations. It is suggested that the battle between censorship and representation has limited the scope of discussions around learning sexuality. In response, the chapter presents an alternative model of sexual learning that combines the lessons of Machiavelli and the *Kama Sutra* in order to imagine an education that can encounter the uncertainties of a changing world.

The chapter on sexualised spaces returns to the larger theme of global shifts in order to argue that sexual propriety is conceived in spatial terms. The rapid shifts in everyday experiences of spatiality – from global networks, to the erosion and/or reworking of the public–private divide, to the cultural expressions of time–space compression – have a knock-on effect on social contracts of sexual propriety. The chapter reviews ideas of the spaces of sex and ends with the notion that a more portable conception of sexual propriety could shape a consideration of the place of intimacy in social relations.

When I began to write this volume, I wanted to re-insert the study of sexuality as a social process into wider debates about society. Returning to the *Kama Sutra* seemed to offer a route into a more worldly account of sexual life, a model of sexual learning that looked beyond the private world of lovers to the public world of citizens. Here was a way of returning to the mysterious relation between private and public, individual and society, without being transfixed by the practised posturing of more recent social theory. Of course, more recent social theory also figures in the discussion. But the detour through another kind of document, especially the ridiculed exemplar of exoticist titillation, gives us all some space to think and rest, and perhaps even doubt and laugh.

In the shift from one century to the next, there are plenty of predictions of earth-shattering change and the galloping onset of some new Armageddon or other. This highly self-conscious sense of being on the brink of something momentous suffuses all kinds of attempts to understand who we all are, where the world is at and, most importantly of all, where all this is going.

This volume also attempts to reposition sexuality in this widely perceived context of change, because if something is going on, it is going on right at the heart of modern intimacy. But, if there is one lesson to be taken from this project, it is that sex is an elusive creature to catch. It is better to take the detour if we hope to get there at all.

In the course of the following discussion, many terms of change make an appearance. These range from the painfully overused and thus overly familiar to the just-coined-yesterday and thus still a stretch to understand. In the end, I hope that this mixture of the already known and the not-quite-learned will focus our attention on the subject in hand. At the very least, assembling these different stories of contemporary life should indicate the overlapping gap in the narratives, the crucial point in the story that is never quite reached. So, this work brushes against some stories old and new. Among the older and more often told, we can include such myths as the birth of modernity and the ascendance of the West, as well as the confusing dispersal of postmodernity. More recent but equally well-known tales include globalisation, the Third Way and the survival of the nation in the era of hyper-internationalised economics and the troubled boundary between the public and the private. Melting in and out of these discussions, more unusual stories of turbo-capitalism, a second modernity and a return to self-disciplining selfhood as a way of combining social obedience with personal fun, drift into more familiar stories.

The terms of the old stories reappear within the discussion. Even without thinking, readers will recognise their familiarity. These are the answers that we already understand, perhaps in fragments or only semiconsciously, perhaps as common sense or by another name – but no longer as a stretch of imagination, because these are the stories that have entered popular understanding. Some of the framing narratives, on the other hand, are less familiar and decided. These terms deserve some introduction. The ideas of turbo-capitalism and of a second modernity both attempt to instil a fresh conception of contemporary events. Both concepts make reference to the debates of postmodernity and globalisation, yet neither is content with the accounts as they stand. For this reason, these attempts to reframe the broad debates of social theory may allow space for the more ephemeral events of sexuality. In fairness, neither term attempts to explain the mysteries and changes in intimacy, or even to explore the relation between large structure and small experience in any detail. But both accounts suggest a tantalising and central role for the arena of sex, an indication that this private business is already at the heart of global social and economic change.

Throughout this work, I use the term turbo-capitalism – as coined by Edward Luttwak. He gives his own definition:

> Its advocates use no such term. They simply call it *the* free market, but by that bit of short-hand they mean very much more than the freedom to buy and sell. What they celebrate, preach and demand is private enterprise liberated from government regulation, unchecked by effective trade unions, unfettered by sentimental concerns over the fate of employees or communities, unrestrained by customs barriers or investment restrictions, and molested as little as possible by taxation. What they insistently demand is the privatization of state-owned businesses of all kinds, and the conversion of public institutions, from universities and botanic gardens to prisons, from libraries and schools to old people's homes, into private enterprises run for profit. What they promise is a more dynamic economy that will generate new wealth, while saying nothing about the distribution of any wealth, old or new.
>
> (Luttwak 1998: 27)

Luttwak argues that this development of a cultish faith in the free market above all other social goals has given rise to a form of capitalism that is quite unlike the state-regulated capitalism that emerged after 1945 and held dominance across developed economies until the 1980s. This is the insistently hungry and unstoppable face of global capitalism – answerable to no master other than its own machinic motor, the endless expansion of free trade. In the process of this expansion, many of the social forms and institutions of previous times collapse, leaving people shorn of the protections of family, community, intimacy and social value. When Luttwak gives a critique of the excesses of turbo-capitalism, he suggests that we also need to relearn ways of being with and close to each other.

Ulrich Beck coins the term 'second modernity' in order to mark the shift from an earlier optimistic process of modernisation to a more recent sense of doubt in relation to the modern project. Against the largely positive and expansive characteristics of the first modernity, at least when viewed from the West, Beck portrays the advent of a far more uncertain time:

> The second modernity, on the other hand, is characterized by ecological crises, the decline of paid employment, individualization, globalization and gender revolution.
>
> (Beck 2000: 18)

Although the list includes some unfixed and even positive terms, the overall sense is one of disruption. This ranges from the new apocalypse talk of ecological doom, through the personal and social crises occasioned by the changing nature of work, to the possibilities of rethinking gender, or the double-edged move towards individualisation and the yet-to-be-decided outcomes of globalisation. Beck is keen to see the new opportunities that arise in this new conjecture. However, he also stresses the importance of recognising the extent of people's disquiet. Otherwise how can we grasp what is going on?

> In the second modernity, the process of modernization is reflexive in the sense that it has increasingly to face unintended and unwanted consequences of its own success. This means that boundaries tend to break down, as social conditions which 'spontaneously' framed the first modernity disappear in the wake of further modernization. Here are a few examples of what I have in mind.
>
> 1   the corporatist internal structure of classes, and therefore of class society as a whole, tends to fade as social inequalities increase …
>
> 2   sexual and inter-generational relations between men and women, adults and children are stripped of their basic pseudo-natural premise, so that a gradual revolution affects the whole world of the small family, with its conceptions of the division of labour, love and home life …
>
> 3   the society of formal work and full employment, as well as the welfare-state nexus associated with it, enter into crisis as production and cooperation lose their clearly defined local ties …
>
> 4   the imaginative world of a private sphere, in the sense of 'normal biographies' exclusively geared to market opportunities, becomes political again …
>
> (Beck 2000: 21)

These are the changes that inform the focus of this work: not only a sense of rapid economic change and extreme gender shift, but also some accompanying adaptation in the spheres and boundaries of social life. Thinking about sex and relearning intimacy are some everyday strategies for survival in these uncertain times. The discussion that follows attempts to explain why that might be the case.

1 Heterosexuality

Position of the chapter – normativity

Position one is the coupling that seeks acceptance more than pleasure. Made legitimate through recourse to such forces as biological imperatives, the need to propagate the species, the sanction of religion, the stability of society and the growth of the economy, this position appears to offer lovers no personal pleasures at all. Instead, sexuality is handed over to the higher pursuits of social ordering and lovers are rewarded by the affirmation that they are good citizens. The over-riding wish to conform to a norm, albeit one that is rarely specified, leaves lovers afraid of unexpected sexual pleasure. If some activity yields a surprise frisson, there is always the danger that it casts lovers outside the protected circle of the norm. If normative coupling becomes too enthusiastic or adventurous, perhaps it stretches the limits of respectable normativity too far?

This chapter examines the history and formation of that most invisible of sexual identities and practices, heterosexuality. Here it is argued that heterosexuality is subject to the same shifts and changes as other social phenomena. Despite our deep cultural investment in the idea that this expression of sexuality is natural, an inevitable outcome of biological imperatives to reproduce, I seek to reveal the variable and ultimately unknowable character of the so-called heterosexual norm. The chapter reviews debates about the uneven benefits of heterosexual living for men and women and ends with the suggestion that a new heterosexuality may be emerging from the social upheavals of our time (for more on the study of heterosexuality, see Rich 1980; Wittig 1992; Segal 1994; Richardson 1996; Jackson 1999).

The *Kama Sutra* limits its attention to the coupling of men and women, or men and eunuchs, or groups of men with one woman, or groups of women with one man. Although the focus is upon pleasure, not reproduction, the logic of heterosexuality bubbles up through every crevice of the text. This is the heterosexuality that assumes male sexual pleasure as its centre – it is the education of the citizen, coded male, that orders this work. This central role is determined by social power, as always – so other less powerful men can appear as side characters, another option among the sexual servicers of citizens.

In fact, there is an account of other practices, including practices between women that have no anchor of male citizenship (see Danielou 1994: 168–96). But overall the sexual theatre of the *Kama Sutra* assumes that sexual interactions are characterised by an imbalance of power – the interaction between male citizens and women of various orders is never between equals. Each party has its own role and capacities. It is this depiction of sex centring on a relatively privileged male subject, with little mobility in sexual roles, that allows the work to become translated as a celebration of heterosexual primacy, albeit through the illicit pleasures of experimentation. Despite this, I want to use the work to begin with a critique of heterosexuality as a hegemonic structure – not least because hegemony steals away the best pleasures of sex. I am using the idea of hegemony here as a way of describing a structure of cultural domination that seeps into everyday life and somehow gains the participation of those who are constrained and dominated.

The *Kama Sutra* presents sexual pleasure as a project requiring diligence and study. Although social roles appear static within the work, sex itself is never given or natural. There is no suggestion that the citizen can relax and let nature take its course, because sexual pleasure must be learned as one component in a total education. Therefore, while, on the one hand, there is an assumption of unchangeable hierarchy, on the other, there is no sexual role that is not the product of intensive cultural work.

What is heterosexuality?

Before we go any further, let us return to the question of what heterosexuality is. Let us begin with the kind of sex that parades itself as natural, inevitable and the fallback for all other sexual experience. Heterosexuality occupies the role of unmarked norm in much contemporary sexual culture – this is the sex that just is, that needs no explanation, that everyone knows about, has access to and can do without learning. This is the primal scene of sex – with one man and one woman, drawn together by their instinctual need to reproduce, unhampered by the confusions of culture or social expectation because the penis finds the vagina of its own accord, as its biological destiny. Perhaps even more than other cultures of dominance, heterosexuality can appear to be beyond critique – after all, are not all human cultures heterosexual? Is there not a point at which biological imperatives constrain cultural diversity and innovation? Heterosexuality seems to be buoyed up by nature and the absolute bottom-line need to reproduce – because without reproduction we will die out. Sex for pleasure, of any variety, can hardly compete with this instrumental requirement. Even liberal and tolerant accounts tend to posit heterosexuality as the unavoidable norm against which all else is judged.

Against this, I want to argue that heterosexuality itself is a term with a history. Although human reproduction has taken place across all eras of human history – which is not the same as saying that everyone has taken part in these processes of reproduction – the particular entity 'heterosexuality' is a historically discrete affair. Despite the extreme pressures to regard heterosexuality as normative, beyond history, in fact, heterosexual activity has been as historically variable as other forms of sexual connection (see Stone 1990; White 1993; Adams 1997).

The great difference between past heterosexualities and past homosexualities is that, more often than not, heterosexual relationships were both statistically and culturally normative. One of the problems with normativity is that it may seem to be unproblematic, unconstructed and, indeed, 'natural'. One does not have to enquire very far, however, to discover an enormous variety of heterosexual identities and heterosexual 'normativities' in the past. Here are three examples:

- Within living memory the socially expected age of marriage has risen by about five years in the US (from 19–21 for women in the early 1950s to 25–27 in the 1990s). What was normal in 1950 would now be scandalous.
- In numerous societies polygamy is a social norm, even if not statistically frequent (e.g. Old Testament Israelite society, various Islamic societies, traditional Chinese societies, some African societies). In others monogamy is given a unique moral validation.
- In many pre-industrial societies the age of commencement of sexual activity was close to the age of sexual maturity. Industrial societies, while continuing to endorse a mythology of the 'normal', have tended to delay the onset of permitted sexual activity (Halsall 2001).

These suggestions come from a proposal to teach the history of heterosexuality – as an antidote to the forgetfulness of celebrations of heterosexual life as the one, true, constant choice for the righteous. The course proposal acknowledges that heterosexual liaisons have been more public and (probably) more numerous throughout recorded history. There is no suggestion here that same-sex liaisons occupied an interchangeable role with heterosexual ones at any point, so the point is not to remember the lost idyll of homosexual normativity. Instead, the proposal seeks to uncover the significant variation in even explicitly normative heterosexual cultures across time – because even such cornerstones of respectable straight culture as monogamy and the absolute boundary between childhood and married adulthood are not universal (Aries 1962; Smith and Smith 1974; Walvin 1982).

The wider suggestion that heterosexuals are, like everyone else, a people with a history places heterosexuality in more general debates about the history of sexuality. Central to this assertion is the idea that an act or series of acts is reified into this entity, sexuality, only at a certain moment. In part, this is an argument that says that sexuality can only function as a naming term within a historical context. If, after Foucault, everyone believes that the homosexual came into existence in 1892 – shifting a series of acts and crimes and sins into a named persona for vilification – then a similar pattern of identification must occur for the more privileged identity of heterosexual:

> [I]f homosexuality didn't exist before 1892, heterosexuality couldn't have existed either (it came into being, in fact, like Eve from Adam's rib, eight years later), and without heterosexuality, where would all of us be right now?
>
> (Halperin 1990: 17)

This naming is strictly relational – *hetero* makes sense only in relation to its other, *homo*. Unlike other forms of sexual naming – size queen, romance addict – *hetero* and *homo* encompass the range of human behaviour. Bisexuality proves the adaptability of human beings, but does not upset the logic of sex being either this or that, opposite or same. Definitions take place between these two poles:

> How is it possible that until the year 1900 there was not a precise, value-free, scientific term available to speakers of the English language for designating what we would now regard, in retrospect, as the mode of behaviour favored by the vast majority of people in our culture?
>
> (Halperin 1990: 18)

If heterosexuality is so normal that it is inevitable, how can it have remained unnamed until the twentieth century? Hidden in Halperin's question is the suggestion that, whatever permutations of male and female sexual interaction took place before this naming, it was not heterosexuality as we understand it. The names homosexual and heterosexual signal the advent of a certain consciousness of sexual choice as identity. Now acts can become identities – but also, sexual habits become socially meaningful in a different way. What you do with your body and in relation to other bodies comes to mean something far more about you, something that could seep into other arenas of your life. The larger point is that sexuality is itself a historical entity, not an inevitable aspect of self in all times, but a historically specific articulation of self that emerges at a certain moment. Heterosexuality appears as the organising term against which pathologised sexual choices can be measured.

What determines the emergence of (hetero)sexuality?

If heterosexuality comes into being only at a particular historical conjuncture, then the moment of emergence may offer some clues as to what is significant and socially necessary about naming sexuality. Sexuality can only become a conspicuous domain apart in relation to other arenas of living. The appearance of sexuality is an indication of a wider reworking of spheres of human activity and their respective power and meaning. Although human bodies evoke sensations of pleasure and discomfort in relation to physical stimuli, the particular organisation of getting sexualised pleasure alters across historical moments and societies. Perhaps even our interpretation of physical pleasure alters through social factors – so that I learn to enjoy the intrusion of kissing because it indicates affection and a promise of impending intimacy. These gestures assume meaning within the larger context of social meanings and relations – in part intimacy is recognisable because it is distinct from other more formal interactions. When searching for the place and meaning of sexuality, there must be an understanding of the interdependence of different spheres of being, one nodal point in a network, rather than a discrete object of scrutiny. Once we place sexual relations in a bundle with other social relations and argue that there is a connection between these disparate areas of human existence, perhaps even a connection in which one set of relations determines another, sexuality comes into the arena of the economic.

Of course, in some ways this is the most familiar account of heterosexuality in the book. When Friedrich Engels wrote *The Origin of the Family* as part of the larger project of understanding the workings of private property and class formation, his attempts to explain the role of the family and patriarchy in the formation of capitalist relations are describing the instrumentality of a certain model of sexual relations. Engels describes family relations that grow around the need to protect and maintain household property, with the unequal relations between men and women giving shape to the class tensions that characterise societies based on private property. This is heterosexuality motored by power, control and the wish for free labour, not romance, desire or physical longing. It is still, however, an account of heterosexual living.

In the end, this account of the instrumental outcomes of heteronormativity excises desire altogether. By heteronormativity I mean the extensive and far-reaching ideological system that seeks to impose a public contract of heterosexual compliance as the only way of living and being – precisely the culture of dominance that forgets sex in favour of social privilege. Despite all the privilege, the implication that heterosexual relations perform a function for wider society and wealth production before performing any more immediate purpose for participants seems to empty sex out of the equation. Later chapters will consider the puzzling relation between sexuality and the more pragmatic goals of social organisation, including economic wealth. For now, our focus is on the variation in heterosexual living across time. If the detail of heterosexual living is made by the imperatives and habits of particular moments, we already accept that even the unassailable naturalness of heterosexual relations must alter over time. It is only a small leap to admit that the heterosexuality that is made unthinkingly and inevitably by the imperatives of biology is, in fact, not one thing at all. Instead, there are all too many different ways that girls can be with boys – and most of the time reproduction plays only a side role in these manoeuvres.

The trick of appearing natural relies heavily on the comparative lack of documentation about the detail of sexual contact – for anyone, but perhaps most of all for straights. Whatever the strategic silences and erosions of the history-writing of the dominant, the various sexual practices of the demonised, vilified and persecuted have tended to be identified for scrutiny and punishment (see Moran 1996). This process has often led to record-keeping of prurient detail – and although there must be large elements of titillated fantasy, there is also some recognition of the variety of human possibility. The everyday practices of the most normalised and mundane forms of living, on the other hand, leave few historical traces. Although every document of power reveals the hegemony of the norm, the lived texture of improvisation and surprise that must characterise any intimate life is rarely part of the document. Without this detail of everyday variation, heterosexual life is reduced to the core components of normative myth – formalised romance as a route to marriage, procreation as a socially necessary outcome, lifetime monogamy as the domestic building block of social stability. So little is said about the sex itself – in terms of acts, feelings, meanings or anything – a reader could be forgiven for believing that, until very recently, the life of a respectable heterosexual contained no sex at all.

This is a central paradox of heteronormativity – that the presentation of the most natural, desirable and inevitable of sexual choices is characterised by a conspicuous desexualisation. While the vilification of minority sexual choices focuses on sexual practice, so that these monstrous people are depicted as dirty, sleazy, excessive and very very sexual, straights are just straight. For all the public celebration of heterosexual living that characterises Western societies, the excessive publicity given to heterosexual life-choices empties them of sex itself. We see the battles and negotiations between men and women, but so little of desire and pleasurable practice. As a lifestyle choice, heterosexuality appears to offer few pleasures, only the security of social privilege (for more on the benefits of heterosexual recognition, see http://www.stonewall.org.uk).

The key question remains – when does reproductive sex become an identity or lifestyle? Although the account of the historicity of heterosexuality describes the emergence of sexual names as identities, the parallel account of how individuals assume these names is missing. Lesbian and gay history has used the suggestion of discursive emergence in order to analyse the growing self-consciousness of this new breed, the homosexual. The category name may appear as a result of the discursive machinery of power, but the name itself offers new possibilities to men who have sex with men – there is undoubted persecution, but there is also an increasing awareness of the identity of this name. There is no comparative document of the increasing self-awareness of heterosexuals – and, therefore, no account of the sense that heterosexuality may become an active choice, a lifetime's quest, a tormenting secret or the driving motor behind the narrative of living. In part, these questions may be answered by considering the role of sex before sexuality – why does activity start to matter to wider social relations? What are the cultural habits that make up the lived identity of heterosexuals?

There is an assumption that as the norm, heterosexuality is completely familiar and knowable – without mystery or glamour. Yet het life remains as uncharted as other sexual existence, staged as family romance but not known as sexual diversity or sexual anything. This is one of the core ironies of heterosexual hegemony – that the will to dominance, normativity, respectability, is itself highly desexualising. Later in the book I will pursue the idea that sexiness invokes risk in good ways – for now the question is whether something so adamantly good for you as heterosexuality can ever be exciting in a sexual way.

Is there such a thing as straight culture?

The question here is how the hegemony of heterosexual choices is maintained. To respond I want to focus on two aspects of the idea of culture – one, the explicit propaganda war, the other, the lived culture of the everyday. Straight culture encompasses both – a widespread multimedia advertising campaign for the heterosexual way of life and a complex self-reproducing system that suffuses the crevices of the everyday. The two aspects reinforce each other to create a resilient official culture. The question is – what relation does this bear to the actual lives of heterosexuals?

A variety of debates in social enquiry have suggested that power elites of various kinds remake themselves through the supplement of culture. A period of insistent attention to the workings of ideology, a period which seems already to have passed, gave rise to work that drew connections between state interests and popular debates, media cultures and the imperatives of the international economy (Larrain 1979; Eagleton 1991). This suggestion, that power sustains itself through cultural display, has led to analyses of the cultures of masculinity, nationalism, whiteness and, belatedly, heterosexuality. This range of work has been marked by the linking suggestion that cultures of power present themselves as the only alternative, so insistently visible everywhere that their version of the world becomes the only one (Said 1978; Hobsbawm and Ranger 1983; Dyer 1997). Perhaps more than any other, the public cultures of entertainment fit this model of propaganda for heterosexual living. Everywhere you look, the world is full of representations of heterosexual people loving, living, surviving their lives. Anyone else only figures as an anomalous diversion from the main story – that straightness is what human existence is all about. We can think of straight culture as the policing of norms through insistent display. Although almost none of this endless display is identified explicitly as heterosexual, the power of being everywhere all the time should not be underestimated. This is what Wittig (1992) describes in the concept of the straight mind.

In the manner of other powerful types, heterosexuality appears frighteningly seductive in its popular culture incarnation. The archetypes of popular romance belong to heterosexuality – so completely that it is difficult to imagine a distinction between cultures of romance and cultures of heterosexuality. Yet the resulting misapprehensions create parallel delusions for both men and women engaged in the quest for happy heterosexuality. Perhaps it is the omnipresence of heterosexual propaganda that makes lived heterosexuality seem such a disappointment.

Learning to be a happy heterosexual

The *Kama Sutra* presents the time of sexuality as one episode in a longer life course. Youth must be devoted to the pursuit of scholarship and is a time for the discipline of books and study. Adulthood is a time to turn attention to the demands of the world – including the sensual world of *kama*. Old age belongs to the spirit and is a time to relinquish the burdens of worldly goods and concerns. Each episode complements the others and life's journey must pass through each stage.

Within the process of sensuous education itself, lessons are highly graduated. The process of education demands attention to the physical type of the partner, to the range of sensations that can be elicited through different activities, and to the growing capacity of your own response. It is through this process that individuals come to *inhabit* their own sexuality – through diligent application. The lesson is that, despite the assumption of absolute and unlearned natural responses, heterosexual life courses also grow and change over time. No-one is born a fully fledged heterosexual – and a major part of adhering to the norm is to adopt appropriate behaviour at different points in your life. So let us reconsider the process of emergence. Once we acknowledge that all sexual behaviour must have a learned component, the adoption of heterosexual identity can be recognised as a rite of passage in itself. Despite the many jokes, straights must also come out in some manner – albeit in less constrained circumstances than less privileged others.

Stage one in the journey is the assumption of identity. For the anxious young would-be heterosexual, self-realisation and public declaration form the often unacknowledged basis of claiming identity. Sadly, strategic deployment of homophobia can play a central role in this process of marking affiliation. Without rehearsing the all too familiar arguments about the supplementarity of gay to straight, and perhaps of all other choices to the master project of reproductive heterosexuality, it is worth noting the extent to which young heterosexual identity is learned as a phobic marking of what you are not. For boys especially, growing up can seem to be little more than an endless display of non-gayness, combined with ongoing and organised violence against those deemed to be gay (for more on this supplementarity of gay to straight, see Butler 1990; 1993). Critiques of heterosexual privilege have described this process with amusement – describing the natural choice of heterosexual living as beset by one crisis after another:

The first identity crisis occurs when an individual enters puberty, and experiences a variety of covert threats, bribes and commands to behave in an acceptably heterosexual manner.

(Penelope 1993: 263)

The suggestion is that heterosexual women hit the extreme contradictions of their existence at certain points in their life course: first, at this initial moment of heterosexual coercion; second, when entering marriage and dependency on a man; third, when realising that their life has become an endless process of servicing others; and fourth, when reaching menopause and recognising the end of their status as reproductive material. Each crisis moment represents an opportunity to refuse the bind of compulsory heterosexuality and to escape into some other less constrained existence. For women, apparently, the stages of heterosexual life reveal only their oppression in increasingly painful ways.

The parallel account for men is more celebratory, although with its own sources of anxiety. Whereas straight women live heterosexuality as a display and service for men, men describe the performance of heterosexuality as an appeal for recognition from each other:

Heterosexual first sex is an induction into adult masculinity for young men in which women, whether sexually experienced or not, play an ambiguous role.

(Holland *et al*. 1998: 179)

Although women are the necessary conduits for the entry into manhood, thus holding power over this anxious rite of passage, women do not hold the social status necessary to confirm successful masculinity:

Young men are not responding to the surveillance power of femininity; they are clearly living heterosexual masculine identities under a male gaze. Young women are living feminine identities, but in relation to a male audience – measuring themselves through the gaze of the 'male-in-the-head'.

(Holland *et al*. 1998: 11)

After coming out as straight, the assumption of coupledom signals an important moment of social entry – although heterosexuality has the power of all dominant cultures to mark all unmarked spaces as its own, so that everyone becomes straight by default, full membership of this elite grouping can require certain badges of affiliation. Popular culture rewards two versions of younger heterosexuality – display of sexual activity in line with dominant norms and the establishment of publicly recognised couples. This recognition has informed campaigns that stage kiss-ins and agitate for same-sex marriage in order to make visible heterosexual privilege (see Sherman 1992; Malone 2000).

An earlier feminist critique of the hegemony of the straight couple concentrated on marriage as the ties that bind. Marriage was, it was alleged, the institutionalisation of male power and privilege – the method by which women were marked as chattel and limited to that status. Marriage split women into two equally untenable roles – the adulthood of married status, in which you were never more than an adjunct to your male owner, or the comparative freedom of being unmarried but endangered and without social recognition. Now that marriage is no longer such a central building block of social order, these ideas seem to have fallen from favour.

However, aside from the legal status accrued through formal marriage, recent experience of changing domestic patterns reveals the extent to which heterosexual coupling as a public statement and status continues to be endorsed and encouraged. In terms of institutional power, it is not clear whether heterosexuality demands conformity or only the appearance of obedience. Who cares ultimately what people do with their bodies? We will pursue this question in more detail in a later chapter. For now, it is enough to suggest that heterosexuality allows some deviation – and that this limited permission makes its hegemonic hold more resilient. If anything, this limited flexibility contributes to the fantasy of an absolutely stable and resilient heterosexual couple as the marriage myth of our time. This is the other side of the demand that heterosexual couples stay together through thick and thin – the idea that healthy relationships require work, including sexual work. The social imperative towards long-term monogamy legitimates sexual experimentation in the interests of happy heterosexuality. This is a concerted effort to re-eroticise heterosexuality, because privilege alone cannot sustain its key institutions.

The core myths of hegemonic heterosexuality have it that people are born this way because it is natural and no doubt or deviation ever crosses their minds. Some others, through bad luck or evil perversion, are outside this happy camp of normality. Some of these people may even 'recover' and become straight (again). But, in the main, heterosexuality is held to be an absolute and lifelong state.

So why is it so easily threatened?

If heterosexual culture has one identifiable characteristic, one thing that is proclaimed openly in many places, it is this sense of threat. For all its power, heterosexuality seems to be a fragile and delicate thing. Heterosexual men can be driven to kill by no more than the imputed threat of another man's desire for them; heterosexual families can be dissolved by the mere suggestion that other ways of living exist. The grand project of propagating the human race through heterosexuality is presented as being under constant attack, always in danger of erosion by the dangerous possibilities of other erotic choices. Much of the social legitimacy that is granted to this form of heterosexual paranoia derives from a particular concern about the making of babies. Although parenting is highly undervalued as a social process – the subject of much debate and anxiety, but little acclaim and status – I want to suggest that the role of parent can operate as a mechanism to proclaim the respectability and instrumentality of your sexuality. Parenting may have no connection to sexual behaviour or identity, but the responsibilities of parenting are used to argue that heterosexuality is more than the mere pursuit of pleasure – unlike other less socially responsible object choices.

There are two important strands here. One is the appeal to biological imperatives – so that the call to make babies is portrayed as the definitive pull of heterosexual behaviour. The second is the suggestion that some sexualities are driven by something other than desire and the wish for physical comfort – and that this other driver is more than the wish for sex in itself. This is an important component of heterosexual identity, the suggestion that it is more than sex and that it lives beyond sexuality. Little has been said about what happens to sexuality in the process of ageing. What there is tends towards the therapeutic – how to keep things going or how to counsel people who cannot. However, in sex, as in all things, time changes everything. Why should the certainties of heterosexuality be excluded from this? Although the name may be retained, who knows what practices come to accompany it?

As well as this adaptation to the demands of different stages of life, the heterosexual life course must also adapt in relation to historical changes – the broad stages represent responses to particular demands and shifts. In order to function, intimacy itself must become a shifting skill. There is some precedent for viewing reworkings of heterosexuality as an element of wider social changes. In particular, reviews of the twentieth century regard shifts in the narration and performance of sexual life as a core aspect of the development of a late-modern sense of self. This may offer an insight into the growth of the particular subcultural community of heterosexuals – and may indicate something of the coming to consciousness of this group:

> After 1910, a vast corps of experts, be they corporate managers, ministers, doctors, advertisers, or marriage manual writers or dance-hall operators, began to offer new solutions to the nervousness and ethical confusion of Americans and in the process devised a new moral code for American society. This new morality stressed instant gratification and fulfillment through consumption and leisure as a means of assuaging the boredom and aimlessness of twentieth-century life and as a resolution to the seeming irrelevance of the older system and the dullness of corporate life and concomitant decline of personal autonomy.
>
> (White 1993: 13)

White identifies other factors in this version of 'sexual revolution' – the rapid growth of cities, newspapers appealing to greater mass readerships through the use of titillation, more leisure for more people and more time to consume, the expansion of all forms of mass entertainments: 'the movies, dance halls, amusements – all were set in sexualized environments in which an ever more middle-class audience could spend its money' (White 1993: 14). Jonathan Katz suggests that it is this rise in consumerism that encourages the idea that sex may be pursued as a pleasurable activity for both sexes (Katz 1983; Matthaei 1997).

Even the defensive strategies of purity campaigns had the effect of opening public discourse on sexuality. By making sexual behaviour and morality into an issue of public discussion and campaigning, advocates of a return to puritan values inadvertently advertised the pleasures of sexual freedom. White also reports that the Kinsey Report shows a greater variety of straight sexual experience from 1890 to 1910 – in particular, far greater percentages of oral sex as a petting experience. The entry into the twentieth century expanded the range of heterosexual experience and also greatly increased everyday investments in heterosexual lifestyles. Now that you could choose a straight lifestyle as a leisure choice, sexual identity became something else altogether.

Another area of discussion seeks to argue that heterosexuality is not uniform across time, place or culture – and that the mode of sexual identity and behaviour that receives so much support and acclaim in contemporary Westernised life has not always been the most celebrated articulation of self in all times and cultures. Largely, this debate has stemmed from a concern to rethink the parameters and possibilities of heterosexuality (for more on alternative forms of heterosexual masculinity, see Hearn and Morgan 1990; Boyarin 1997; Seidler 1997). Can heterosexuality encompass a different set of ethical concerns, or develop fresh habits of intimacy to adapt to the political and social changes in wider life? If we are all in a process of relearning what it is to be a man or a woman, will this not have consequences for the sexual interactions between so-called men and women?

> Neither the assumption that that some (even most) people prefer to have sex with people who have different genitals than they do, nor even the tabooing of certain or all same-sex genital acts, constitutes heterosexuality. Only the premise that same-sex desire is [abnormal], that it constitutes, in Foucault's words, a separate species of human being, creates this category.
>
> (Boyarin 1997: 14)

However, like other dominant cultures characterised by invisibility, heterosexuality is about more than sex itself. It is also about the everyday cultures that make the norms of heterosexual life. Therefore, an analysis of its structures and power effects must give attention to the lived cultures of heterosexuality. More than the act itself, whatever that mysterious act may be, heterosexual life is made in the in-between of social recognition and approval. Here we can think of the culture of heterosexuality as the everyday habits that lead to heterosexual coupling as the only respectable expression of sexuality. Other kinds of sex may be tolerated, but they are not a continuation of respectable living. In a later chapter I will discuss the role of maintaining heterosexuality in wider ideological projects. For now, the point is that heterosexuality occupies the space of acceptable outlet – if you must exercise desire, this way is permitted and can be reintegrated into the business of society.

In terms of analysis, the difficulty is identifying where this culture of heterosexuality resides. Once we accept that straight living is made through many sources and influences, only some of which are explicitly sexual, then all aspects of cultural reproduction could be regarded as part of this culture. (For some accounts of the role of popular culture in reproducing heterosexual identities, see Radway 1987; Ingraham 1999.) Although a number of critiques have attempted to reveal heterosexuality, as we know it, as historically specific and culturally limited, no more than another minority choice rather than the only choice, placing the perpetuation of straight living in the wider bundle of reproductive ideologies – the assemblage of popular culture and state intervention, social rewards and punishments, the whole interconnected structure of social activity that encourages social relations to be made again in the same manner, protecting existing privileges and disparities at the expense of social change – all of that implies that certain interests are protected by this process.

If heterosexuality has its own cultural forms, what do straights wear, read, watch? It is possible to regard the vast majority of popular culture as an intensive advertising campaign for heterosexual living. Despite the complexities and disappointments, the laughter and the tears, romance and/or the promise of sex pervade mass-produced forms of entertainment – and the romance in question is heterosexual. Recent writings have suggested that every community forms itself through the creation and dissemination of its culture, that we learn identity and social interaction in part through this vocabulary of belonging (D'Emilio 1983; Gilroy 1987). However, although predictably, these ideas are most developed in relation to minority or non-dominant communities – the cultures of migrants, not hosts, of black people, not white, and of lesbians and gay men, not heterosexuals. The community cultures of dominant groups are only now emerging as subjects of study and discussion.

A key lesson in this process is the realisation that dominant groups are less likely to explicitly mark cultural products as their own. Instead, privilege might entail a sense of entitlement, which allows ownership without declaration – belonging does not need to shout out its claim, because everyone recognises the entitlement of the in-group. Are pop songs part of straight culture, except in the all too rare instance when they declare otherwise? Is Hollywood a multi-million dollar campaign to show the pains, pleasures and ultimate inescapability of heterosexuality (of certain sorts)? Is all commodity-culture inevitably recouped into the project of promoting heterosexuality, unless it declares itself as part of the niche marketing of the gay community?

On the other hand, any cultural product we point to must belong to others too – the power of being everywhere means that there is no safe haven of community (whatever straight culture says). Queer readings have revealed the vulnerability of the most orthodox and unlikely documents to appropriation and creative interpretation (for more on queer appropriations of mainstream popular culture, see Burston and Richardson 1995; Penley 1997). This raises a whole new set of questions – if even the documents of heterosexuality can be reworked to pleasure queer audiences, how does the culture of heterosexuality maintain its tight and frightened hegemonic grip? This volume will go on to suggest that wider social changes are transforming heterosexuality into something less powerful and more uncertain. Cultural proliferation may be a factor in loosening the hold.

Is heterosexuality good for men or for women?

The most sustained critique of heterosexuality as an institution has come from feminist debate, which argues that this sexual arrangement is another aspect of the systematic subordination and exploitation of women:

> Heterosexuality is not, as it appears to be, masculinity-and-femininity in opposition: it *is* masculinity. Within this masculine heterosexuality, women's desires and the possibility of female resistance are potentially unruly forces to be disciplined and controlled, if necessary by violence.
>
> (Holland *et al*. 1998: 11)

Lifestyle surveys show that men appear to fare better from their heterosexual couplings – at least when we view this form of sex as leading to a certain form of domestic arrangement. Young women are far more likely to live away from the family home than young men – who wait for another woman to replace their mother, in predictable sitcom style (see the *Independent*, 27 January 2000, 'Family Life: Young men staying at home even into their thirties: Young women showing greater independence than men as figures say nearly one in three males aged 20–35 still lives at home'). After divorce, men's health and well-being declines significantly – although it is less clear that women's improves (see the *Observer*, 12 August 2001, 'Divorce: can it feel this good?').

Critical thinking about heterosexuality has rightly focused on the negative consequences of women's subordination and the marginalisation and disenfranchisement of other sexual choices and I do not wish to deny or underplay the ugly outcomes of heterosexual hegemony here (see Richardson 2000). However, the model of analysis that sees heterosexuality as a veil for the exercise of an abusive power takes its tools from accounts of other kinds of social structure. For some forms of structuration it is arguable that people cooperate only because of their investment in maintaining privilege at the expense of others disprivilege – nation could be thought of in this way, whiteness certainly has little currency except as a marker of racial privilege – but is this really the case with heterosexuality (on the contract of race, see Mills 1997)? Although heterosexuals themselves express much dissatisfaction with lived heterosexuality, can their erotic lives be reduced to an exercise of power and privilege?

Perhaps as much as free domestic labour and sex on demand, we could think of men's dependency on heterosexuality as an indication of the still evolving emotional politics of gender. Straight men are less likely to sustain deep emotional bonds outside their sexual relationships. They are far more likely to regard their sexual relationship as the focus of their intimate life – if not the only, at least the major arena of intimacy, that strange but necessary component of well-being for inhabitants of atomised late modernity (Giddens 1994). Women, famously, sustain themselves in other and more various ways – and most importantly through their relationships with other women (Sheehy 2000). Heterosexuality clearly contributes to the well-being of straight men – more than just the sex, men seem to need the wider trappings of this sexualised arrangement. Whereas straight women can instigate versions of domesticity, intimacy and affection independently of their relationship with a man – however much they may wish for the special romance of a 'successful' sexual relationship – men seem to be having a much harder time learning to adapt to these different circumstances. We could take this as a confirmation of the allegation that men love heterosexuality for instrumental reasons, that this is about power, not love, or even desire.

But, aren't men also subject to the same smashed dreams and disappointing boredoms as women? Although men appear to obtain material and emotional service from their engagement in heterosexual relations (of certain kinds), this augmentation does not render men immune to dissatisfaction. However good heterosexuality can be for men, it never actually makes them invulnerable (on masculine vulnerability, see Pfeil 1995; Seidler 1997). As the world changes in ways which impact on the sexual lives of industrialised economies, fresh sources of anxiety appear for heterosexual men. Many of these become the policy questions of our time – what do work, family or community mean in the era of male obsolescence? Working on and at sex is a way of working on these issues.

Of course, the converse of the suggestion that heterosexuality services men is that it is a disservice to women. There are plenty of everyday indications of Western woman's dissatisfaction with the state of contemporary heterosexuality (see the television programme *Ally McBeal* and most women's magazines). However, at the heart of all this outpouring, it seems that, more than ever, straight women are invested in the possibilities of what heterosexuality could be. Otherwise, how do we understand this long lament for the promise that is never fulfilled, for the perfect man who never appears, for the sweet satisfaction of a love that never quite arrives? As usual, academics seem to miss the point when they concentrate only on the pains of women's heterosexual experience. Of course, there is abusive male power, continuing exploitation, all kinds of sad skewed power imbalances – and this work will go on to examine some of these issues – but, however bad all of this is, it is rarely all that there is.

One key theme of this book is the idea, the faint hope, that all kinds of sexuality could be good for all kinds of people. Plenty of what follows is a demonstration of how this is not the case – and that, instead, sex remains a cause of suffering, a point of weakness, a promise that does not deliver. Despite all of these failings, this is written because I want to believe that things could and will be different – not least because so many people care about the quality of their intimacy, sensuality and capacity to touch other human beings.

Is heterosexuality changing?

The structure of heterosexuality is determined, or at least adapted, by the shifts in wider society. The manner of living together and leaving relationships has opened up dramatically in recent years – with fresh pains as well as fresh possibilities. Despite resistance and limitations, there has been a shift in the character and balance of roles within many heterosexual relationships. Most of all, women's demands for equality, enfranchisement and respect in all arenas of life have changed the framework of heterosexual romance – sexual success for heterosexual men will depend, in part, on their ability to meet and support these aspirations. There are indications that heterosexuality has adapted greatly to changing expectations in recent decades – but whether this has altered the practice of sex is another matter. The practice of physical intimacy remains largely mysterious. Recent work has attempted to provide more comprehensive documentation about the detail of sexual practice, largely in response to the urgency of sexual health needs. This imperative to answer the immediate demands of public health concerns, however, has constrained the kind of information that is collected. The introduction of a major survey of sexual behaviour in Britain explains the emphasis of the work:

> Future historians may wonder at the absence of information on the psychological and pleasurable nature of sexual relationships and at the descriptive rather than explanatory nature of the enquiry.
>
> (Johnson *et al.* 1994: 8)

However, despite this absence of any more textured account of how sexual life feels, this survey does uncover significant trends, especially in the conduct of heterosexual life:

> Three trends were identified: a progressive reduction over the years in the age at which first intercourse occurs; an increase in the proportion of young women who have had sexual intercourse before the age of sexual consent; and a convergence in the behaviour of men and women.
>
> (Johnson *et al.* 1994: 69)

The gender disparity in heterosexual practice is eroding. Although this takes no account of the cultures of gender that surround the acts, it is an indication of a shift in possibility. If women are participating differently in heterosexuality, then perhaps what it is to be heterosexual is changing too. We know from some surveys that people are more likely to have more partners – or at least that they are more likely to claim this. We know that attitudes to some sexual diversity and experimentation are altering (*Financial Times*, 28 November 2000, 'Social attitudes survey: Britain likely to get more permissive'). But we do not know much else. What are all those straights doing behind their respectable front doors? Does sexual practice change over the course of a heterosexual lifetime? How much uniformity or diversity is contained within the term 'heterosexual'? If we are trying to chart changes, surely we need to know what we are starting from?

Much of the most honourable debate within feminism has attempted to imagine more fulfilling sexual experiences for all women – free from discrimination, violence, prejudice or exploitation. This desire charts the continuity between the struggles of lesbian, bisexual and transsexual women and heterosexual women, with the sexual freedom of one group always depending upon the others. Feminism, despite its shortcomings, divisions and backlashes, has overhauled all our emotional lives, whether we like it or not. The impact may be variable, but the flicker of these other possibilities is there all the same. As heterosexuality changes, there is always the glimmer of a chance that this change will be for the better – if only we can survive the turbulence of the change:

> Many men are driven, by a lack that can manifest itself in overt rage and violence. It has become a commonplace in the therapeutic literature to say that men tend to be 'unable to express feelings' or are 'out of touch' with their own emotions. But this is much too crude. Instead, we should say many men are unable to construct a narrative of self that allows them to come to terms with an increasingly democratised and reordered sphere of personal life.
>
> (Giddens 1992: 117)

However much energy is spent describing and analysing the constraining and hegemonic force of heterosexual culture – and I believe that these accounts describe the workings of the social lives of developed economies fairly accurately – the daily existence of heterosexuals is not characterised by a sense of stable and unassailable privilege. Instead, the language of crisis suffuses popular and policy debates. Anyone would think that heterosexuality was going out of fashion. This sense of attack is one aspect of the male rage described by Giddens – which, to his credit, he re-identifies as an unsophisticated strategy to encounter, if not negotiate, change. This narrative of male displacement and ensuing rage is among the more familiar stories of heterosexual change. The changing status of women in all spheres of life has threatened masculine power in the home – and, by implication, in the bedroom. There is a tacit acceptance of the radical feminist critique of heterosexual living here – if the rage occurs at the loss of power, then perhaps it is the case that the mourned-for relationship was based around power, not love, as alleged. The demand for equality and respect seems to make heterosexuality unworkable, for a while at least, while straight men learn to adapt and appreciate the values of intimacy.

Alongside the outcomes of women's changing consciousness, actual and perceived, come more tangible signs of change. Male rage in the West has become a subject of study in relation to economic change, not relationship difficulties. The backdrop to women's entry into public life has been a very considerable set of changes in the world of work, the autonomy of nations and the status of labour. The home life that reproduced and supplemented a previous era of work – with the male breadwinner supporting the young family in return for the sexual and domestic service of an economically dependent wife – has become a minority pastime, one more exotic fetish among many. In a new era of post-Fordist working practices, the particular pleasures of playing the male breadwinner are a very expensive habit – by force, even men choose help with the bills over the entitlement that comes from being the only wage in the house. Younger men know that women must work too (*Independent on Sunday*, 17 December 2000, 'For the man who has everything …; women are becoming more powerful by the day, yet predicted crisis in masculinity hasn't happened. In fact, men are finding that the new world order suits them rather well.').

The real yelp of male rage and policy concern is that these new economic arrangements have led to irrevocably different domestic set-ups – not adaptations, but something else altogether. Without the cement of economic dependency and social disprivilege, straight couples break up – even when they are married, even when they have children. In the process, men can become distanced from the enriching processes of family – and society as a whole realises that the old-style family performed a multitude of unpaid tasks (Castells 1997).

In the Britain of recent years, this anxiety around changing domestic arrangements has been expressed largely as a nostalgic lament for what has passed. As I will discuss in a later chapter, the long reign of the new right played heavily on this fear and resentment of a changing world of sex. The more recent ascent of a highly moralistic centre-left inherits this concern about the demise of the family, albeit with a more understanding voice:

> Many families today experience huge strain. Relationships are breaking down at a rapid rate; more and more children are growing up in disrupted families; birth rates are in decline; and there is a serious tension for many between the demands placed on them to be good parents and spouses and to be high achievers in an increasingly competitive workplace. Our very notion of family itself appears to be threatened.
>
> (Wilkinson 2000: 111)

Helen Wilkinson and her colleagues at Demos have argued that the new holism of the Third Way – the dreamed-of centre-left consensus that will rule for a thousand years – must incorporate creative responses to family change:

> Families are the foundation of civil society, where we first learn moral values. Families generate social capital – the trust and relationship skills which enable individuals to cooperate. Family breakdown is a major factor in declining social capital and wider social dysfunction. The state has an interest and a role to play in preventing this.
>
> (Wilkinson 2000: 112)

This proposal for a Third Way in family policy echoes the other third ways in its attempt to straddle traditionalism and radicalism, to be champion of both authoritarian family values and flexible personal changes. As a result, this account celebrates marriage and the traditional family in the whole-hearted and excessive manner that we have come to associate with the right – marriage becomes the model of all good social relations here, a precious entity to be nurtured and protected by state policy. With marriage, the family is depicted as most effective when built around the heterosexual couple – only this formula can guarantee the stability that children need to become productive and law-abiding citizens. Alongside this cheerleading for old-style domestic relations comes an acknowledgement that households have changed – marriage may be best, but social changes have made other ways of living. People co-habit in straight or gay couples; couples break down, whether or not they are sanctified by marriage; adults raise children alone or in couples that change membership over time; families are reconfigured through divorce and reconstitute simulacra of the traditional family by amalgamating children of past relationships into the care of the current partnership. These shifts make the new social arena that the Third Way attempts to address – it is these changes in private choices that make up the bigger patterns of public life.

This is an interesting acknowledgement, because now the private choices of sex and affection are seen to create the crises of social cohesion. Instead of remaining private and unconnected to the larger business of government, society is depicted as the outcome of collected personal choices – and, as a result, personal choices become a key site for engineering social change. Rather than trying to shape and contain the scary forces of the global economy, fostering different kinds of personal relationship seems to offer an easy route to crime reduction, cutting care costs, ameliorating poverty through social support, and combining the essential messages of traditionalism and empathy in government. Even more than rightist appeals to family values, this Third Way focus on the centrality of particular family formations to healthy social relations transforms the mythical ideal family into the prime political agent – the audience to which all political rhetoric is addressed and from which all political mileage comes.

However, although this elevated status brings some family issues into public debate, others remain noticeably absent. Issues around the economic and time pressures on family life enter the discussion as the constraints that determine personal choices, but trickier issues, such as desire and the variation of sexual longing over a lifetime, are elided. While the vulnerabilities of sexual life may open new possibilities for governmental practice, sex is too unruly to fit easily into such instrumental projects.

Despite the adherence to conservative conceptions of family life and relationships, the proposals for another route in family policy do introduce some positive benefits for those interested in increasing both personal freedom and group well-being. For the project of this book in particular, this re-evaluation of the role of intimate life in other social relationships opens new possibilities of understanding the interaction between private and public lives. This is a conception of the family that recognises that important aspects of everyday experience, such as sense of security and well-being, stem from the quality of personal relationships – and perhaps most importantly from the affective relationships that we choose, and through which we choose to nurture others. Instead of being relegated to the status of an idiosyncratic hobby, here, sexuality, among other affective connections, can assume a pivotal role in social stability and our resilience in the face of change. If heterosexuality is changing, this change is part of wider shifts – and this book argues that the significant shifts in the arena of sexuality include a decline in the status of the West. We live with all these indications that sexuality – even in its most mainstream manifestations – is changing, perhaps all the time. It is like a slow-moving glacier we stand on and move with – believing we are on solid ground even as the scenery changes all around us.

Every time I save this document, a question comes on screen, 'Do you want to replace the existing heterosexuality?' The discussion that follows attempts to provide an answer.

2   History

Position of the chapter – universality

This is the position that arranges bodies into the timeless essence of sexuality – that absolute kernel of human experience that transcends all context, all cultural influence, any trace of passing fashion – to grip limbs and genitals into that same special feeling that all lovers have felt throughout time. Despite the unpromising premise that there is nothing new under the sun and that every gasp and caress is no more than a repetition of rituals so old they have no origin, in fact this is some exciting position. In this embrace, all lovers feel their easy connection to the eternal.

In this chapter I discuss attempts to document and understand sexual behaviour across different times. The study of sex in history has taken a number of forms and the chapter reviews the investments of various approaches – from the assertion that sexuality is characterised by a common essence in all locations to the view that historical variation reveals sexuality to be a product of culture not nature. Here, I return to the suggestion that we are witnessing a period of significant change in cultures of sexuality and argue that attention to history can aid understanding of these contemporary events (for more on debates about sex and history, see Bartlett 1988; Nestle 1988; Halperin 1990; Scott 1993).

Before anything else, and certainly long before I can persuade you that sex will be the key to all sorts of exciting new forms of social and political understanding, there must be some agreement about what this 'sex' is. The difficulty is not in distinguishing sex and gender – that debate about the difference between biological traits of sex and the social structures that give meaning to the cultural construction of gender has been rehearsed effectively elsewhere (for an early exposition of this distinction, see Rubin 1993). Neither is it in the slippage between act and identity, from coupling to lifestyle. The question is the failure to agree any common definition of sex. Even at the point of contact, when doing the deed itself, there can be confusion about when it is happening, when it is over. Across short time spans and other people's experience, there is no way to verify a standard referent. Across longer time spans, little is left apart from the heavily coded traces of a million fantasies. How can anyone know what went on or what it meant?

Is there a history of sex?

The question can seem obvious – of course, all human activity has a history. Some histories may be better documented than others – and some may be deemed more trivial and less worthy of extensive study – but no aspect of human life is beyond history. Everything takes place in the context of its moment.

However, this question can trip up some of our lately learned cleverness. In as much as there is a longer tradition of scholarship, the question has been answered by examples of sex throughout history. The history of sex is written as a series of vignettes depicting the sexual theatre of each epoch. These are the habits of intimacy in Ancient Greece, these are the rituals around sexual contact in Victorian England – or, in more orthodox versions of historical documentation, these are the loves of great men and this is their secret impact on great events (Aronson 1994). The impulse has been to agree too quickly that sex is recognisable and inevitable – and then to get to work to discover its hidden location in more secretive times. In these accounts, there is no doubt that we know what sex is, or that this is what sex has always been. Like food and sleep, sex is a constant throughout human history – one of those things that we weak creatures cannot do without. Historical writing must only uncover this constant thread to reveal one of the great enduring themes of human existence.

More recently, the question has been heard differently – not so much has there been sex in history, but does the concept of sex itself have a history? This is a very different kind of question – can we conceive of this most natural and instinctive of activities as a historical construct? The earlier discussion about the invention of heterosexuality prepares us here. While bodies have bumped throughout time, perhaps this bumping becomes sex only in certain circumstances? Perhaps the requisite circumstances vary across time and place?

Clearly, bodies have touched in some manner throughout time, and some accounts of this touching may appear to be poignantly familiar to us, the contemporary audience – however distant in time and place. The question 'does sex have a history?' attempts to defamiliarise these most emotional of experiences – and asks what commonalities can exist across such gulfs of social experience:

> Sex, like being human, is contextual. Attempts to isolate it from its discursive, socially determined milieu are as doomed to failure as the *philosophe's* search for a truly wild child or the modern anthropologist's efforts to filter out the cultural so as to leave a residue of essential humanity. And I would go further and add that the private, enclosed, stable body that seems to lie at the basis of

modern notions of sexual difference is also the product of particular, historical, cultural moments. It too, like opposite sexes, comes into and out of focus.

(Laqueur 1990: 16)

So this is another form of sexual knowledge that is torn between good sense and soft hearts, between the well-learned lesson that all human experience is made through context and the obstinate desire to find some enduring and constant emotion at the heart of the human condition. The suggestion here is a little more than the trite exclamation that everything is historical – there is an attempt to nudge us out of our familiar sense of physicality as an absolute baseline of sexuality. The first layer of understanding shows that sex is different in each moment, made by its own context. The second layer uncovers the larger realisation that sexuality may not be a changing constant throughout human history, dressed in the garb of its time but always there. Instead, sexuality itself emerges at certain times in relation to the invention of the privatised body.

Contemporary mythologies of love and sex can posit these attributes as essential components of the human condition – and our investment is in the idea that all people in all times have wanted and needed exactly these same things. Popular understandings of the past tend to assume that people are people, with the same wants and needs wherever and whenever they live. It is hard to imagine that codes of intimacy, physical pleasure and emotional attachment have been constructed differently for other times, perhaps so differently that a contemporary reader could not recognise this bundle of activity and feeling as sex. However, once we accept that social meaning is made through a complex contract in any moment – informed by historical traces but adapted by the constraints of immediate context – sex must be part of this contract of the moment. The expression of sexuality must be determined by wider social structures – it is how this happens that is difficult to chart.

Of course, the initial admission that sex must be defined and made in the moment of activity is the easy part. Although it goes against the fantasy that sex is an eternal essence that binds all lovers across time, the suggestion of a private contract of recognition taps into another myth of sex, i.e. that the moment of interaction is absolutely unique each time, beyond recognition, repetition or communication. Acknowledging the historicity of sex gives lovers back the special secret of their affair – because the complex destiny that brings two unique individuals together in that moment can never follow the same path twice. What is more difficult is conceiving the process through which this determination of meaning takes place.

Looking for clues, signs and other mementoes

Historical understanding demands some comprehensible documentation – and although the range of acceptable sources expands to include any mark or trace that can be deciphered, without these codes to break there can be no historical translation. However, even if documents can be found, there is a question about what emerges as the relevant and conspicuously sexual component of the information. How does a contemporary reader recognise the traces of sexual life in documents from another time and place?

Think about the manifestations of sex in different moments. Some recent work has outlined the manifestation of sex in earlier periods – contributing to the varied and emerging sub-discipline of the history of sexuality (Marcus 1966; Bray 1982; Hitchcock 1997). That work has tended to use multiple sources, from official records and from everyday culture, in order to depict sexual culture as textured and multiple. The difficulty is, still, how to find records of actual sexual behaviour. The official depictions of law courts can reveal quite detailed and intrusive narratives – but here the sex has already been reworked into an offence (Norton 1992; Moran 1996). Often the narrative comes from non-participants – or when participants speak, there is an erasure of their desire and agency, perhaps in response to the fear of official punishment. Other kinds of document – erotic literature, popular song – provide another order of information, more aspiration and interest than actual practice (Rotenberg and Mirsky 2000; Neret 2001). Inevitably, what we are left with is an account of public discourses about sex, with little sense of how these discourses relate to everyday sexual behaviour. Tim Hitchcock explains this dilemma:

> We need to question more rigorously the silence which preceded the development of a language of sexuality. We need to look again at the unrecorded sexual behaviour which came before the rise of mandatory heterosexuality and 'natural' sexual difference.
>
> (Hitchcock 1997: 7)

But, as his work shows, looking at unrecorded sexual behaviour is no easy task. Again, we are left with a variety of other records and a space to speculate about sex. Unlike many other areas of historical enquiry, the attempt to write plausible histories of sexual life must reconstruct an account of largely undocumented activity. There is little evidence of what took place, between whom, where, when or why, let alone any clues to what it all meant to those taking part.

Of course, there are well-known historical stories that can accommodate an account of sex. Instead of demanding a self-conscious document of sex itself, this is a way of insinuating knowledge about sex from more general and well-documented historical accounts. Yet the danger remains, how can a construction of the sexual past avoid ordering evidence according to the sexual codes of the present? David Halperin comments on the intransigence of this problem:

> That some people might not have a sexuality to express, or might have sexual

experiences unassimilable to modern sexual categories, was seldom a practicable conclusion to draw from the evidence uncovered in the course of the research.

(Halperin 1990: 7)

If you are scrutinising documents for evidence of an activity that you expect to recognise, then what is unrecognised escapes analysis. If there is no necessary continuity between contemporary sexual understandings and past cultures of sex, intimacy and the body, recognising the relevant material in historical documents may be no more than luck or guesswork:

> One of the problems with the new sexual history is that it is in danger of becoming a history without a proper subject. The history of sexuality is at the same time a history of a category of thought, which, if we follow Foucault, has a delimited history; and a history of changing erotic practices, subjective meanings, social definitions and patterns of regulation whose only unity lies in their common descriptor.
>
> (Weeks 2000: 130)

The attempt to historicise sexual behaviour risks losing its object of study altogether because the process of de-recognising the apparently familiar risks dissolving all possibility of defining an object of study. If we cannot rely on our ability to interpret material or recognise significance, then meaning is hard to find. In response, historians of sexuality have returned to the story of our contemporary sexual consciousness – the history of sex becomes the particular history that leads to this conception:

> Homosexuality and heterosexuality, as we currently understand them, are modern, Western, bourgeois productions. Nothing resembling them can be found in classical antiquity. A certain identification of the self with the sexual self began in late antiquity; it was strengthened by the Christian confessional. Only in the high middle ages did certain kinds of sexual acts start to get identified with certain specifically sexual types of person.
>
> (Halperin 1990: 8)

Key terms are specified here. Sexuality is divided into *homo* and *hetero* in the moment of other modern, Western, bourgeois productions. Modern because this narration of self from activity is possible only with the larger change in cultures of the self – as I will go on to discuss. Western because the ascription of identity from sexual acts occurs within the modernity of Western ascendance – and the particular conception of sexuality as space apart can take this form only in the separating spheres of Westernised living. Bourgeois because all these processes are enabled by the social changes of technology and economic development – and the Western self is a prime product of the long, perhaps never quite finished, bourgeois revolution.

There are a number of central assumptions here:

1   that sexuality can form an identity name – and that this is what distinguishes sexuality from just sex;
2   that sexuality is a version of self-narration and therefore requires a machinery of self to exist;
3   that sexuality is a historically specific concept that organises the bumping of bodies into a particular cultural experience.

These three sets of issues and the questions that they raise have become central themes in recent explorations of the history of sexuality:

> The invention of homosexuality (and, ultimately, of heterosexuality) had therefore to await, in the first place, the eighteenth-century discovery and definition of sexuality as the total ensemble of physiological and psychological mechanisms governing the individual's genital functions and the concomitant identification of that ensemble with a specially developed part of the brain and nervous system; it had also to await, in the second place, the nineteenth-century interpretation of sexuality as a singular 'instinct' or 'drive,' a force that shapes our conscious life according to its own unassailable logic and thereby determines, at least in part, the character and personality of each one of us.
>
> (Halperin 1990: 26)

The wider debate about the historicity of sexuality addresses these issues and links sexuality to the development of a larger culture of self. This literature is shaped by the concept of self as a discursive construction. Jerrold Seigel (1999) presents the intellectual history of selfhood as revolving around the three modes of the material or bodily, the relational or social, and the reflexive or self-positing dimensions of self. The emergence of sexuality links aspects of each mode – at once a manner of narrating physicality, marking relations to others and between different spheres of sociality, and as an arena of that key technique of selfhood, interiority. Intuitively, sexuality would seem to represent an essential component of modern conceptions of self, particularly the self who is conceived as the bounded subject of possessive individualism. What remains largely unwritten is the connection between the birth of the subject as a bounded individual who lives a segmented existence and the articulation of sexuality as a key characteristic of that subject's humanity. However, in relation to the concept of sexuality, an older scholarship of individualism may illuminate a later debate about desire and subjectivity. The literature seeking to outline the birth of the individual has focused largely on England. The argument has been that the cultural event of possible individuality has enabled many other social changes – most importantly, the changes in economic life that gave rise to early capitalist formation (Macpherson 1962; Cassirer 1964).

With this development, other changes occurred – some have been documented as the spread of the concept of an inner life or of a developing consciousness of individual life story. If sexuality is the changeover from a series of activities to a narrative of personal attribute, then the advent of the individual is part of this process. After Foucault, this story has more often been told as the emergence of a modern culture of self – and there are clearly overlaps between the concepts of self and individual. However, my interest in the account of individualism comes from the idea that this cultural event could create new economic relations. By implication, the organisation of sexuality is acknowledged to have a shaping effect on other aspects of social arrangement. It is worth reviewing this process in relation to some of the key terms of modernity – and to show that the new cultural possibilities that emerge from material changes must themselves have an impact on material culture:

> We can trace the emergence of an increasing social and epistemic privatization that leads to the idea of the individual, for better or worse, as we understand it today. The development of a palpable awareness of self can be followed through the changes by means of which it is produced, beginning in the Middle Ages when information first begins to accumulate – the increasing number of family and self-portraits; the increasing popularity of mirrors; the development of autobiographical elements in literature; the evolution of seating from benches to chairs; the concept of the child as a stage in development; the ramification of multiple rooms in small dwellings; the elaboration of a theater of interiority on drama and the arts; and most recently, psychoanalysis.
>
> (Stone 1996: 19)

What is being described is the changing machinery that enables the conscious narration of self – not one absolute shift in technology or social relations but a gradual accrual of various techniques of staging self. The representation of the individual and the increasing importance of a self-conscious presentation of the visual self form one aspect of this process. However, equally important is the shift in everyday spaces and habits of occupying domestic space, with buildings and furniture enabling ever-greater individualisation (Bryden and Floyd 1999). Alongside both these trends, the longer-term development of a language of selfhood that describes the life-course as a journey towards self leads right up to the present-day scrutiny of all our psyches. Sexuality takes the role of the privileged illuminating component of the sovereign self – one of the essential secrets that can unlock the meaning of interior life and public display. Sex is the key to this double-faced mystery of selfhood, because sex is one enabler of the bargain of privacy. Once interiority becomes a mark of subjecthood, the dangerous magic of the hidden becomes the best secret of all (Steedman 1995).

Within this larger history of emerging and increasingly self-conscious selfhood, sexuality exemplifies some central aspects. In this account, determination is a two-way process – the self takes shape in relation to a variety of forces, from the change in economic activity to the spatial relations of domesticity. Yet the emerging possibility of selfhood also wields its own determining influence, enabling the larger shifts of economic development and national expansion. The question becomes – does sexuality have its own motor of history – or is it an ephemeral phenomenon determined by something more basic? Do the practices of sex constitute a closed system, altering across time in response to the dynamic of their own internal disequilibrium? Or is sex always made by a context beyond the thing itself – an outcome of the complex system of social meanings and practices of any moment? Like so many other either/or questions, neither option is quite right, of course. Despite the various mythologies of sex as a separate sphere, it is unlikely that bodies ever meet, touch, bump and grind, free from the habits and expectations of their social context. Yet, equally, sex is not some final moment of determination – the predictable outcome of a series of functionalist structures. There is something resilient and other about the sexual, some aspect of this experience which is not a performance of an extended economic structure or the choreographed finale of a dance of etiquette. In this, sex resembles other aspects of everyday culture, neither completely autonomous of social structures nor a passive object of more powerful forces (see Sayer 1987).

What is at stake in this convoluted debate is the nature of social determination; the degree and type of resilience of such everyday cultural forms as sexual practice reveals something more basic about how the world is shaped. Because, whatever larger economic and political forces are inscribed on sexual practice, in other ways attitudes and practices around sex effect change in themselves. This is the argument of the puritanical right – that sexual freedom is most dangerous because it will encourage people in the pursuit of other, more dangerous, freedoms. It has also been an argument of the liberationist left – but this moment seems far away now (for a view from the right, see Scruton 1986; for an account of sexual politics from the left, see Chapter 3). Academic analyses of everyday cultures have saved their best and most affectionate energies for the detail of ordinary life, both because the secrets of all social life are inscribed in these details and because these details illuminate something about the building blocks of all social life. Understanding the logic of people's most mundane and precious moments is the first step towards understanding the changing selfhood that makes new social relations – the detail promises to reveal the kind of agent we have all become.

Sex is that kind of detail. Hidden in the strange and various investments of contemporary sexual behaviour there may be a clue as to what makes contemporary social relations. Charting the history of sex provides a model of how this relation is articulated. The question of what motors this process, however, remains. If the struggle over the means of production makes the history of economic relations, does some other process make the history of sexual interaction? Or, if the actions of nation-states through war and diplomacy create the narrative of international relations, does some other set of dealings set the plot of interpersonal relations? When we analyse these large historical processes, there is an assumption that the dynamic of change comes from within the object of interest – to see economy, you look at economic relations; to see statecraft, you look at government. Does the realm of the private and intimate demand a different approach, or is there an arena of the sexual which makes the history of sex across time?

Accounts of the structuring process of sex borrow from other traditions, squeezing the contradictory evidence of sexual life and its variations into the functionalist requirements of economy or state or nation. Although this approach offers a mechanism to connect one realm of experience with another, the complexity of lived cultures rarely fits tidily within such abstractions. The problem is moving from broad and plausible hunches to an account of how the myriad spectrum of behaviour comes from larger social determination. In the end, the new history of sex plumps for this conclusion – sexual behaviour cannot be reduced to a simple effect of any larger structure, but some aspects of the organisation of sexuality can be traced alongside other developments. Perhaps each adapts and reinforces the other?

It is worth considering why we have invested in the sameness of sex across time. Despite all this academic good sense, it is hard to accept that love songs of another time do not speak to our own special passion. How can these words and images from other times and places touch us so deeply? How can we be wrong when we feel our most secret intimacies depicted so accurately by those we will never meet? This is one of the recurring themes of this work – the idea that sexuality is special, unlike other orders of experience, and that it is like this because of our excessive investment in it.

In part, I argue that this is tied to the pursuit of knowledge – and that, after the limit of the soul, sexuality has come to function as the unfathomable secret of human existence. Sexuality comes to represent the ultimate object of knowledge – the core of the body and of the spirit, sensation and emotion, lust and love – but also the teasing reminder of how far from perfect knowledge we are.

Although good academic sense proves that sexuality cannot be the secret core of humanity which transcends time and place, doesn't desire convince us that it is, again and again? It is as if sex is recognisable and similar for everyone, whenever they are alive. What kind of scholarship wants to smash this magical dream? The rest of this book argues that sex is, actually, special – for this time, if not for all times.

Can we understand secrets and fantasies across time?

The available documentation of sexual life tends to take the form of secrets and fantasies. We can pretend that this is not the case, if only to hide our shame at intruding so rudely into someone else's best and most private space, but traces of sex are not like other historical traces:

> Somewhere in the late eighteenth century, confession as penitence became confession as interrogation. It was channelled into diverse discourses – from the case-history and scientific treatise to scandalous tracts such as the anonymous *My Secret Life*. Sex is a 'secret' created by texts which abjure as well as those which celebrate it. Access to this secret is believed to disclose 'truth': sexuality is fundamental to the 'regime of truth' characteristic of modernity.
>
> (Giddens 1992: 21)

The suggestion is that it is the change in documentary style that makes this entity, 'sexuality'. Sex is one of the truths of the interiorised self – not the only one, but a privileged access to the kernel of the private self. The belief that this central truth can be uncovered and deciphered seeps through the culture of sexual documentation:

> Erotic pleasure becomes 'sexuality' as its investigation produces texts, manuals and surveys which distinguish 'normal sexuality' from its pathological domains. The truth and the secret of sex were each established by the pursuit and the making available of such 'findings'.
>
> (Giddens 1992: 21)

This is an account that places 'sexuality' cleanly in the realm of institutional categorisation – modernity is structured around a will to know that gives rise to a variety of inspecting machineries, including social science. Once the diverse range of erotic pleasures becomes the object of this judgmental scrutiny, practices become sexuality, split into normal and pathological forms. The abjuring texts become central to conceptions of sexual history. The will to chart the history of diverse sexual practices – and in particular to reveal that same-sex relations have been present in all times – has led to a variety of interpretative leaps. Often these jumps of reading owe as much to wishful thinking as to historical documentation. The proof of recognisable lesbian affairs or sadomasochistic practice or even of companionate heterosexual marriage can seem so stretched through the unpacking of codes, secrets and unspoken inferences that nothing much can be judged apart from the commentator's own agenda.

Of course, all historical interpretation contains this element of over-reading – many documents may be overlaid in order to cross-reference and consolidate, but the narrative of any individual life requires this leap of imaginative reading. Braver commentators have acknowledged the role of fantasy in this dialogue (Bartlett 1988). But beyond our modern push towards endless self-narrative, is there not still a wish to know things more clearly? Even the pleasures of performing self do not compensate for giving up on the possibility of knowledge. However, each document type seems to bring its own pitfalls. Let us consider some examples.

Public records, the most proper of historical records, the stuff of record offices and official documentation, have presented the history of sexuality as a series of misdemeanours and public contracts. Between sinful crimes and marriage, there is little sense of how people gain pleasure from their bodies. Private diaries, those more intriguing, juicy and revealing documents, are impossible to substantiate. Fantasy and event are indistinguishable, with no line between private recollection, guilty confession and made-up bravado. Oral history and reminiscence offer the legitimacy of first-hand data, but include all the trickery of modern-day storytelling. Every attempt to pin down documentation comes up against these cultural disguises that surround sex and its secret.

Lesbian and gay history, in particular, has sought to produce documents of community life – to make records where none exist. Central to this project has been the collecting of personal testimony. Telling stories becomes the way you know the truth of sexual life – this is where all the best secrets are spilt (Plummer 1995). However, despite the undoubted value of these community endeavours, even the apparent immediacy of first-hand accounts raises some problematic assumptions.

Assumption one is that first-person narrative is the stuff of truth. You would have thought that queer cultures, more than others, would know that performing the self, especially for an attentive, younger, oh-so-serious audience, is only distantly related to that mysterious thing, truth. That naive social gambit 'tell me about yourself' is an open invitation to work on your self, to pull together all your best resources of fantasy and popular culture, half-memory and learned-later knowledge – inevitably the narrated self that emerges is a document of today, not yesterday. This is a lesson learned by all collectors of reminiscence. Assumption two is that people tell the truth about sex. Who would not rewrite their sexual history, given the opportunity? Assumption three is that the interpretation of oral testimony is more direct and less ambiguous than the deciphering of written texts. Assumption four is that any of us 'knows' our sexual experience in a form that we can narrate to another.

Although we learn many important things from listening to sexual reminiscence, including an insight into the assumption and performance of sexual identity and the public meanings of sex, the final truth of the act itself is not available through testimony. When we hear all those sexual stories, perhaps we are listening for something else altogether?

How important is the story of the past for sexual understanding?

If sex is so difficult to uncover, always escaping into its privileged status as secret, why bother with the thankless task of history-writing at all? All too often, the cover of being 'history' has been used to make, sell and swap straightforward (and not so straightforward) pornography. Bodice-rippers use the iconography of period drama to titillate and educate. Corsetry can turn a book into a historical novel rather than a fetish magazine. As with other almost academic pursuits, most notably that of popular anthropology, the appearance of study has allowed all manner of most unseemly scrutiny. The pursuit of knowledge permits and demands very close and attentive looking at every detail, without the limits of decorum, modesty or good manners.

As with all forms of historical enquiry, a historical understanding of sex enhances our understanding of the present. In terms of the high excitement and intense anxiety that surround sexuality in the early twenty-first century, historical research can offer a number of reassurances and comforting reframings. In times when same-sex liaisons draw persecution and discrimination, a longer view can reveal the large diversity of sexual practice across societies and eras. When changes in sexual etiquette are used to incite panic, accounts of other times can show that changing sexual cultures do not lead to destruction. When the present causes us fear and anxiety, the lessons of history reveal the outcomes of earlier processes and prepare us to learn the consequences of today.

There is a question about how much any of this matters – after all, what is done is done. Unlike more earth-shattering and earth-shaping histories, sexuality remains largely private and individualised in our time. Why bother worrying about the sexual habits of the ancients or early moderns or, even, our near ancestors, the Victorians? A key motivation in excavating the sexual past is to develop a framework for understanding sex today. The past stands in as a practice run – not only a space that needs to be documented, but also a finished story in which we can chart the components and see the ending. The promise of historical enquiry is that it will yield a model of knowledge – economy plus social convention will interact with local cultures and organised religion to construct the individual narrative in this way, rather than that. Once you have an idea of this process, the present can be comprehended as a determining system – an ongoing story that will one day have an outcome.

Recent accounts of global change themselves hint at the sexualised logic of history. Turbo-capitalism is such a sexualised image – voracious, unstoppable, with a great big extra power motor that bowls over everything in its path. Perhaps the lived outcomes of the processes encapsulated in that metaphor are also turbo-charged. If we are witnessing such epoch-changing events, can it be that sexuality is not also altered? Not randomly, but in response and relation to these other global shifts? Although the various critiques of the dream of absolute determination have lead discussion away from the identification of any determining forces, however partial, historical work can offer ways of plotting the shaping forces at work in social settings (Sayer 1987). None of this is fail-safe, and some is an act of faith. However, there is something about the deductive process in historical accounts – perhaps particularly in such speculative areas as sexuality – which lends itself to contemporary translation.

So much has been written about the rapid changes of recent life that it is hard to remember what is happening and what is hype. However, it seems safe to suggest that something has been taking place – and although these shifts may be no more speedy or earth-shattering than previous movements in global relations, they are significant. Against this, gay history has often assumed the existence of a transhistorical sexual identity – this is 'our' past, the truth of a long-standing community forced into silence and hiding by bigotry and persecution:

> Much of the most interesting work on sexuality in feminist and gay and lesbian studies has been historical in character rather than devoted to contemporary issues. This has led to significant tensions between historical studies which emphasize continuity, often framing the past in terms of current categories, such as gender or gay, and the present oriented social constructionism of sociological and anthropological approaches to sexuality which treat categories such as women or gay as contemporary categories.
>
> (Parker and Gagnon 1995: 10)

Rather than replicate this debate about whether contemporary categories of sexual identity have existed throughout time, this chapter has focused on the idea that sexuality is itself a historical category. Rather than focus on minority sexual identities, it is argued that sexuality has been constructed as a field into which a range of individual insertions occurs. This has been the lesson learned from Foucault – that sexuality emerges as a varied discipline of self. This contract makes us all, but can encompass many variations of disciplined subjecthood. If anything, it is this network of differential positions that characterises modern sexual identities:

> Sexuality is not the most intractable element in power relations, but rather one of those endowed with the greatest instrumentality: useful for the greatest number of maneuvers and capable of serving as a point of support, as a linchpin, for the most varied strategies.
>
> (Foucault 1979a: 103)

Foucault argues that there is no universal strategy for the instrumental deployment of sexuality – instead, sexuality plays a role in many objectives and through many means. The emergence of the homosexual does not take place as a moment in the larger and ongoing project of heteronormativity as such. Rather, the figure of the homosexual emerges as one outcome of a machinery of power and knowledge, a machinery that links and shapes a series of social categories. Foucault summarises these disciplinary structures that emerged at the beginning of the eighteenth century as 'a hysterization of women's bodies; a pedagogization of children's sex; a socialization of procreative behaviour; and a psychiatrization of perverse pleasure' (Foucault 1979a: 104–5). Through this network of processes, women's bodies have come to be seen as filled with a sexuality that constantly threatens to become pathological, children have become repositories of a latent sexuality that must be controlled through education, the reproductive couple has been coaxed and harried into becoming an instrument of economic and social goals, and, in the separation of normal and pathological sexual behaviour, the pathological has taken the status of medical affliction. The much-discussed invention of the homosexual is one moment in a chain of revised meanings. Rather than some spontaneous emergence of new demons, some more subtle shift across the terms of maturity and sexuality, of domestic and public life, comes to bear. The outcome is a consolidation of masculine privilege through adaptation. At the beginning of the twenty-first century, the traces of these four themes can still be seen in the public organisation of Westernised sexual life. Later chapters will revisit these issues – and perhaps the consideration of historicity will illuminate those discussions.

How can we narrate sexual acts?

The question that reappears through all the many diversions of sexual history is – what is sex anyway? All attempts at understanding the meaning and practice of sex stumble at this question. Once sex is revealed to be contextual, not natural, there is no biological certainty to fall back on. Sexuality is as changeable as other aspects of social living – and as enclosed in the meaning systems of its time.

In the course I teach, we spend an early session trying to define what sex is – to list the activities that count and those that do not. Certain themes come up again and again – an initial fixation on genital contact, an expansion to include more diffuse practices of petting and courtship, a confusion about the competing determinants of act and response. Is it what you do, or how it feels and makes you feel that make it sex? And is everything sexual the same as sex itself? Much discussion centres on the importance of orgasm – is this what makes it sex? And if it is, how do we account for the strange and various ways that people reach climax?

Ultimately, it becomes difficult to settle on anything more than an agreement that sex is what people experience as sex – while recognising that sex can happen without this naming of experience. After this debate, every brushed shoulder on the bus, lingering glance in the street, breathless teenage expectation, becomes part of the sexual act. Pretty soon juicy fruits and hot baths, exciting pictures and clean pyjamas seem to be part of sexual experience too. The demarcation between sex and other sensual experience is hard to maintain – and the demand of orgasm does not fit many people's accounts of their sexual lives. In the attempt to identify sex as more than what feels nice, we are left pointing to what feels very nice – knowing all along that sometimes sex does not feel nice at all.

We try to retreat back into easy liberalism – what does it matter? Sex is whatever you want it to be. But, of course, if it is worth studying, then we must have some idea of what it is and where it lies. If not an absolute object, at least a vague area, there must be some route-map to the study of sexuality. Otherwise, there can be no study at all. The drift into including all human life in the arena of sexuality – a suggestion that clearly has some truth to it – prevents any focus on the particular business of sex. There must be some way of marking the boundaries between sex and other kinds of interaction.

In order to unpack this difficult discussion, I have used references to more recent histories, because these events seem close enough to understand and interpret. Luckily, the history of the relatively recent past throws up a tasty example of the role of definitions of sex in big-boy versions of history.

The strange spectacle of the Starr Report suddenly threw confusions about the definition of sex into the centre of public debate. Kenneth Starr led the team with the difficult task of investigating the allegations of sexual and constitutional misconduct levelled against Bill Clinton, then president of the United States. Although the world media may have pretended that what was at issue was the constitutional role of the President of the United States, the world's audiences were gripped by the peculiar detail of the interaction between Clinton and Monica Lewinsky. Most entertaining of all was the strange formality of the legal wrangling about what constituted 'a sexual relationship'.

In the report of the investigation, the account begins with a statement of certainty. There is no doubt here about what constitutes sex – and the evidence is plain and verifiable.

> Physical evidence conclusively establishes that the President and Ms Lewinsky had a sexual relationship. After reaching an immunity and cooperation agreement with the Office of the Independent Counsel on July 28, 1998, Ms Lewinsky turned over a navy blue dress that she said she had worn during a sexual encounter with the President on February 28, 1997. According to Ms Lewinsky, she noticed stains on the garment the next time she took it from her closet. From their location, she surmised that the stains were the President's semen.
> (Starr 1998: Section B.1 Physical Evidence)

Blood tests confirmed that the stain was 'the President's semen' – and this became the framing 'fact' of the discussion of sex. The tested fact of the semen stain made this sex, conclusively – even though the stain was on a dress, even though no-one knows how it got there. The whole sorry affair was obsessed with the mystical status of the President's semen – he withheld his orgasm despite her entreaties, in response she made a fetish of his emission, saving the traces beyond any normal concern for hygiene or good fashion sense.

During the media furore I speculated – what if Clinton was wearing the dress? Does the trace of semen still prove the existence of a sexual relationship? What if he came on the dress without her even being there? What kind of a date ejaculates on your dress anyway?

Despite the firm assertion of the opening paragraph, the report is less conclusive about the nature of sexual relations. In the beginning it seems as if the trace of semen is the determining feature – but the meanderings that follow, and the strange details of what did take place, make this less and less certain.

When giving his version of events, Clinton avoids the term 'sexual' altogether. Instead, his admissions centre around the idea of intimacy – a more old-fashioned and romantic term, with warm connotations of closeness and sharing:

> Testifying before the grand jury on August 17, 1998, seven months after his *Jones* deposition, the President acknowledged 'inappropriate intimate contact' with Ms Lewinsky but maintained that his January deposition testimony was accurate. In his account, 'what began as a friendship [with Ms Lewinsky] came to include this conduct'.
>
> (Starr 1998: Section C.1.b Sexual Contacts, the President's accounts)

The inclusion of the qualifying 'inappropriate' is important here. The spectrum of intimacy allows us to imagine a gradual progression from friendly closeness to inappropriate physicality – as if the different incarnations of intimacy blur into each other, without any volition from participants. The concern to define sexual relations does not include discussion of inappropriate, and, by implication, appropriate, contacts – the concern is only to pin down whether or not what happened is sex. The shift to an idea of inappropriate intimacy opens the question of what is permissible where and between whom. For Clinton, it also opened up the possibility of a common-sense denial:

> The President refused to answer questions about the precise nature of his intimate contacts with Ms Lewinsky, but he did explain his earlier denials. As to his denial in the *Jones* deposition that he and Ms Lewinsky had had a 'sexual relationship,' the President maintained that there can be no sexual relationship without sexual intercourse, regardless of what other sexual activities may transpire. He stated that 'most ordinary Americans' would embrace this distinction.
>
> (Starr 1998: Section C.1.b Sexual Contacts, the President's accounts)

The defence is that the electorate is fixated on the spectacle of heterosexual intercourse – and, therefore, this must be what constitutes sex. As well as his brass-necked audacity, there is something admirable in Clinton's appeal to popular belief. Penis in vagina, perhaps that is what most Americans understand by sexual relations – maybe everything else is an addition or an extra or a side-dish, but never the thing itself:

> The President also maintained that none of his sexual contacts with Ms Lewinsky

constituted 'sexual relations' within a specific definition used in the *Jones* deposition. Under that definition:

[A] person engages in 'sexual relations' when the person knowingly engages in or causes – (1) contact with the genitalia, anus, groin, breast, inner thigh, or buttocks of any person with an intent to arouse or gratify the sexual desire of any person … 'Contact' means intentional touching, either directly or through clothing.

(Starr 1998: Section C.1.b Sexual Contacts, the President's accounts)

According to what the President testified, his understanding was that this definition 'covers contact by the person being deposed with the enumerated areas, if the contact is done with an intent to arouse or gratify', but it does not cover oral sex performed on the person being deposed. He testified:

[I]f the deponent is the person who has oral sex performed on him, then the contact is with – not with anything on that list, but with the lips of another person. It seems to be self-evident that that's what it is … Let me remind you, sir, I read this carefully.

(Starr 1998: Section C.1.b Sexual Contacts, the President's accounts)

In the President's view, 'any person, reasonable person' would recognise that oral sex performed on the deponent falls outside the definition:

If Ms Lewinsky performed oral sex on the President, then – under this interpretation – she engaged in sexual relations but he did not. The President refused to answer whether Ms Lewinsky in fact had performed oral sex on him. He did testify that direct contact with Ms Lewinsky's breasts or genitalia would fall within the definition, and he denied having had any such contact.

(Starr 1998: Section C.1.b Sexual Contacts, the President's accounts)

Although one of the most notable heterosexual scandals of the twentieth century, the so-called Lewinsky affair succeeded in making the heterosexual proclivities of the world's most powerful man into a strange perversion.

Based as they were around the avoidance of intercourse, the described interactions illustrate an alternative theatre of sex in which roles and actions are both more stylised and more fluid. What went on between these two people is very far from the official script of heterosexual sex. In one reading, he was almost exclusively passive – exposing himself and waiting for pleasure to be given. In another, the focus was upon her pleasure and he gave up his own desire to his service to her. Nowhere in the narrative is there any sign of the biological imperative that corrals men into penetration. And despite his reputation as a greedy womaniser, there is little indication of a reckless pursuit of personal pleasure. His shameless and detailed denial embraces the role of her object – no more than the meat on which she performs. The public rituals of heterosex cannot explicate the strange dynamic of this case.

After all the scrutiny, what sex is seems more uncertain than ever. For all the intensive discussion, scrutinisation and speculation, it is hard to pin down the moment when this interaction goes from being sexual to being sex. And this is in relation to an event that has thrown up huge reams of documentation and in which the key protagonists were subject to careful and public questioning. If we cannot identify the moment of sex here, what chance do we have of reconstructing the sexual behaviours of less notorious players?

Does it matter if we cannot?

Without some possibility of narration, sex is consigned to the always unspoken realm of absolute privacy – unthinkable, elsewhere, sublime and impossible. Although there is some attraction to this properly romantic notion, so that sex constitutes some new sublime for our time, absolute silence hardly describes the culture of sex in any time or place recorded (for more on the politics of the romantics and the strategic place of the sublime, see Thompson 1998). Something is always said. The question remains – what is the relation between these representations, suggestions, rumours and fictions and the actual acts of sex in any time?

Perhaps the past is another country – lost in its own culture and context, beyond our foreign understanding. But, in the manner of other boundaries, we can imagine as much familiarity as strangeness in our encounters.

Familiar themes re-emerge in our attempts to grapple the essence of sexuality to the carpet. Is this the same eternal essence that we have sought through all time? Or is this the kernel of the sea-changes of our turbulent times? Do we look to the past for reassurance of what we still are? Or to understand how far we have come? In one quite obvious way, the manic interest in all matters sexual can be regarded as another aspect of *fin-de-siècle* madness (see Showalter 1991).

Whether we take turbo-capitalism or globalisation or the advent of the mythical Third Way as our hook, plenty of contemporary discussion tells the history of the present as the beginning of a whole new era, the shift into a new paradigm. The suggestion makes sense because everyday experience seems to confirm the idea that we are witnessing rapidly changing social relations that remake all our lives. Most often this is told as the fragmentation of known stability – rapid movement of people, break-up of families, the loss of affective bonds of community, an end to mutual dependence between employer and employee (Luttwak 1998; Soros 1998; Giddens 2000). Alongside nostalgia for old, lost ways, inevitably new habits and possibilities appear. However, there has been so much understandable attention to the immiseration caused by globalisation that it is easy to forget or underestimate the glamour and attraction of these new possibilities. So imagine for a moment that some of the more pleasurable aspects of contemporary living also arise from this paradigm shift moment.

We could regard our time as a new era of self-fashioning, in which a fresh mythology of self-authorship pervades people's dreams and aspirations. This is a world in which the new entrepreneurs become the new rich – in an unexpected and dramatic rewriting of the role of entrepreneur. The break-up of old ties gives rise to fresh and perhaps freeing performances of identity, because even the much-missed entities of family and community have always held their own punishing disciplinary regimes. Similarly, the loss of working-class affluence and stability is a form of release from class identity – although who would have known that this freedom from class would be worse still. Alongside turbo-capitalism, social science has identified the rise and development of other parallel phenomena. These can be summarised as gender shift, plastic sexuality and identity through consumption. These are the multiple processes that give rise to new forms of gender roles and relations; the emergence of a deep belief and investment in the malleability of sexuality and the role of sexuality in achieving personal fulfilment; and the growth of techniques of self that rely on performance, style and the adornment of commodities. The study of sexuality can allow us to consider whether these other processes are outcomes or contributors to turbo-capitalism.

Turbo-capitalism can be seen as a time of all-round reappraisal – a time of significant shifts in many areas of social life, with rapid relearning of many sorts. We can consider the contemporary heat and excessive interest in matters of sexuality as an aspect of this global shift. Whatever our investment in historical understanding, it is quite likely that previous models of relations and determination will be adapted by new structures – because this has been a time of significant shift in processes of capital, formations and workings of nation-states and international relations and cultures of self. Feminist writing has pointed to these large-scale changes in the private lives of the West (Faludi 1992; Segal 1994).

Our task is to provide route-maps for some key areas of sexual culture and to suggest their relation to wider social changes. This chapter has approached the history of sex in two ways – one, by questioning our ability to comprehend sexual experience across time, the other, by suggesting that sexuality is itself a historically specific concept. The implication has been that it is more fruitful to consider the emergence of sexuality as a historical event than to worry about our uncertain ability to document real sex lives. I want to argue that there is some benefit to accepting a failure of understanding and that sex stages that limit particularly effectively.

When we think of narrating the strangeness of nearby, with imperfect linguistic mastery, so that comprehension of any sort is an effort of attention and interpretation, we see a model of scholarship that demands diligence and promises disappointment. Unlike versions of education that pretend to explicate, organise and package up the world once and for all, this is a much older attitude to study. Here the student must learn attentiveness in order to fail properly – and the moment of education is captured in this diligent failure, as opposed to the non-educative failure of laziness. The study of recent cultures of the everyday, which mainly promises to be up to the minute, flash-bang exciting and glamorously star-studded, holds the possibility of this other scholarship. The following chapters suggest some lessons in studious patience and distraction.

3   State and economy

Position of the chapter – instrumentality

In this position, all parties achieve just enough pleasure to keep going – the main benefits are to other people altogether. In part, this is about the pleasures of servicing the greater good – so personal pleasure is extended to become a much more socialised experience. However, the particular piquancy of this position also arises from an acceptance of constraining discipline. The hotness comes from allowing only the smallest release, under duress – and the excitement comes from the frisson of taboo, so that we can all be naughty teenagers forever.

In this chapter I return to the impact of social forces on sexual choices and behaviour and review debates that suggest that, far from representing a space of free choice and expression, sexuality is subject to control and manipulation by economic imperatives and state interests. The economic advantages that are gained by various sexual cultures and the connections between consumerism, work and docility are considered. In the second part I reconsider British debates about hegemony and sexual cultures and review recent developments in government interest in sexuality. The key debate within the chapter is the question of whether sex can be subject to instrumental concerns that are determined by larger social forces (see Weeks 1989; Parker *et al.* 1992; Singer 1993).

Despite all the talk of spirit and training, the *Kama Sutra* offers a highly instrumental account of sexuality. This is not the instrumentality of reproduction – the making of babies hardly troubles the many variations of coupling that are described and advocated. Instead, this is *kama* as an all-round life skill. The training is designed to utilise the benefits of sexual skill to best effect – and best effect goes beyond pure and immediate pleasure. The instrumentality of the *Kama Sutra* falls into two types – the immediate wish to maximise pleasure for both parties and through this to render your partner pliant to your wishes, and the impetus to use sexual skill to impact upon wider social relations beyond the bedroom. Both forms rely upon the effects of sexual technique and knowledge, so attention to the wider world does not exempt the student from studying the *Kama Sutra*. However, the acquisition of sexual skill is never quite the end in itself that is implied. Instead, after the injunction to couple within or below your caste and not with the wife of your friend, we are presented with a long list of permissible exceptions to these rules. Each exception is allowed for worldly and instrumental purposes.

Although this detracts from the romantic version of eastern eroticism so celebrated through the translations of the *Kama Sutra*, the exceptions give an insight into the role of sex in wider negotiations of power and position. This is an acknowledgement that the networks of sex overlap with the networks of public life – there is no suggestion here that sex is a realm apart. We need only look at some of the allowed instances of sexual contact, the exceptions to the main rules, to grasp the impact of sex on other aspects of life:

> This woman has gained the heart of her great and powerful husband, and exercises a mastery over him, who is a friend of my enemy; if, therefore, she becomes united with me she will cause her husband to abandon my enemy.
>
> (Burton and Arbuthnott 1993: 120)

It is true that the text identifies the realm of public power as the domain of men – and, by default, the parallel realm of sexuality which impacts upon these public relations becomes the domain of women. Each instrumental exception identifies a woman who becomes fair game because of her social connections and role – she is the secret route to public struggles. But despite this imbalance, underneath the skewed gender roles, there is a larger lesson about sex and politics.

If, instead of a domain of men and a domain of women, we think of human endeavour as split between public struggle and intimacy, the instrumentality can be seen as a trick between arenas rather than between men and women. The point is not to use women as an alternative route to the structures of power; it is to use the other value system of *kama*, the peculiar weaknesses and empowerments of the realm of intimacy:

> By making this woman my friend I shall gain the object of some friend of mine, or shall be able to effect the ruin of some enemy, or shall accomplish some other difficult purpose.
>
> (Burton and Arbuthnott 1993: 120)

Sexuality offers an alternative politics of alliance. Although the public world makes no explicit acknowledgment of its impact, difficult purposes can be achieved through an appeal to these alternative values:

> This woman loves me ardently, and knows all my weak points; if therefore, I am unwilling to be united with her, she will make my faults public, and thus tarnish

my character and reputation. Or she will bring some gross accusation against me, of which it may be hard to clear myself, and I shall be ruined. Or perhaps she will detach from me her husband who is powerful, and yet under her control, and will unite him to my enemy, or will herself join the latter.

(Burton and Arbuthnott 1993: 120–1)

The demands of sex also threaten to upset the achievements of the public world – not least because the lover is a different character with different attributes in each realm. While the skills of the lover may entice collaboration in the aims of public betterment, withholding a lover's touch may lead to punishments that register in public life.

Hidden in this discussion is an account of why sex is important to the world of big politics, the realm of economy, state and nation. Much of what has been written in this area assumes that sexuality is shaped by the larger events of the world – so that intimate life shows the markings of economic change or state intervention, more superstructural froth to some more basic structure. Part of the argument of this section suggests that sex has some impact upon those larger endeavours and that the secret routes of intimacy have repercussions in the world of public affairs.

> The time has come to think about sex. To some, sexuality may seem to be an unimportant topic, a frivolous diversion from the more critical problems of poverty, war, disease, racism, famine, or nuclear annihilation. But it is precisely at times such as these, when we live with the possibility of unthinkable destruction, that people are likely to become dangerously crazy about sexuality. Contemporary conflicts over sexual values and erotic conduct have much in common with the religious disputes of earlier centuries. They acquire immense symbolic weight. Disputes over sexual behaviour often become the vehicles for displacing social anxieties, and discharging their attendant emotional intensity. Consequently, sexuality should be treated with special respect in times of great social stress.
>
> (Rubin 1999: 143)

The obsessive heat around sexual matters that characterises contemporary public life reveals the faultlines in our social order. Although Rubin does not account for why sex takes on this symbolic weight, as opposed, for example, to food, her argument identifies an indisputable tension around sex in contemporary cultures. The extreme anxieties caused by rapid social change have, in recent times, been articulated through highly charged debates about sex. This can stretch from the policy concerns of the Third Way, to concerns about the boundaries of nation and blood, to confusion about the sexual status of children. Each instance of concern about sex – and a concern that ranges beyond any rational conception into the realms of crazy fantasy – illuminates a larger social tension.

This chapter suggests that the solutions to these sexualised problems also offer an insight into what might soothe other social ills.

Is sex a slave to money and power?

There are two streams of instrumental pressure in debates around sexual policing – one is the interest of the economy, of capital, and the other is represented by an idea of the state or government. Often, these two can be collapsed or confused, with an assumption that the state is little more than a function of capital anyway. The following discussion will attempt to disentangle the two arguments while acknowledging their interconnection. The key overlap, of course, is the account of sexuality as a malleable entity reshaped for non-sexual ends.

This kind of determination talk can become so familiar that we forget what is actually being said. So, think for a moment of your own most intimate desires, the irrational and intoxicating impetus that drives you towards another's body, the added sweetness of life with sex – and then imagine all this as a detail of a financial plan or a government programme – worse than this, a plan or programme not written by you. In this account, sex loses its own rationale – it is no longer an end in itself. Instead it is a trick that uses our enjoyment and emotional investment to fulfil some other goal, to make us conform, behave, buckle down.

All the talk about desire being remade for instrumental ends, the implication that capitalism and/or government meddle in people's otherwise free and natural sexual choices, assumes that capital and/or the state require certain sexual identities and behaviours, or at least require some more than others. So this is the first big idea in the sequence – everyday sexual behaviour plays an unforeseen and functional role in larger economic and political projects. This suggestion raises, of course, a series of questions. What kinds of sexual behaviour receive this sanction and why? How are individuals cajoled and coerced into adopting the favoured behaviour? What are the penalties for disobedience?

None of the existing discussions can account for the continuing variety of sexual expression – even in situations in which there are clear privileges for favoured lifestyles and harsh punishments for dissenters. The ability of individuals to wilfully pursue their own erotic satisfaction, even when against the grain of societal rewards, appears to undermine accounts of instrumentality. Whatever master plans exist, individuals resist – we all fervently hope. Rather than discount the possibility of sex being shaped by other forces altogether, the discussion that follows tries to allow room for individual agency while exploring the impact of economic and political constraints.

This chapter straddles two related debates – one that suggests that sex is constrained by economic concerns and another that suggests that the state actively intervenes in the sexual expression of the populace. The suggestions are connected – both assume that sex can be reworked, channelled and disciplined by larger forces and for instrumental ends. However, where one set of debates focuses on the processes by which good workers and consumers are made, the other is concerned with the even more nebulous notion of the good citizen. These attributes – good at working, good at buying, good at behaving – present a necessarily simplified account of social living. Critiques of these various theories of determination have pilloried this reduction of human lives to mere functions of larger structures – and, as a result of this, attempts to chart the process by which a social structure determines another activity appear clumsy and dated (Thompson 1978). Who believes that the world works in such a simplistic way any more? However, despite this fall from fashion, I want to retrieve the suggestion that sex is made through larger forces and through particular interests.

Whatever the complexities of the process, the question remains important and interesting for a number of reasons. First, the issue of determination replaces sex in a historical and social context and retrieves its formation from the omnipresent grip of nature. Second, raising the question of interest in relation to sexual behaviours upsets the fiction of sex as a realm apart, somehow beyond the dirty deals of other social relations.

The assumption of the question needs to be unpacked before we even look at the arguments – what does it mean to suggest that economic relations require back-up from affective relations or sexual behaviour? The previous chapter has raised the question of determination and the boundaries between separate spheres. Here the issue is to plot in more detail the possible chains of influence from one arena of life to another. Although there is no overall theory of determination here, certain themes emerge in the descriptions. Sex fits in around the regimes of work. Sex informs the conception of fulfilment through other means – and, equally, consumption becomes sexualised as a substitute eroticism in itself. This debate about capitalism and sex spans plenty of time and ground – and has been a theme in left discussion forever, despite its more recent fall from favour. In other times, liberation movements of various persuasions have demanded sexual freedom as a central and non-negotiable tenet. What is freedom without the freedom to love, after all (see Marcuse 1966; Reich 1970; Weeks 1985)?

For our more knowing times, sexual freedom can seem to be too innocent and too complicated a goal. We know very well that freedom in this regard is complicated – that one person's freedom can become another's abuse, that the illusion of hedonistic free-play can veil ugly social relations, that an activity as highly socialised as sex can never be experienced as freedom in any easy sense. However, the question about the constraints upon sexuality remain. Even if there is no demand for sexual freedom, do people not want to preserve some autonomy in their sexual lives? Is not the incursion of economic concerns or state imperatives regarded as an unwarranted liberty? Most of all, do people not wish for some element of privacy and tolerance in their sexual lives? Even if sex is not regarded as the marker of absolute freedom, there is an expectation that sexual choices belong to the individual and are not the proper subject of state scrutiny (see Chapter 7).

In terms of political organisation, the question has been whether the pursuit of sexual freedom (and we will come back to what that might mean) can be integrated into other forms of political agenda. Most of all, the question has been whether the self-indulgent quest for sexual pleasure can be reconciled with the more urgent struggle for basic living standards or social equity (Phillips 1983).

At its worst, this debate has degenerated into a caricature of sexual politics as no more than an excess of bourgeois culture – never progressive, and sometimes dangerously reactionary. Once again the left has chosen sour-faced pleasure-hating as its arena of choice (for an account of this, see Ollman 1979). Against this, others have suggested that certain disciplines of sex are essential to social order and the everyday terror required for profit to be made. Here repression takes place in both public and sexual arenas – social order is maintained through this dual agenda (Reich 1970). The implication is that the ideological and actual policing of the public sphere requires the additional docility engendered through the shame and repression of desire in the private sphere.

More recently, greater analysis of consumption and the channelling of pleasure for politically conservative agendas has changed the shape of the debate. Commentators have suggested that as long as people continue to work and buy in a disciplined manner, their sex life is of no interest or consequence to social order and the pursuit of profit (Singer). In fact, quite the contrary, sexual experimentation and diversity can itself offer another great opportunity for sales. This can be seen most clearly in the area of explicitly commodified sexual services. In this marketplace, greater sexual awareness and better knowledge about varied and alternative practices gives rise to new areas of economic exchange:

> Market segmenting has also been a useful strategy for expanding the market for sexual services. Part of this involves a logic of specialized sexualities, each of which can then be fetishized in its differences through a capital- and commodity-intensive erotic aesthetic … The economic advantage of specialized sexuality is not only proliferation (more kinds of sex, more kinds of supportive instrumentation), but the creation of a differential economy of access and availability, a kind of erotics of supply and demand, which allows certain sexual practices to be proferred at premium prices, given their presumed relatively limited availability.
>
> (Singer: 48)

Finer gradations of difference in sexual taste facilitate the formation of niche markets – each requiring specialist equipment, publications and confirmation of community. The mainstream take-up of sadomasochistic iconography illustrates the potential of the cross-over market – with leather and rubber fetish gear widely available, although often of poor quality and highly priced, revealing the low production values and large mark-up in the market for sexual equipment. In Britain, this proliferation has taken place during a period in which the British state has defended its right to prosecute those engaging in consensual sadomasochistic activity (see Thompson 1994a; for an account of the whole case, see http://www.barnsdle.demon.co.uk/span/span1.html). This official and explicit taboo has developed while the popular representation of SM has increased and general awareness of SM practices has become widespread (see Madonna's (1992) infamous book, *Sex*). These processes seem to have occurred in parallel, without explicit acknowledgement of each other – much as I would like to argue that the state intervenes to make some practices appear more transgressive and therefore more saleable, Operation Spanner, the policing operation that arrested a group of gay men for engaging in consensual sadomasochistic sex acts, was never a widely publicised affair. If anything, this incursion into our freedom to choose our own sexual pleasure has taken place covertly, too embarrassed to proclaim its quest to protect the nation's morals. Linda Singer offers an account of the commercial possibilities of sexual taboos:

> The very division of sexualities becomes an erotic mechanism of perpetual stimulation and incitement and also maximizes sites of profitability, positions within the economy from which profits can be made: experts, aesthetes, procurers, and prosyletizers.
>
> (Singer: 48)

Singer describes the thrill of commodification as sexual proliferation – more, and of more types, the endless thrill of the new. This is a return to the root of commodity fever – the mystical aura and frenzied pursuit, described by Marx, owes its heat to the language of sexuality.

This account of sexual markets also allows another conception of the sexual actor. Here, rather than the rather vague constructions of discourse, there is an indication that some roles are made through the market. There are new kinds of sexual-economic actors to be because the market has changed – so profitability extends beyond familial respectability and debased sex work to include a variety of other roles. Of course, the new roles may overlap with the old, so that the proper wife may learn to extol the benefits of her peculiar tastes, perhaps as an aid to marriage. Or the aesthetes who specialise in the most practised and ritualised services may sell their wares through the standard markets of prostitution.

This kind of account echoes the earlier accusation that the pursuit of sexual pleasure is a celebration of bourgeois values – although it might be more accurate to say that this sense of entitlement to bodily enjoyment belonged more to aristocratic cultures. Overinvesting in sex makes people forget to fight for freedom – instead of political organisation, we all seek out individual therapy, counselling, the perfect relationship. By making good sex the best and most elusive object, we all forget that fulfilment could entail greater goals.

Citizenship and sexuality

Debates around the concept of citizenship have centred on the question of how to combine both rights and responsibilities, or how to reach a balance between the two. Whereas rights accrue to the individual as a means of exercising freedom, responsibilities imply that the individual must fulfil some obligation to society. If rights let you do what you want, responsibilities tell you what you must do (for an introduction to these debates, see Lister 1997). The relationship between individual and state is a tussle between these two pulls. Histories of state intervention into sexual practice have fallen into the second model – injunctions to obedience for some wider social good, often calling for abstinence from certain practices or some other limiting of sexual expression.

In Britain, the machinery of the state emerges as a scrutinising presence in a variety of everyday locations. This is the inspecting state that watches and collates, that wields power through this documenting and surveillance and that hails citizens as a series of characters in the theatre of national order. This is the state that learns to create the disciplined subjects of Foucault's account. Sexual practice is part of this disciplinary order, covertly in the manner of social engineering in health and sanitation, and overtly in the figures of the homosexual and the prostitute. These are the criminalised creations that mark the boundaries of respectability – at the defining edge of the contract of familial and national order. This is not a boundary that requires absolute prohibition; instead, sex law is framed to render deviance visible. This can be seen in the framing of the Contagious Diseases Acts of 1864, 1866 and 1869, which attempted to register prostitutes and enforce medical inspection as a means of containing the spread of sexually transmitted diseases among servicemen. Rather than outlawing sex work, this legislation enabled state scrutiny of women's bodies and movements (Walkowitz 1992). Similarly, Labouchere's infamous amendment to the Criminal Law Amendment Act enabled a greater criminalisation of gay men – by changing the punishment for sexual contact between men from life imprisonment to a maximum of two years hard labour, the amendment enabled easier and more numerous convictions (Bartlett 1988; Fisher 1995). In both instances, the linked figures of homosexual and prostitute are made more conspicuous by the exercise of law. The more recent framework of the 1967 Sexual Offences Act, which still forms the basis for much sex law in Britain, outlaws sexual contact between men in public, with public defined as a space in which a third person may be present. The notion of the public has, problematically, included hotel rooms and bedrooms used by couples while others are in the building. Although the Sexual Offences Act is remembered as the legislation that decriminalised consensual sex between men (over the age of 21, now amended to 18, but still awaiting amendment to 16 and parity with heterosexuals), this act has also led to more convictions of gay men and the development of a new machinery to scrutinise the boundaries of this very limited private space (Jivani 1997). In effect, decriminalisation has led to new levels of homophobic vigilance in the quest to keep public space clean of this depravity.

In the light of these intrusive interventions, debates have focused on limiting the power of the state in curtailing the personal freedoms of sexual choice. This has involved both a resistance to criminalisation and the conspicuous making-visible of legislative and popular understandings of sexual diversity and a claim to the right to privacy and protection from the scrutinising intrusion of the state. More recently, there have been attempts to imagine a more positive version of sexual citizenship – to develop a way of thinking that attends to entitlement and an expansion of individual possibility under the protection of the state (for an account of these debates, see Richardson 2000).

The ideas about state and economy that we have reviewed so far do not allow for this positive citizenship that brings the benefits of rights. Broadly, these are accounts that endorse the idea that the state is a function of capital, however mediated this relation may be – government intervenes in order to meet economic imperatives (Therborn 1978). This is the body of thought that depicts the state as an extension of the ruling class, a social machinery that allows those with wealth and power to safeguard their own positions. In relation to the policing of sexuality, this idea has been most fully developed in the work of Wilhelm Reich. Reich sought to link the insights of psychoanalysis to the revolutionary politics of Marxism. Writing through years that saw the rise of popular fascism across Europe, Reich argued that sexuality became distorted by the requirements of capital, and that this distortion opened the door to authoritarianism. Reich argued that the emergence of patriarchy had taken away any pleasure in work or other activity – so that now activity was motivated by a sense of fearful duty. This alienation from the self-justifying pleasures of human activity gives rise to 'impotence and fear of life' – and this, according to Reich, 'forms the psychological basis of authoritarian dictatorship' (Reich 1973: 8).

Reich argues that capitalism represses and disciplines sexuality in order to suppress the power of orgasm. Once alienated from their orgasmic potential, individuals submit easily to the drudgery of work without pleasure or empowerment and cease to demand the satiating fulfilment of sex in any aspect of life. What is lost in this desensitised sexuality, the sexuality that takes its constrained and guilty release in the snatches of time around the working day, is the vision that sensuality could be achieved in other spheres of life, including work:

> The structuring of masses of people to be blindly obedient to authority is brought about not by natural parental love, but by the authoritarian family. The suppression of the sexuality of small children and adolescents is the chief means of producing this obedience.
>
> (Reich 1973: 8)

For Reich, both social and political evils must be addressed by retrieving the disrespected power of sexuality. Only by relearning a non-alienated relation to sexuality can we resist the intimidation of authoritarian regimes, be they in the form of the totalitarian states, or the Church, or academic organisations, among communists, or parliamentary governments (Reich 1973: 11). Cultures of sex are the key to organising for greater liberty in this account.

There has been a fall from favour of this libertarian model of sexual politics. As we have discussed, this politics is too heavily linked with the demands of the sexual revolution and the associated descent into permissiveness. The call for a general end to repression is rarely heard in contemporary debate. Instead, more recent attempts to imagine sexual freedom have sought to operate within the broad terms of citizenship. In some cases, the objectives of equal rights for lesbian and gay people and freedom from discrimination on the grounds of sexuality have been pursued through the machinery of the state itself, although in Britain this has more often been a tactic within local government (Cooper 1994). Alongside this engagement with the formal structures of the state, there have been suggestions that citizenship may require an attention to the business of sexuality. This argument is exemplified in Ken Plummer's concept of intimate citizenship.

Plummer refers to T. H. Marshall's theorisation of citizenship as revolving around three areas. These can be summarised as the right to justice under law, the right to be politically represented and the right to basic welfare and well-being. To these three, Plummer proposes to add a fourth, the realm of intimate citizenship, a form of citizenship that can answer the new needs arising from the changing structures of social life:

> For some, natural hierarchies of order and dominance, of a fixed place in the world with a fixed agenda, of a stable story, are visibly crumbling. Now, and I suspect increasingly in the future, people may have to make decisions around the *control (or not) over* one's body, feelings, relationships; *access (or not) to* representations, relationships, public spaces, etc.; and *socially grounded choices (or not) about* identities, gender experiences, erotic experiences.
>
> (Plummer 1995: 151)

This is the arena of intimate citizenship, the spaces of choice and ethical judgement in relation to bodies and contacts, ways of being and ways of touching. Plummer suggests that the social changes of recent years leave us facing new dilemmas in these areas, dilemmas that reach beyond the scope of existing discourses of public citizenship. Negotiating this new terrain demands new forms of social understanding and agreement, a suggestion that is taken up in later chapters of this book.

Does the state care what people do with their bodies?

It is not clear that capital or the state has an interest in the acts of sex themselves. The complex mesh that polices sexual behaviour, stretching from the unspoken contract of social norms to the state persecution of minorities, seems to operate more through ideas of public identities and allegiances than through an explicit prohibition of particular acts. And, as we have discussed above, the state may police in a manner that appears to contradict the market – and equally, the market may show no interest in selling the sex that is most highly valued by the state. Although monogamous heterosexuality remains the most celebrated life-choice in political speeches by all parties, little energy is exerted selling accessories for this sexual choice. Although many aspects of consumer culture encourage and reward heterosexual living arrangements, there are few attempts to sell the pleasures of heterosexual sex as sex. Instead, commodified sex aids extol the pleasures of group sex, public sex, SM sex, voyeurism, swinging, unexpected casual encounters and excitingly scripted scenarios that must be paid for in advance – nowhere is there any sense that the supposed social benefits of marriage could be sold as erotic adventure.

Even at this level, there is some disparity between the interests of the state, as explicitly stated, and the interests of (some sections of) capital – what makes easy cash doesn't seem to be the same as what might make an orderly society. Equally, the easy cash of the leisure industries may transform people into greedy consumers who lack the discipline to be good workers. In part, I want to suggest that the sex police are more interested in maintaining public norms than in crushing all diversity of practice. Investment in the closet is an issue of public culture – the closet is itself an admission of diverse sexual behaviours, so what is at issue is not the behaviour in itself, but the punishment that can come from speaking this diversity publicly.

To explore the manner in which states may intervene in sexual behaviour, let us consider another kind of example.

> [W]hereas state regulation in the Maoist period focused on policing 'bad' class subjects and 'deviant' sexual subjects as a way to normalize national identity, the state in the era of market reforms turns its attention to problematic economic and political behaviour. This is not surprising, given the emergence of important new categories of people such as investors, professionals, sex workers, tourists, and urban consumers.
>
> (Ong 1999: 63)

It is helpful for us to consider such an explicitly interventionist state model – Westerners understand the hand of the state clearly when speaking about Maoist China, in ways that seem harder to grasp in relation to so-called Western democracy. Whatever the shifts in the world order, Westerners remember their well-nurtured fear of the totalitarian regimes of the East. This is a model of state regulation that is easy to understand – the ruling elite adheres to an explicit master plan and enlists the participation of large sections of the population in order to adapt overall behaviour. In the process, the pleasures and value of individuality are lost and many suffer for their attempts to resist. Although this account cannot help but play on this mythology, I want to consider Ong's example as an indication of the impact of global capital on cultures of sex. Rather than describing the authoritarian state and its accommodation of sex cultures, this is a point about the sexual imperatives of globalisation. Nations of many political persuasions, despite local misgivings, find the project of national government adapted by the demands of the global economy. The key point here is the tension between local political demands and the pressures of the global.

What Ong describes is a shift from state intervention for the purpose of national order and the construction of obedient subjects of the national project towards state intervention designed to best enable market-led behaviour. Whereas previously social order was seen to be best served by encouraging uniformity and limiting the irrational impulses unleashed through sexual freedoms, now sex occupies a more ambiguous role. While, on the one hand, the development of an illicit market for commodified sex brings new threats of criminal disorder, on the other the circulation of more varied sexual services and practices enhances the entry of everyday cultures of the market. Potentially dangerous subjects gain new value as bearers of market cultures:

> However, these new subjects are critical to the booming Chinese economy both as producers and consumers, and the loosening sexual mores are considered part of a general liberation from the oppressive past and an aspect of the economic 'opening' (kaifang).
>
> (Ong 1999: 63)

Even semi-legal sexual activities can contribute to economic growth. If we believe Singer, the existence of weakly policed taboos can create better business opportunities. A sense of increasing sexual freedom becomes the sweetener that makes the difficult process of economic liberalisation more palatable. After all, how threatening is sexual diversity compared to the risk that people might resist the incursions and disciplines of the market? This is Ong's conclusion – that sexual permission (of the sort that enhances the entry of the market) can be welcomed by a state that wishes to encourage new kinds of economic subject:

> Policing not sexual freedom but political ideas and economic norms that might weaken the power of the nation is the focus of state concern as the new transnationalized spaces within the body politic destabilize a coherent national imaginary.
>
> (Ong 1999: 63)

The changes brought by global processes decentre the power of national government and offer individuals access to many new styles of being. In this context, perhaps fostering an addiction to commodified sexual experience is a way of limiting more politically or economically disruptive behaviour? This is not to say that all sexual diversity and expression is tolerated; China, in particular, has sought to limit the range of commodified cultural expression, with devastating results (see Shanor and Shanor 1995). However, there is a sense that the desire to dance with the forces of global capitalism, to become open and receptive to the market, also enables participation in the rituals of commodity-centred heterosexuality.

Policing implies an active campaign of intimidation, a force that is unleashed for some particular end – and that end has largely been theorised as an interest. Again, there is an assumption of easy instrumentality – if I kick this transsexual, the wider population will work harder at their jobs; if the government celebrates marriage, there will be less resistance to social injustice. But, of course, the chain through which these goals could be met, even theoretically, is anything but straightforwardly linear. The confusing disciplines of commodity-culture can remake the boundaries of permission and policing, until it is hard to discern the line between prohibition and encouragement.

Can the state ever successfully control sexual activity?

The questions of earlier chapters re-emerge here. Sex remains so secret in its actual lived detail – who can tell how the public stories fit the hidden behaviour?

When George Orwell used sexuality as both the method of discipline and the first point of resistance in the novel *1984*, he was indicating something peculiar about the status of sex (Orwell 1954). Even in the most regimented of future nightmares, in which desire is effectively disciplined and allowed in controlled outlets, a more unruly version of sexuality juts out to disrupt this absolute regime. Although this is 'just' a story, the temptation to have sex of your own choice stands in as an emblem of all that is beyond total control.

The example of liberalising China is important here – economic compliance is more desirable than sexual uniformity, and, contrary to earlier thinking, constraining sexual expression may not ensure the right kinds of economic and political subject. Ong seems to suggest that access to some commodified forms of sexual freedom is a veil for the loss of more significant rights – an argument that seems to echo very old leftist critiques of the decadent West. Where Ong's account differs is in the inclusion of versions of this opinion from mouthpieces of the Chinese state – the official account almost says that sex is an acceptable and controllable freedom, unlike the desire for justice and 'democracy' (for an account of sexual repression, see Evans 1997; for the tension between human rights and economic liberalisation, see Santoro 2000).

Consumer culture benefits from sexual diversity. Uniformity may keep people scared and unwilling to experiment in any arena of their lives – maybe even accepting the excesses of brutal authorities by forgetting their own capacity for pleasure. But uniformity is poor turf for commodification. Everything we have learned in recent years about shopping shows how important market segmentation has become (Bowlby 2000). Not only in the marketing of everyday products, but also in a host of other calls to the general public, differentiation has shown itself to be the only game in town. The varying constraints and encouragements in sexual culture show the signs of these competing calls – towards uniformity and towards a differentiated market.

Recent popular-right thought has argued that capital and state are in direct opposition – with the progressive and democratising force of capital facing constraint from the despotic tendencies of old-fashioned nation-states. In the era of turbo-everything, it is worth considering this suggestion. If the rapid and shape-changing intensification of capitalist relations is eroding identities, relationships, communities and all other affective bonds all over the world, then, by default, people must find other ways to be.

Most discussion of the role of the state or capital or international relations or some other unquestionably real and public political structure in sexual practice has begun from the assumption that sex is somehow pre-social and is therefore shaped, belatedly, by social forces. Although there is no sense that sex has an essential nature – because we have all learned those critiques only too well – there is a covert assumption that sex is there to be worked upon by the social. We might manage to stretch our imaginations enough to see entities such as class, race and gender as constructions that are hailed through the social, having no independent or previous existence – but sex, surely that is always around in some form or other? While the commentaries never quite suggest that sex is timeless and natural, there is a sense that sex runs through all contexts and is altered by the forces of the moment, but always existing independently of them.

We have discussed already the investments in seeing sex as timeless, rather than historically figured. Here we look at the consequences of viewing sex as part of the terrain across which the social is written. Of course, alongside all this talk of sex as a constant feature of all societies, there is a strong implication that sex is part of the ephemeral froth of living. On the one hand, the notion of biological impulse (not necessarily driven by reproduction, but still springing from the body in some pre-cultural form) makes sex part of the raw material of social ordering. On the other, the belief that the important business of economy and politics makes social relations, with other less central cultural activities such as sex taking shape in relation to these primary relations, makes sex part of the changeable superstructure of life. Is sex down in the basement or up in the attic? Either way, it is clear that the important story (storey?) is happening elsewhere – but the order of the narrative does change our understanding of the role of sex in social relations.

What if superstructural effects, such as sex, rewrite the hard drive of economy? Of course, this is an old and familiar suggestion. No-one thinks determination is a one-way street any more. The debates of most of the twentieth century reveal that culture, the social, the outcomes of hard material relations, all impact upon the material structures from which they spring. Determination is not a once and for all process – operating in a moment and then stuck in stasis. Instead, we all learn that the world is made in a continuous and dynamic set of relations – what is made one minute moves on to remake the next. All of which means, in a move which vindicates the troubled project of cultural studies, that culture matters because it also makes the world (see Hall and Jacques 1989).

The next step is to recognise sexuality as another component of this active culture – something else that is both shaped and shaping. The overall impetus is the same – shifts in the culture of sex may occasion shifts in other spheres of life. It is worth pausing over this suggestion. After all, once a critique becomes orthodoxy, it can be hard to remember the details of the original insight. Everyone knows now that culture matters – but who can explain the mechanisms through which superstructure transforms base? So, a short review may be timely. Let us take a detour through some events of the recent past – across a terrain that promises to remake all our intimate lives.

New Labour and the knowledge economy – cultural analysis and the Devil's work

This book approaches the key themes of the 'Third Way' through the prism of sexuality and intimate life. Although the focus is the private and secretive realm of the sexual, again and again we return to the background story of how the world has changed and is changing. The high excitement around globalisation is one part of this background story. Another aspect is the response that globalisation talk draws from the great and the good of the rich world. I am based in Britain, so I will take the British experience as my focus – but various characteristics apply to other developed economies, and I will try to indicate these connections.

A starting point is the titillating suggestion of the Third Way – not only beyond left and right, Washington and Moscow, but also beyond male and female, straight and gay – excitingly some other way altogether (on the excitement of the Third Way, see Giddens 1998; 2000; Hargreaves and Christie 1998; Blair and Schroeder 1999). So, as well as the explicit political project and its attendant style of economic management, I want to think about the wider lifestyle promise of the phrase 'the Third Way'. Because the Third Way promises to be the route you have not yet thought of, more than you hoped for or imagined, the brand-new experience of raised consciousness and playground porn. It is that expectation that draws people into the invitation to participate – as if this could be your best adventure, more than a vote or a programme of social policy, something like a new erotic high.

Although I am being facetious and optimistic, the appeal to the most intense levels of emotion is intended. If there has been an agreed shift in the manner of mainstream politics in British, it has been this recognition that Thatcher moved people, and now everyone else must attempt to do the same. Promising mere economic well-being is nothing like enough for our media-literate electorate, according to the new orthodoxy. In fact, those old-style rational arguments and lists of information come a poor second to the touchy-feely responses to such intangibles as TV appearances and image connotation. The unhappy lesson that we have all learned is that people will often neither understand nor care about many aspects of government, but that, despite this, how they feel will influence how they vote (Diamond and Silverman 1995).

There is a superior anti-media version of the critique of emotion politics. At its most simplistic, this critique implies that the important substance has been lost from political debate, and instead the electorate is being actively dumbed down through poor information and pin-up politics. Image has become everything, it is alleged – and in the distraction of this circus, bad things are done in our name. At best, this critique places the role of the media within a wider account of the media as industry (Herman and Chomsky 1994). But, as has been pointed out all too often, New Labour takes its approach from the ideology critique of leftist intellectuals (*Marxism Today*). The project is to create an alternative popular common sense – to seduce people using the tools of Thatcherism for another end. We need to review this attempt to learn from the debates around everyday culture and to appeal to people's most intimate places if we are to learn anything about sex and politics.

The sexy promise of the Third Way

In part, the Third Way becomes a cultural product as a strategic response to the right – both new and old, whatever the commentaries say (Giddens 2000). It is a response to the new right in the wish to appeal to populist agendas and a response to the old right in the wish to establish a right to rule. The outcome shows both influences – rabble-rousing and aristocratic – and sex plays its role in both themes.

Much has been said already about the impact of populist right-wing agendas on cultures of sex (Smith 1994; Weeks 1995) – so much, in fact, that we can forget that anything went before the shift to family values and individual responsibilities (and punishments). For this reason, it is worth reminding ourselves of the radical and risk-taking flavour of the project to change consciousness. Before this, changing popular consciousness was the burden and prerogative of the left. The right already owned the consciousness of the population through the falsity of ideology – no more active cultural project was necessary. Instead, the onus to appeal to hearts and minds, to change beliefs and expectations, to change society through changing consciousness, fell upon the left (Laclau and Mouffe 1985). Everyone else, apparently, was happy with things as they were.

The left has never been very happy with this burden. Its key tenets of equality and justice for all are taken to be self-evident goods. As the political expression of the will of the masses, the left has assumed itself to be beyond populism. Despite the learned discussions about ideology, the cultural project of the left has rarely touched the hearts and minds of urbanised, industrialised populations. Hence the disappointing prospects for global revolution or the parliamentary route to socialism – however extreme the contradictions of social relations, harnessing resistance into one united mass will has been no easy task.

Instead, depressingly and surprisingly, the right has reinvented cultural politics. Alongside the economic and political projects of monetarist orthodoxy, coupled with an authoritarian state policy that favoured policing over welfare, the emergence of the new right was characterised by an aggressive cultural war (Levitas 1986). Whereas previously, post-war parties of all faiths in the rich world had assumed a certain consensus about, say, a desire for full employment and social insurance to protect the vulnerable from poverty, the new right took a hammer to that belief set. This process has been extensively discussed and documented – the point here is to remember that this was a departure from previous political culture and that this departure was enabled by a propaganda war, a battle for hearts and minds (for more on the monetarist experiment, see Minford 1980; Friedman 1991).

Sadly, right-wing populism once again proved to be more effectively attuned to popular feeling (on earlier right-wing populisms, see Forgacs 1986; Betz 1994). While the left offered critiques on the cheapness of the rabble-rousing, the rabble continued to be roused. At the same time, political debate was reshaped by changes in the media – technology, ownership and audience (Gerbner *et al*. 1996). Appealing to emotion became the key to electoral politics.

In Britain, the cultural project that swung the electorate rightwards was organised around certain key themes – hot spots of feeling that strung together less appealing practices. There were public enemies to be decried, controlled and ultimately destroyed – scroungers, trade unions, criminals, foreigners here and abroad, sexual perverts and loony lefties. There were popular values to be defended – family, nation, law and order, self-reliance (for more on Thatcherism, see Gamble 1988). The terrain had been set by these successes of the right. This is not an excuse to berate the ascendant centre-left for accepting the agendas of the right. The point here is to learn from our Third Way wallah friends. The moment of British cultural theory that excited so many produced engaged analyses of the most worldly and annoying of social and political processes. These accounts attempted to construct a political understanding that could recognise and appreciate the role of popular imagination in any struggle or outcome. This is the shift that demands attention to private and emotional responses. Although there is little explicit discussion of sexuality in the analysis of Thatcherism, this is an account of hegemony that understands the irrational heat that informs popular consciousness.

When Hall grudgingly applauds the well-judged populism of Thatcherism and other new right projects, the lesson for the left is to understand the essential role of emotional hot spots in any hegemonic project. Forget the bourgeois civility of policy debate, because most of the electorate feel excluded from this distant process. Instead, build party allegiance as a team of shared feeling, tied together through the irrational but resilient tug of heartstrings:

> Thatcherite populism is a particularly rich mix. It combines the resonant themes of organic Toryism – nation, family, duty, authority, standards, traditionalism – with the aggressive themes of a revived neo-liberalism – self-interest, competitive individualism, anti-statism.
>
> (Hall 1988: 48)

This is the push towards image politics that so many despised, the point at which Britain learns that elections are won through an appeal to emotion and identity. New Labour is the result of this lesson – the outcome of a rethink that took on board that the right appeared more pleasurable and infinitely safer than even the most soft left agenda. This admission has changed the cultural project of the left – because now techniques are learned from your enemies, they are the experts in this field. In many ways, this is a highly exciting and visionary project, one of those freeing moments when it feels as if the old doctrines have lost their hold and all kinds of new and undecided things could be possible. What is more troublesome is the extent to which the political agenda remains that set by the new/old right.

So, at last, enter sexuality. Sex had been only covertly politicised previously – too much discussion could encourage transgression rather than obedience, too public an interest could disturb the carefully policed boundaries of the private and of the public. That stuff was not the business of mainstream politics – perverts came under the proper business of policing; everyone else knew how to keep their doings to themselves. Of course, none of these things were assured. Cultures of sex were changing – in part through the impact of other political changes. Post-war affluence has built opportunities for more leisure, more disposable income, youth culture and more sex all round. As any account of the post-war period will tell you, people's expectations changed. Perhaps, most of all, everyone started to want and expect more pleasure.

Although none of this has come about through explicit legislative change, the demand for individual fulfilment has had an impact on party politics. Like it or not, there has been a widespread and wide-reaching shift in sexual cultures in the post-war period. As well as expecting more material affluence, better welfare provision and increased prosperity and opportunity, people also expect that society will adapt to the changes in everyone's individual lifestyles. Sexual diversity has been only slowly and grudgingly accepted – but the significant shift to serial monogamy as the majority lifestyle choice has altered lots of other expectations.

As others have noted, this shift in sexual expectations has heralded wider changes in what people want and expect from their lives. The celebration of youth has dismantled the hierarchies of age and obedience, and for some, offered significant rewards for cockiness, risk-taking and irreverence. The emergence of a popular culture that belonged to the young working class remade class identities – now, more than occupation, class also became a matter of cultural literacy, style, deportment, with the markers of working-class identity acquiring the same diligent display and kudos of aristocratic cultural forms (for a well-known account of the take-up of working-class styles, see Hebdige 1979). Widely available and reliable contraception has facilitated heterosexual experimentation – and although later feminist commentaries have suggested that this freeing held some danger and ambivalence for women, there is little doubt that straight sex became more open and, apparently, more frequent. The mainstream accounts of this permissive culture include factors such as the trial of *Lady Chatterley's Lover* and the changing legislation in relation to gay male sex (Haste 1992).

Overall, the shift towards an expectation of individual fulfilment has come to permeate mainstream politics. Although there is little explicit mention of sex, the larger promise that life will yield immediate and personal pleasures belongs to the growth of leisure generation. Given this, it seems inevitable, with hindsight, that the burst bubble of the 1970s, when individual fulfilment became so elusive, would be associated with this earlier rush for goodies. The varied pains of that decade – from recession to industrial disputes to humiliating IMF intervention – were amalgamated into one narrative of national decline, precipitated by the greedy, oversexed and underdisciplined children of the 1960s (for an account of the effect on national consciousness, see Burk and Cairncross 1992). The answer of the new right – which was not yet recognised as new – was to rein in all this excess. Whereas, before, we had seen economic planning as a method to enable personal freedoms – all the benefits of Keynesian prosperity – now enforcement of individual discipline was proposed as a route to economic liberalism. Almost without anyone noticing, sexual propriety re-entered as a prerequisite for social order.

Of course, the right profited from the rightly and deeply felt dissatisfaction of many voters – the monsters were real enough and the horrors of inflation and unemployment, industrial decline and an insecure currency hit the British electorate both materially and emotionally. The promise to return to greatness, security and order appealed. But the appeal also depended on the hidden insight that many in Britain had felt, and still felt, excluded from the high jinks of the 1960s. Yes, there had been a party happening, but for whom? In particular, a whole range of people resented the claim of sexual freedom and personal fulfilment – because these things were clearly never meant for them. The new right picked up on this underlying seam of support and constructed a number of inter-related mythologies to mobilise this resentment (for more on the appeal of authoritarianism, see Reich 1970).

Sex becomes a shorthand for many other fears

Anna Marie Smith describes the process of creating new demons in her account of race and sexuality debates in the era of Thatcher. Unlike previous regimes that condoned the persecution of lesbians, gays and other sexual minorities without ever acknowledging that such sexual diversity existed, Thatcherism built a populist agenda around the spectre of new enemies. Part of this process was an active politicisation of homosexuality – an introduction of overt attacks on sexual minorities, as opposed to the polite silence of previous prejudice, and the widespread reporting of the dangers of gay activists who had infiltrated such key locations as schools and local government. From almost nothing, because there was almost no mainstream political discourse about homosexuality before this, Thatcherism created the folk demon of the bad queer as dangerous contaminant of the nation, in large part through the infamous legislation of Section 28, a paragraph of local government law that makes it an offence to use public money to promote homosexuality as 'a pretended family relationship'. In other words, to suggest, through public institutions, that lesbians, gay men, bisexuals and transgender people might have warm and complicated and valuable emotional lives, just like everyone else:

> The Section 28 supporters explicitly linked the promotion of homosexuality with the promotion of multiculturalism. They drew extensively upon already normalized racist metaphors around disease, foreign invasions, unassimilable 'other' cultures, dangerous criminals, subversive intellectuals, excessive permissiveness and so on. Most of the commentators on Section 28 failed to note these important genealogical linkages. They did not recognize that Powellian and Thatcherite racism had become a hegemonic discourse – that it had become so normalized and so intertwined with political discourse that all other demonizations tended to be shaped in terms of its codes, tactics and metaphors.
>
> (Smith 1994: 22)

The Thatcher government politicised sexuality through the mobilisation of long-standing cultures of racism. Almost before we had learned to analyse the everyday and mundane cultures of popular racism, the right had understood that demons could be interchangeable. Faced with an absence of mainstream political rhetoric that could be explicit about sexual practice, Thatcherism whipped up electoral homophobia through reference to well-established anxieties about racial diversity. And sure enough, the British electorate recognised an abject 'other' by any name (on the abject, see Kristeva 1982). What could be better than finding new people to hate?

> Thatcher's decision not to translate her entire moral agenda into actual policy allowed her to occupy an imaginary political 'centre' without paying a large price for the discrepancy. Because there was no credible political voice that was

more right-wing than her own leadership, she was relatively insulated from the charge that she had not completely realized her promised moral revolution.

(Smith 1994: 31)

In the end, it made little difference whether behaviour was changed or not. The point was not to realise the vision of a national space cleansed of dangerous diverse identities, only to capitalise on the popular support for this as an idea. Although Section 28 served to heighten plenty of everyday bigotry, the prohibition against giving local authority funding to any project or activity that portrayed homosexuality as a pretended family relationship also brought protesters for lesbian and gay rights back out on to British streets and, despite intentions, probably increased the visibility of same-sex choices to many.

Smith suggests that this contradiction is already accommodated in the strategy to mobilise the most grudging elements of popular imagination. This is a caricature of right populism, of course, but the caricature catches something of the truth. The embattled and disenfranchised, figured here as male, faces an array of enemies who have had it easy, unlike him. The new right articulated these antipathies: 'You work hard without complaint, but prosperity is stolen from you by these whingeing trade unions. You belonged to a great empire, but your manhood and pride has been stolen by the soft touch of privileged do-gooders. Immigrants come to take your jobs and women, and you are left with nothing at all. And in all this disarray, others have enjoyed the good times that should have belonged to you.'

Sexual disappointment inhabits each myth: 'There is a leisure economy – but not for the likes of you. There were unquestionable privileges for white men – but not now and not for you. There is sexual adventure – but always for others and at your expense. And despite all the many promises that you could take part in the pleasures and freedoms of this new society, you have never been able to do this and probably never will. More of the same will not include you – for you, better times can only come by turning back the tide.' The resurgence of the right mobilises these same mythologies, as can be seen in the troubling successes of the far right in the British elections of 2001.

This is exactly what the new right also began to do. Rather than granting any new and substantial rights to anyone, the new right began by clamping down on the excesses of others. Rather than increasing opportunity, that soft old left tactic, the right argued that we needed to increase policing. Rather than enabling greater personal liberty, the right appealed to the longing for authority and got down to telling people what they could not do.

It has taken the best part of two decades for the left to understand these processes. What New Labour has begun to understand is the depth to which people resent the interfering patronage of having good done for them – that peculiar double hatred of liberal permission and the exhortation to participate, because this is freedom and it is good for you. The right rolled up with a far tastier version of open authoritarianism

– shoring up populist values against change, telling people to stay the same and resist the new and the different because they know best, not these meddling do-gooders. Before New Labour, the left could never quite grasp this resistance to making things better – why would anyone resent more freedom? New Labour has adopted the methods of cultural studies to comprehend this strange non-instrumental response. At last, someone takes seriously the idea that culture is ordinary. Structures of feeling stop being vague depictions of nostalgia or guilt, and start to be route-maps for a new populism.

The analysis this builds centres around such hot and unpredictable topics as sexuality. If you want to identify what matters to most people, go for the areas of confusion, excitement and violence – when did sex not fall into this list? Whereas the allegiance to personal liberty decreed that sex was not an explicit part of government, because this was a private and personal matter, the right had shown how much mileage had been lost by this tactic. If anything, the right had swung into ascendance on the accusation that all the failings of the left stemmed from a failure of sexual discipline – a softness that let everything slide.

The allegiance to sexual liberality appeared to be the left's least appealing quality – up there with tolerance towards ethnic minorities and attempts to rescue the young poor from a descent into crime as key vote losers. At a time when the world seemed to be becoming more dangerous and uncertain because of widespread shifts in sexual practice, celebrating this emerging diversity irritated more than it consoled. However unlikely it seems, the right did succeed in portraying old, staid Labour as champion of perverts, home-breakers and other loose-livers – and all this was extrapolated from the only loosely adhered-to doctrine of personal liberty.

Once this was understood, New Labour set about reworking the dangerous connotations and consequences of this belief in personal liberty. This is where the complaints about covert rightism come in – New Labour covets the populist authoritarianism of the new right and the envy shows in many of its approaches and policies. But let us keep an open mind for a moment at least – because the reworking of the idea of personal liberty is not the same as a wholesale adoption of rightist anti-liberty. Giddens makes this argument – in response to the accusation that recent centre-left electoral machines represent a shift to the right:

> They [New Labour and the New Democrats] have shown that the left should listen to the anxieties that worry ordinary citizens. The traditional left's indifference to issues such as crime and family breakdown damaged its credibility in other areas where its policies were strong.
>
> (Giddens 2000: 50)

There is a significant suggestion here – more than the much repeated idea that the left must relearn its approach to the everyday concerns of the electorate. The suggestion is that issues such as family breakdown, the supposedly trivial arena of changes in sexual and domestic arrangements, in fact, have more impact on consciousness and political choices than mainstream agendas such as the economy.

It is only with this admission that the left can appreciate the depth of the right's cultural impact. Despite the extensively felt material hardships of the new right years, the attention to the cultural manifestations of uncertainty assured continued electoral success. Although this has never been said explicitly, by anyone, this is a reversal of standard left explanations of social dynamics. Even after base and superstructure, policies are designed around the assumption that if you adapt the economy, or the political machinery, or the provision of essential services, then the cultural manifestation of social behaviour will adapt in response. So, better welfare will take the sting out of changes in family life, more effective economic management will lead to greater affluence and, eventually, curb crime.

The attention to everyday cultural concerns turns these expectations around. So, if you address issues of personal responsibility in relation to family and crime, this creates a climate that can enable more effective economic management. Rather than assuming that culture is made by something more solid and basic, such as the economy, this approach assumes that an intervention into cultural experience is necessary to any other larger change. Reworking the idea of personal liberty so that it is tempered by personal responsibility is part of this approach:

> The New Democrats and New Labour have given particular attention to family life, crime, and the decay of community – a conscious attempt to relate policies of the left to what are seen as prime concerns of ordinary citizens. We need a third way approach to the family, distinct from those who simply ignore the issue on the one hand and those, on the other, who want to turn the clock back to a time before women went out to work. Changes in the family are related to antisocial behaviour and crime. Responding to anxieties about crime is seen as vital to third way policies
>
> (Giddens 2000: 4)

Again, this is one of those moments that has many left-leaning fellow-travellers reaching for our sick-bags – all those most embarrassing aspects of New Labour, the sermonising, the cheap moralism, the unreflecting paternalism, the constrained cultural choices and human possibilities. But, again, let us pause to consider what works in this approach. Most obviously, the key themes are taken from the right – family, community, crime. This has been the terrain of the right for some time. Maybe not community – the appeal to ordinary people, as opposed to welfare scroungers and extremists, hailed the population as a series of identical households, recognising their common interests even after the demise of that encumbrance, society. However, the larger point holds – the Third Way takes up the key themes of the new right and reworks them as integral parts of a left tradition. All of that cultural studies undercover work around new times suggests this strategy – the soft, old, libertarian left is just surprised by the audacity of the total takeover (see Hall and Jacques 1989; McRobbie 1994).

However, more than the themes themselves, although they are significant, the attention to the risks and tensions of everyday life marks a change in rhetoric and style. Rather than rush ahead to identify the underlying causes of these disruptions – because government has a role in managing the underlying shifts of society – the new approach is to give weight and space to the experience of fear. Whatever we may feel about the appeal to bigotry and traditionalism, this is some big lesson to learn. And the lesson is – pretending to always know best has been part of the problem. For all the rushing to provide quick fixes, popular dissatisfaction has not stemmed from a failure to find quick enough solutions. Instead, the suspicion has been that our elected representatives do not have the first clue about the problem, how it feels, why it matters and, importantly, why it is so hard to fix. Thatcherism recognised some of this, but gave space to the experience of disjuncture only to promise to return everything to how it once was. Blair pushes the approach a step further – listen to how often he admits that we do not know the answers, that we live in times of change that are uncomfortable and unpredictable – that doubt is our shared experience.

Although Giddens rightly identifies the anxieties that surround changes in family life and also acknowledges that women will never return to their role as domestic angels, he skirts over the issue of sex. We hear about family break-up and women in the labour market, about lone parenting and new narratives of family life. We even hear about the growth of single living. But the place of sex in all these changes is rarely spoken.

Third Way thinking responds to the upheaval in everyone's personal life that is occasioned by new cultures of sex and intimacy. Unlike previous left accounts of the private and intimate, the Third Way acknowledges that the fruits of sexual freedom are not always straightforwardly enjoyable. In this there is a danger in veering towards the view that there is no pleasure or value in the pursuit of sexual freedom – and at these moments New Labour most resembles its new right predecessors. However, allowing space and articulation to the discomforts of these social changes catches the moment cleverly. Most people probably do not want to go back to the old days and ways – but they do feel the pains of new ways that are still being learned and adapted. Unlike Thatcher, New Labour avoids scapegoating the broken home – because which home remains unbroken these days? What New Labour recognises is that people remain deeply troubled by marital breakdown – even and perhaps especially when the marriage is theirs. Although relatively few people in Britain will experience lifelong monogamy, many believe that it is a good thing – maybe they even believe it is what they want, however much their behaviour militates against it.

New Labour recognises and gives space to people's fears and discomforts about changing cultures of sex, but never once suggests that we can go back to how things used to be. Although the outcomes of changing sexual cultures have been identified as a key source of contemporary angst and social disharmony, it is worth remembering that this same cultural shift has enabled the growth of Third Way thinking. The chapters that follow trace the ramifications of these widespread uncertainties on cultures of sex at different levels, from national identity to the requirements of citizenship to notions of propriety. New routes through sex and politics are part of learning to live with the threats and possibilities of the global.

4   Fragments of identities

Position of the chapter – performativity

In this position, pleasure comes from the style of being rather than from any technique. This is a manner of sexual engagement that loves theatre and spectacle. Instead of accepting the body as a limit to sexual activity, performative sex expands the boundaries of sexual expression to encompass anything the human mind can imagine. Consequently, the pleasure taken reworks the possibilities of the body, beyond particular roles or body parts. At its best, this position can come to inflect all other arenas of life.

This chapter reviews recent debates concerning the mutable and malleable nature of social identities. This discussion is informed by larger debates in recent social theory and here we consider the impact of economic restructuring on the conception of sexuality. There is a discussion of the idea of 'queer' and its currency in contemporary social explanation. The chapter ends with the suggestion that recent shifts in the global order have shaped new forms of flexible being, including a flexible staging of sexuality (see Seidman 1996; Simon 1996; Califia 1997; Phelan 1997; Queen and Schimel 1997).

This chapter considers the rise and emergence of new articulations of sexual identity. Of course, this statement begs some questions. Following on from previous chapters, there is an assumption that sexual identities emerge and change – and that these shifts are connected to other social forces. But also, and perhaps more importantly, here we examine the contention that sexual identity is articulated, that this is another performance made up of various repertoires of self-expression. The opening statement above indicates a belief that these performances are becoming more numerous and more varied – perhaps that some historical shift has allowed greater sexual diversity to be articulated. This chapter will examine the context that gives rise to this belief and attempt once again to suggest that sex is shaped and enabled by the more general events of history.

There has been a shift in social science from attention to absolutely determining structures and static relations to more negotiated versions of self. In particular, this has been a way to give space to the recognition that individuals have some agency in their articulation of self. In part this arises from a culture of capital which privileges individual, private and inner life and the separation of different spheres of existence. The wide-ranging debates about the now-dated term of postmodernism refocus on the constitution of individual identities – another story in which a world of stable certainties and long-standing relations fragments into far more uncertain, shifting and segmented forms of existence (Harvey 1989; Soja 1989; Jameson 1991).

Postmodernism makes us think differently about the assumption of identity. Now it seems that no-one has access to stable social relations and therefore the identity names of modernity (class, race, gender?) are both complicated and enhanced by other social processes. These processes exemplify the strange contortions of postmodernity – style, consumption, affinity, performance. Although this is not a chapter about 'queer' – because this term has been more effectively discussed elsewhere – the impact of queer theorising cannot be avoided in discussions of sexual identity (see discussion of Butler in the Introduction; Seidman 1996; Phelan 1997; Queen and Schimel 1997). In relation to sexuality, the term 'queer' has occupied a particular and privileged status in identity debates – however, many aspects of the concept 'queer' are echoed in other forms of theorisation, including many resolutely unsexy and even sexless arenas of thought. The discussion that follows attempts to place 'queer' within larger debates about identity and agency and to think again about what gives rise to these many reformulations of our intimate selves.

As a result of this focus on recent debates, this chapter ends up being the place of trends and high jinks – all the consideration of ponderous talk and flashy theorisation is squashed up together here. This can, unfortunately, make for heavy going. As an aid to the overburdened readers, I will stop at times to re-orient both myself and them. There are some key arguments to follow:

1   the intellectual climate bears some relation to the economic and political climate and academic trends reveal something about the spirit of a time;
2   discussions of sexuality are informed by this more general debate and therefore reveal the influence of wider forces;
3   accounts of identity-shift expand our sense of possibility and, in turn, have an impact on wider social relations.

I will go on to review these debates, including the intersection between postmodernism and queer theory and practice, and the relation of both to debates about the impact of globalisation. Before moving on to this, let us consider the high interest and heated debate that has surrounded the idea of identity. Kobena Mercer places the obsessive scrutiny of 'identity' in the wider context of postmodernism:

Just now everybody wants to talk about identity. As a keyword in contemporary politics it has taken on so many different connotations that sometimes it is obvious that people are not even talking about the same thing. One thing at least is clear – identity only becomes an issue when it is in crisis, when something assumed to be fixed, coherent and stable is displaced by the experience of doubt and uncertainty. From this angle, the eagerness to talk about identity is symptomatic of the postmodern predicament of contemporary politics.

(Mercer 1994: 259)

For our purposes, the postmodern predicament can be extended to include other descriptors such as turbo-capitalism or globalisation. The focus for this chapter is the manner in which people think of themselves and their significant attributes in times of rapid change. In fact, the preoccupation with the term 'identity' as the root and solution of all these uncertainties seems to have transmuted into another set of debates. However, the wider question of how people are conceptualised as agents in social structures – not least to themselves – remains central to any discussion of sex, politics and life as we know it.

The debates around postmodernism – which also seem to have abated or relocated in the expansive tent of globalisation – formulate the question of identity in particular terms. In part, as Mercer points out, there is a nostalgia for some previous moment of more knowable and less changeable aspects of identity. Most obviously, economic changes, from de-industrialisation in developed economies to the mobility of capital via global networks, remake identities based on occupation, in many cases destroying work-based sources of status and self-naming and offering nothing in their place (Gorz 1982; Rifkin, 1995; Sennett 1998). Linked to this sense of economic uncertainty and change, the nostalgic account also assumes a previous era in which people were not so geographically mobile and in which work-based identities filtered out to give status and recognition in a locality where everyone knew each other. Without the anchoring force of stable sources of employment and a static population, who you are, and, importantly, who you are to other people, becomes more difficult to judge (Sassen 1998).

More positive accounts of postmodern experience suggest that new forms of identification emerge to replace and adapt the roles that are tied to economic activity. In part, these take the form of more open and flexible adoptions of identity names that appeared to have become solidified in economic determination. So, once gender is freed from the instrumental demands of families reproducing capital – and freed by assorted forces, including economic change, the impact of feminism and the growth of leisure – the old binaries of man and woman can be rethought as an array of exciting possibilities (Matthaei 1997; Baker 1999). These new possibilities are enabled also by new political formations – and another reading of postmodern fallout suggests that the losses of a certain conception of class politics come alongside fresh articulations of other political forces. Kobena Mercer argues that the demise of the certainties of Marxist triumphalism and promised progress of modernity opens the possibility of other kinds of agency. Now we can

> appreciate the diversity of social and political agency among actors whose antagonistic practices have also contributed to the sense of fragmentation and plurality that is said to characterize the postmodern condition. ... it is my impression that 'identity' is currently invoked as a way of acknowledging the transformations in public and private life associated with the presence of new social actors.
>
> (Mercer 1994: 288)

These new social actors are represented by the various non-class political movements around gender, race, sexuality, disability, but also by the non-identity organisations around ecology, neighbourhood, consumer rights or freedom of information. All of these other political motivators increase in influence at a time when the traditional left has faced major challenges (Laclau and Mouffe 1985; Aronowitz 1996; Klein 2000). Theorists of postmodernity have located this shift as stemming from an epistemological break and from a different economic logic. Broadly, these overlapping accounts identify the 'Death of grand narrative' and the 'advent of time–space compression' as the motors and explanations of change. These themes have been developed in many other commentaries (Harvey 1989; Jameson 1991; Massey 1994). However, both accounts of the strange, and possibly on-going, phenomenon of postmodernity impact upon our understanding of sexual practice and identity.

The 'death of grand narrative' approach places the construction of knowledge at the heart of consciousness; the break between eras is marked by a crisis in how we know. This view describes a long era of modernity during which human endeavour constructs a sense of order and control over many aspects of existence, both human and non-human. Humanity ascends to the central and pivotal role within the universe, and risk is managed through a belief in the ordering and predictive power of knowledge. Although modern experience manifests the underlying uncertainty beneath this vision of order, in the many scary and exhilarating cracks in the cultures of modernity, the implication is that overall the myth just about holds. It is the advent of this new and unavoidable postmodernity, a time and/or place in which the fiction of the big, explanatory story can no longer hold, that displaces faith in knowledge and knowability (Lyotard 1979; Friedland and Boden 1994).

This version of postmodern apocalypse gives rise to a parallel optimism. If the old and stifling order is dying, or at least breaking up with room for movement, then other spaces, identities and stories become possible. The display of momentary innovation gains a new social status, as meaningful as any role given through larger social structures. In the opening of this possibility, sexuality regains its mystical promise, a chance to live all our secret truths (Squires 1993; Beck and Beck-Gernsheim 1995).

Alongside this shift in the register of knowledge and self-articulation, proponents of the 'time–space compression' account identify a parallel shift in the material conditions of, at the very least, formerly industrialised societies in the era of global economy. In this vein, David Harvey famously describes the condition of postmodernity as an extension of tensions within modernism – with flexible accumulation replacing the comparative stability of Fordist organisation. Instead of the order and predictability of mass production via the rigidity of the assembly line, with its necessary investment in the community formation of the workforce, flexible accumulation limits its ties to any location or group of people, preferring to shift production and resources to the next best deal whenever it can. The implication is that this different model of accumulation and regulation leads to different approaches to aesthetics and reason. The regime of regulation demanded by flexible accumulation dismantles the Fordist household in favour of more fragmented and flexible domestic arrangements, so intimate life is also remade through this process. Hidden in this account is a suggestion that flexible accumulation also requires a certain kind of subject – not only in order to work in new ways, but also to consume in new ways and through this to become a new breed of political animal.

Of course, attempts to understand everyday culture have been interested in the effects of economy on subjectivity forever. And however recent and trivial the studies of sexuality may appear, the concern to chart the relation between new economic and social relations and the business of everyday emotional and sexual life is there in the work of the most favoured uncles of cultural theory. The intensive discussion of the concept of hegemony that is referred to in Chapter 3 reveals the influence of Antonio Gramsci on theories of culture and politics. Gramsci was leader of the Italian Communist Party (PCI) from 1924. His major theoretical works, in which he considers the role of the revolutionary party in the encounter with the state and develops his ideas about the place and value of intellectual work and engagement with popular consciousness, were written from 1926 while imprisoned. Although Gramsci devoted his imprisoned energies to describing and understanding the new moment that allowed fascist ascendance, he also struggled to grasp all aspects of the subject at that time. Most importantly for this volume, he considered Fordism to be an intervention into the sexual lives of workers. He argues that the success of new rituals of production depends upon the creation of new forms of subjects, with this subjectivity including areas beyond the workplace:

[I]t is worth drawing attention to the way in which industrialists (Ford in particular) have been concerned with the sexual affairs of their employees and with their family arrangements in general. One should not be misled, any more than in the case of prohibition, by the 'puritanical' appearance assumed by this concern. The truth is that the new type of man demanded by the rationalisation of production and work cannot be developed until the sexual instinct has been suitably regulated and until it too has been rationalised.

(Gramsci 1971: 296–7)

Gramsci revisited the debate about capitalism and morality precisely at a time when new forms of productive process were spawning new movements towards moralism. Despite the high-minded rhetoric surrounding Fordist family planning, Gramsci reminds us that capitalism knows no virtue except the virtue of profit (on the social engineering of Fordism, see Nevins 1954). While employers may inhabit the guises of puritanism for popular effect, this is just a front for a more old-fashioned instrumentalism. Fordist practice requires a regulation of the entire life-world. There is no room in this plan for the haphazard pleasures of popular home life, with its traces of peasant pasts and carnivalesque release (Thompson 1968: 441–6; Stone 1990). This reproduction requires more than simple attendance at work and sustenance of the body, it demands a regulation at home to mirror the regulation at work. Without this total culture how could anyone maintain the dullness of routine and the anxiety of scrutiny?

> These new methods demand a rigorous discipline of the sexual instincts (at the level of the nervous system) and with it a strengthening of the 'family' in the wide sense (rather than a particular form of the familial system) and of the regulation and stability of sexual relations.

(Gramsci 1971: 300)

The point here is that the disciplining of sexuality complements and reinforces the disciplines of the workplace. Importantly, Gramsci acknowledges the space of allowable diversity within this project. What is important is the construction of suitably disciplined subjects; sexuality must be accommodated within the requirements of the Fordist regime. However, despite an expedient drift towards the values of marriage and sexual arrangements sanctioned through other social institutions (including organised religion), the Fordist subject can encompass some diversity of living arrangements. Family may be a variety of systems, and, by implication, the disciplining of the sexual nervous system may take a variety of forms. The requirement is only that this discipline complements the order of work:

> It is in their interests to have a stable, skilled labour force, a permanently well-adjusted complex, because the human complex (the collective worker) of an enterprise is also a machine which cannot, without considerable loss, be taken to pieces too often and renewed with single new parts.

(Gramsci 1971: 303)

Within this desire for stability there is the recognition that life must have its pleasures, that there must be space for satisfaction in any disciplinary complex (see the discussion of Foucault in the Introduction to this work). Gramsci came to the conclusion that state-sanctioned monogamy becomes the employers' lifestyle of choice, for their workers if not for themselves, because this arrangement offers the least problematic outlet for the unavoidable wish for sexual release:

> [I]t seems clear that the new industrialism wants monogamy: it wants the man as worker not to squander his nervous energies in the disorderly and stimulating pursuit of occasional sexual satisfaction. The employee who goes to work after a night of 'excess' is no good for his work. The exaltation of passion cannot be reconciled with the timed movements of productive motions connected with the most perfected automatism. This complex of direct and indirect repression and coercion exercised on the masses will undoubtedly produce results and a new form of sexual union will emerge whose fundamental characteristic would apparently have to be monogamy and relative stability.
>
> (Gramsci 1971: 305)

Monogamy emerges as the only arrangement that can allow working people the regular comfort of sex. Working life leaves no room for sexual adventure; that is another privilege reserved for the more leisured classes. Monogamy becomes the manner by which the less lucky retain the sustenance of intimacy in lives colonised by the greedy rigours of work.

In the changing economic circumstances of the late twentieth and early twenty-first centuries, Fordism has lost its central organising role. The variety of names for the mixed bag of working practices that have emerged in its wake – flexible accumulation, turbo-capitalism, leisure and service economies, McDonaldisation, postmodernity – identifies a move away from any possibility of one overarching working order (see Harvey 1982; Lash and Urry 1987; Soja 1989; Massey 1994; Ritzer 1996; Luttwak 1998). Capital disperses in many directions and new subjectivities emerge to answer each trajectory. In different ways, each account of change illuminates developments in thinking about sexual identities.

The decentralisation of traditional aspects of identity makes space for sexuality to assume a new importance. As the world of work contracts, in status if not in time spent, more personal and intimate choices become more significant. Yet, freed from the family as the base industrial unit, sexuality becomes more openly dispersed and tied to different instrumentalities. Sexuality, more than other identity traits, typifies the optimistic promise that the death of certainty leaves room for flexibility, multiplicity, innovation and experimentation. The point at which postmodern arguments seem to seep into and anticipate queer is in the idea that the self is made through performance, from the adoption of roles to the consumption of objects (see the discussion of Butler in the Introduction to this work).

The various debates around 'queer' and other formulations of more dispersed and fragmented sexual identities echo a larger debate around the fragmentation of social identities. In its more generalised guise, this discussion spans across developments in economic structure and political relations. However, the general debate rarely acknowledges sexuality as an aspect of this fragmentation – and, equally, discussions of queer rarely refer to the role of the economy and non-sexual politics. But if the forces of turbo-capitalism have been remaking all our social relations and senses of self, then there must be some impact on sexuality. Some of these processes have been reviewed in previous chapters. This chapter will extend this discussion to the construction and performance of identity.

Queering the terrain of social identities

There is little in this discussion about the actual nitty-gritty of the deed itself. Although the celebration of performance heightens the visibility of some practices – so that queer is identified with piercing, tattoos, new drag, fetish gear and bought accessories – it is not clear that sexual practice shifts with outward display. Instead, the perception that we all are in the midst of some momentous change, something that will remake the boundaries of human existence, extends to conceptions of sexual life. The possibilities cut both ways – every opportunity for experimentation comes from the loss of some valued security. However, if we follow the suggestions of other areas of debate, sexual possibilities emerge as a strategy to balance safety and danger, order and pleasure.

If postmodernity allows us all to play with meaning and improvise new identities with relative ease, free from the killjoy demands of context or social structure, then sex rolls up as a key identity of play. In one sense this is a follow-on from the new social movements described by Mercer and others. However, sexual identity is more than the explicit political demands for tolerance, equality or space to express oneself. Unlike the challenge to the left orthodoxy of feminism or black or gay politics – all that serious burden of history debate that suggests that new subjects appear to turn the motor of progress – sex opens up other investments in identity games. More than those promises of modernity-style emancipation, sex signifies a leap into personal fulfilment without the boring detour through sublimating individual desires to group agendas. This is another version of the politicos' complaint that sex steals energy away from the hard work of struggle. The difference here is the emphasis on what is gained in the increasing belief that happiness is achievable through a pleasure-seeking individual life. For all the pain and anxiety of losing modernist certainties, the promised compensation of immediate satisfaction lights up postmodern existence, however elusive this compensation is. Sex becomes one realm of life that is emblematic of this new framework of expectation.

We can read the debate about queer, and the related and recent interest in transgender and other identities in movement, as one aspect of the discussion about life in postmodernity (Bornstein 1994; Califia 1997). This discussion posits sex as a prime location of postmodern variation. If we want to understand the move into postmodern living as self-articulation and consumer-style pleasure-seeking, then the shifting sexual cultures of recently developed economies offer the most accessible and easily comprehensible example. To examine this premise we need only review some of the key themes of postmodern theorising.

First, and to continue an earlier discussion, let us consider economic changes. Proponents of the view that postmodernity is a distinctive phase of the development of international capitalism, as opposed to some free-form shift in consciousness and meaning-production, argue that the postmodern era spawns new economic forms. If flexible accumulation remakes the nature of work and the working day so that we expect no more than transitory fragments of paid employment, undertaken whenever there is a demand, then the spaces of sex in our lives adapt accordingly.

Second, if the seductive fictions of global corporate culture encourage us all to take refuge in our fantasies of a self created through commodities, then the articulation of sexual desire comes to be framed by this process. If this fantasy is enabled by the speeded-up geography of new regimes of accumulation, then our favoured commodities, including our favoured mode of presenting the commodity of our selves, all bear the marks of this new era.

Third, if aesthetic choices have become so self-referential that we no longer distinguish between original and copy, then sexual selves are all equally authentic – and inauthentic. If there is no recourse to grounding metanarratives of reason, being or meaning, then the moment of performance becomes the only test of self.

The unexpected rise to orthodoxy of queer thinking (in certain circles at least) is an indication of these larger resonances. It is helpful to begin with a consideration of the rapid and expansive hegemony of queer over anglophone accounts of sexuality. Recent years have seen a growth of academic work that questions the fixity of bodies and sexual identities and instead privileges contingency, fragmentation and performance as the defining terms of sexual naming (see Butler 1990; 1993). This work has become so normative in its success that it can be difficult to remember the initial terms of debate. The critique of biologism, foundationalism and fixity is so well rehearsed and so widespread – so omnipresent in academic discussion – that the sorry object of critique is forgotten altogether (for a review of social constructionism, see Gergen 1999).

However, not all discussion in so-called 'queer theory' operates around this organising agenda of queer as an anti-foundationalist critique of identity. There has been a parallel body of work that suggests that the construction of modernity occurs around an always troubled *homo–hetero* opposition. Here, the suggestion that homosexuality forms a necessary, but uncontainable, supplement to a mainstream culture that is always presumed to be heterosexual serves to queer the mainstream. Straight culture, and especially the most cherished aspects of high culture coded as straight, is revealed to be cut through with the unsettling presence of homosexual desire, practice and people:

> The *special* centrality of homophobic oppression in the twentieth century ... has resulted from its inextricability from the question of knowledge and the processes of knowing in modern Western culture at large.
> (Sedgewick 1991: 33–4)

Sedgewick argues that western culture in the twentieth century is obsessed with the dangerous possibility of homosexual connection, and guards against this possibility through a complex network of homophobic violence. At the heart of this is the deep-rooted fear that the supposedly fundamental distinction between *hetero* and *homo* is, in fact, non-existent. Sedgewick analyses celebrated literary works of the English-speaking tradition in order to argue that this anxiety is manifested through the mobilisation of certain thematic binarisms – all attempting to distinguish *hetero* from *homo* in a manner that renders the dangerous and disguised homosexual knowable:

> The closet is the defining structure for gay oppression in this century.
> (Sedgewick, 1991:71)

The leap of this work is to suggest that the core workings of power in recent Western societies are structured around anxieties of sexual identity. Networks of power among men may take wealth and influence as their desired objects, but the interactions that enable this circulation of social effects create a culture of ambiguous and ambivalent sexualised connection:

> If such compulsory relationships as male friendship, mentorship, admiring identification, bureaucratic subordination, and heterosexual rivalry all involve forms of investment that force men into the arbitrarily mapped, self-contradictory, and anathema-riddled quicksands of the middle distance of male homosocial desire, then it appears that men enter into adult masculine entitlement only through acceding to the permanent threat that the small space they have cleared for themselves on this terrain may always, just as arbitrarily and with just as much justification, be foreclosed.
> (Sedgewick, 1991: 186)

Becoming a man in ways that confer social sanction and power always waivers dangerously close to becoming a man who is too invested and connected with other men – if you love other men so much, why don't you marry them? Learning manhood, most especially the socially privileged manhood that seeks to shape the world, demands an instrumental camaraderie with other men. Men learn to recognise each other, to find their place in the pecking order, to love and respect and value other men above any woman or child, to seek affirmation and selfhood through the recognition of other men – yet all this while avoiding the slip into loving men too much. Any insinuation that contact with other men is a source of sexual pleasure, rather than a mutual contract of strictly non-sexual masculine entitlement, collapses the whole bargain. This is the danger that Sedgewick places at the heart of modern Western cultures – and this is what makes homophobia into a central organising structure of these cultures:

> The result of men's accession to this double bind is, first, the acute *manipulability*, through the fear of one's own 'homosexuality', of acculturated men; and second, a reservoir of potential for *violence* caused by the self-ignorance that this regime constitutively enforces.
>
> (Sedgwick, 1991: 186)

This is an account that assumes masculine privilege and power – and therefore homophobia structures this coming to power because it is imagined as a threat to, and of, masculinity. However, for our purposes, the most interesting suggestion here is that the policing of sexuality should occupy this central role in replicating the structures of power. Sedgwick is identifying an organising paradox in the construction of political allegiance – and that paradox is the dangerous reliance on something that is always too close to intimacy. Our discussion so far has indicated that this anxiety about the relation between public and private loves still haunts contemporary culture.

It is, however, at least a matter for debate whether masculine power networks have operated in the same manner from the early twentieth century to the early twenty-first. Sedgwick is describing a particular era of anxiety – a moment at which the importance of men's networks and the emergence of publicly gay male identities both became sites of high anxiety. The obsessive playing over of homosexual possibility is a symptom of this shifting terrain. The danger is felt so acutely because these things are not yet decided.

However, the strong implication is that a similarly central homophobia continues to structure contemporary social relations. The contemporary suggestion extends the anxiety to both (all?) genders – yet there is no indication of how the central prohibition against distorting homosocial relations into their close cousin homosexual encounters transfers to women. The strength of Sedgwick's argument has been in her insistence that the heat around male-to-male sex lies in its deep affinity with the power generated through other male-to-male connection. Our earlier discussion of heterosexuality indicated that the construction of masculine power has changed, even if male privilege has not been eradicated. Networks of women, on the other hand, have never generated the same powers as those of men. Given this, it is hard to see how a similar prohibition against woman-to-woman sexual contact could ever incite the same excessive violence as that against male homosexuality. The point here is not to assert that things have moved on and everyone is more tolerant of everything nowadays. There is far too much painful evidence that this is not the case (Loffreda 2000). Instead I want to think about homosexual panic in the new century.

One of Sedgwick's key points is that men of privilege suffer from homosexual panic because assuming the habits and trappings of power seems to run perilously close to seeking the sexual company of other men. The questions here are first, does the assumption of powerful identities follow a similar logic now? And second, is homosexuality still the unspoken secret at the heart of cultures of power?

Homosexual panic seems such a historically specific term. The high anxiety around male-to-male contact recalls a particular social structure, a world in which men mix endlessly, exclusively and intensively with other men. Now the public world includes many kinds of people. Despite continuing discrimination, women appear in many roles and spheres. Although this creates new forms of anxiety about sex, social life and work, the fear that the circuit of power may be collapsed by the articulation of men's desire for each other seems to have abated. Instead, although there is plenty of everyday homophobia in the world, the high anxiety of panic appears to have spread out to include more diffuse sexual anxieties. The fear that power may be indistinguishable from illicit intimacy remains, but in different guises.

If anything, recent times have been characterised by the most intense sexual panic – around sexual diversity, sexual contact with children, the commodification of sexual experience and the blurring of the boundary between state violence and erotic practice. The obsessive scrutiny described by Sedgwick reappears, but with a far greater variety of taboo objects. Now, in a time when so-called productive social relations rely so heavily on the skills of intimacy, there is a constant danger that protocols of power and influence will become indistinguishable from the rituals of sex. In part, this remains an anxiety about the possibility of sexual contact and desire between men. But this is no longer the central organising trope of Western cultures of control. Instead, sex between men takes its place in a more diffuse theatre of sexual anxiety.

For Sedgwick, homosexual panic is the mirror image of an emergent patriarchal order among bourgeois citizens. It is the dangerous closeness and interdependency that generates a fear of being too close and too dependent. New orders of power continue to privilege men, but are less insistent about the role of all-male networks. The assorted manifestations of global forces, in particular, can give a sense of great human diversity. It takes all kinds of people in all kinds of roles to sustain the interests of capital across the global economy. Of course, much of this corporate melting pot is fictional. By and large, powerful players remain powerful. Few others get to influence the global arena – and when they do, it is often in the role of instrument to established powers. However, it remains the case that the erotic energies of public life have been transformed across the twentieth century. The corrosive contact that we all most fear has also changed accordingly.

My argument is that globalisation in the West colonises the everyday life-world of most people. The resulting changes in working patterns and social organisation require a mobilisation of previously private human energies. When we hear that the flexible workplace requires feminine skills, or when we learn to network and form happy work relations as a route to productivity, the skills of intimate life have entered the public arena. More than this, intimacy, or at least the performance of the rituals of intimacy, becomes the lubricant of the new economy. Before we know it, we are all selling sex to keep any job and to keep the peace. In this context, all kinds of non-instrumental sex can become dangerous.

Of course, the question remains: why is homophobia such a resilient cultural form? Despite widespread changes in attitudes to same-sex relationships, the structure and actuality of homophobic logic continues to inform the wider culture of sexual panic. When public hysteria breaks out about the issue and identity of paedophilia, an older tradition of queer-baiting informs both belief and practice. When there are fears that too deep a love of violence will lead to sexualised wounding, the threat of this decline is figured as the most obvious and everyday perversion of homosexuality. In all its most dangerous and exciting incarnations, sex is coded as queer.

And this, of course, has been the argument of queer theory and politics. The informing and always present role of the perverse is stigmatised by power as an alien outside, rather than acknowledged as the defining supplement it is. If there is a contemporary equivalent of homosexual panic proper, perhaps it is fear of the queer in all its most ludic and expansive versions.

Playful politics, theoretical excitement and the possibilities of new identities

This chapter has reviewed the impact of postmodernism on our ideas of identity and suggested that this debate can be seen as part of the larger realignment of a globalised world order. This highly philosophical discussion of the nature of identity and its relation to sexual behaviour has been associated in an unlikely, and perhaps opportunistic, manner with developments in sexual politics and, in particular, with a new activism that celebrates the performativity of sexual identity and politics. Queer activism has emerged as a strategy through which to assume and refuse identity – and in this it is a response to a much longer politics of sexuality. The invention of the homosexual creates the possibility of an identity, not just an act – and as many commentaries have shown, this invention takes place through criminalisation, medicalisation, a solidifying of the power of dominant culture over dissenting sex (Foucault 1979b; Halperin 1990).

Paradoxically, the creation of this identity gives rise to a point of resistance and possibility of community. This is the insight that becomes the orthodoxy of the history of sex, if so embryonic a discipline can have its own doctrines. Hidden in this doctrine is a caricature of identity politics as a bargaining agenda, and most of all of the tactics of the so-called respectable gay lobby. Critiques of this approach have questioned the benefits that can be gained from embracing the identity terms of the dominant culture.

Against these attempts to gain respectable recognition on the terms of the heteropatriarchy, an alternative approach to political empowerment has emerged. This is the performative politics that has grown out of AIDS activism and the refusal of quietly respectable versions of gay identity. Queer proposes a wilfully unrespectable and disrespectful performance of opposition – perverse but trying to be non-normative and inclusive. In this, there is almost a pull back to acts rather than identities. We can all be fornicators or refusers of the straight contract (Smyth 1992; Aronowitz 1996; Phelan 1997).

In this politics that seeks to refuse identity as the basis for organisation or action, we can detect the traces of a number of other contemporary social trends. These ideas are linked to an opening up of our ideas of the organic. Now that the body seems less stable and limiting, it is adaptable through technology of many kinds from medicine, contraception, enhancement, to more radical alteration (Kirkup *et al.* 2000). And it is tied to a larger shift in which people expect change and development in their sexual experience across the life-course. Alongside the shifts in work and family that we have discussed in previous chapters, the leisure economy has become more central to people's sense of themselves. In particular, phenomena such as club culture, male consumption culture, dance and drug cultures, have all had an impact on the birth of queer, because these are the spaces in which people learn to truly value the performance of their fantasy selves (Simpson 1994; Thornton 1995; Nixon 1996).

All these trends move towards a more agent-centred account of sex and sexual identity – echoing New Right discourse, with its buzzwords of consumer choice, individuals and their absolute rights, freedom from the constraints of that tired fiction, society. This everyday appropriation of the philosophy of performative identity almost by accident echoes the heady debates of queer theory.

Within this unlikely alliance, certain themes link the two endeavours of political campaigning and theoretical discussion:

1   The refusal to accept biology as a defining feature of sexuality – and, as the argument develops, of gender.
2   The assertion that identity is variable, changeable, multiple and fragmented – for everyone, across the same lifetime.
3   The celebration of identity and sexuality as a matter of performance, something to be actively made through style and action.

Point 1 grows from a feminist literature that disputes the commonsense connection between sex and gender, and the assumption that both are made through some biological essence. One formative account of this argument is *Thinking Sex* by Gayle Rubin, later hailed as a fairy godmother of queer, and it is worth reviewing here. Rubin's suggestion is that although feminist debate has provided a critique of the biologism of patriarchal reasoning, the implied connection between sex and gender in much feminist theorisation remakes the determining role of biology. This is because even as gender is extricated from biology and shown to be a cultural construction, sex is affirmed as the base and biology that makes gender categories in the first place.

Despite the difficulty of giving up on the commonsense of bodily definition, Rubin argues that we must try to unlearn our addiction to biological arguments in the last instance if we are ever to unpack the social workings of gender. Alongside this, she makes the case that we must develop a separate politicised account of sexuality – and recognise that this sphere has its own dynamic. From this work comes a range of discussion that suggests that despite the constant and politicised references to the body and its imperatives, cultures of gender efface the material body in order to replace it with a monolithic and unified will of the biological.

Once the idea that cultural formations of gender occur independently of biology takes hold, this, in turn, becomes a new orthodoxy, in feminist debate at least. Large bodies of work explore the manner in which gender is organised to meet social imperatives, with the biological playing no deciding role (Fuss 1990; Fausto-Sterling 1999). From this, it is a short step to imagine cultures of gender that encompass more play and innovation. If the limiting call of biology is a fiction, then maybe everyone is more variable and flexible than we thought. Or maybe they could be.

Without the anchor of sex to make sure that gender always means the same thing in the same ways, it was possible to extend the boundaries of thinking about gender roles. Although queer and sex-positive versions of feminist thinking have berated earlier work for being too stuck in the mud of miserable oppression and creating new constraining norms to live by, in fact the wish to imagine fresh ways of inhabiting the names man and woman informed all kinds of feminist thinking. More than anything, feminist thought of many varieties through the 1970s and 1980s was characterised by the belief that contemporary regimes of gender were open to adaptation through individual will and action. It is this debate that gives shape to the later affirmation that biology has no role in sexuality and sex (not gender) roles:

> To make sex/gender and sexuality the effects of discursive practices, even at the level of the body, appears more productive, but only as long as the body, the material is conceived as a drag or a limit as well as a potential. The kind of drag it is cannot and should not be predetermined, given a shape or a content.
>
> (Martin 1998: 31)

Point 2 echoes and anticipates the larger debate about structures of identity. In terms of sexuality, in particular, the dethroning of biology opens speculation about how sexual choices are made, sustained and altered. Instead of the all-encompassing will to reproduce explaining all sexual behaviour in humans, now there is the possibility that sex is as changeable as other cultural choices – and more than this, that it is chosen on the same basis as these other more obviously malleable practices.

Although this argument is made as a timeless account of how sexuality just is, always and in all places, if we could but see it, it is worth considering the historical context of the argument. The wider literature on identity acknowledges this construction – identity becomes more central to social meaning alongside changes in economic arrangements that displace work-related statuses and meanings; time–space compression increases the opacity of power relations so that people invest in personal identity as an alternative index of value; and as traditional communities fragment and disappear, individual identities become the nodal points linking new networks of support. Sexuality appears in this account as part of the wreckage that people cling to and rework – there is a greater investment in sexual identity as other aspects of identity slip away from control. Performance emerges as one way of retaining pleasure in identity.

While there is some evidence that this is taking place – although more obviously for some than for others – this account assumes that sexuality always remains the same kind of thing. People's investments change, but the conception and construction of sexuality remains the same. Instead, I want to suggest that sexual identity shifts as much as other identity formations – and that these shifts are all interconnected:

> The analytic and political separation of gender and sexuality has been the rallying cry of a great deal of queer theory that seeks to complicate hegemonic assumptions about the continuities between anatomical sex, social gender, gender identity, sexual identity, sexual object choice, and sexual practice.
>
> (Martin 1998: 12)

In this account, queer theory seeks to celebrate the uncertainty that causes so much anxiety to others. It is precisely the falling away of seemingly natural chains of meaning and the widespread realisation that anatomy is no guarantee of social meaning that queer theory rallies around. The hope is that we can all make carnival out of disarray, because the old ways have fallen apart anyway. Other literatures offer suggestions of how people find their feet on shifting terrain – and offer a tentative model of subject formation in an era of rapid change. Aihwa Ong, who has considered the process by which globalisation enables new forms of subjectivity, suggests:

> 'Flexible citizenship' refers to the cultural logics of capitalist accumulation, travel, and displacement that induce subjects to respond fluidly and opportunistically to changing political-economic conditions.
>
> (Ong 1999: 6)

Ong describes the processes by which certain communities learn to inhabit the rapidly changing terrain of globalisation, in particular, in the close-to-home negotiation of the local. Although her work is not concerned with sexual cultures, we could transfer her conception of the flexible citizen to the arena of sexuality. In particular, queer could be seen as advocating a version of flexible sexual citizenship – as much a strategy to navigate difficult and changing terrain as an outright celebration.

I am attracted to this suggestion – that sexual identity shifts to negotiate wider social changes and that these new sexual identities then themselves impact upon other social relations. Ong describes the innovations that enable some communities to survive the disturbances of global shift and not only survive, but sometimes thrive. There is no pretence that the new is always better – what is described is frightening and unpredictable, a dangerous journey to be navigated with attentive care. But despite the loss of change, there is something else afterwards – all is not lost in the process of change.

Perhaps the emergence of new sexual identities could be seen as part of this process? Although we live with the pain of lost certainties – longing for lifelong monogamy that few will ever experience – new opportunities to thrive appear. Whereas the account of queer identities reads as if these are ahistorical and always present possibilities, a more historically specific version of events may be hidden in the story. If changes in the role and nature of work and in the boundaries of nation impact upon the space of intimacy, then, no doubt, people learn some strategy of living within this change.

We could read the emergence of this alternative account of subject formation as itself a historical event. The components of queer thinking reveal an affinity with a number of themes from recent social theory – all of them attempts to grapple with our changing present. The moment of queer that celebrates the manufactured over the natural restores technology to its central place in the making of sexuality. More than sex gadgets and love machines, this is recognition that sex is always more than just bare bodies (Wolmark 1999; Kirkup *et al.* 2000). The celebration of performance shows an understanding of the shifting structures of contemporary identity, from work to family to gender to consumption. The reassessment of the sphere of sexuality as a differently politicised arena shows an affinity with the accounts of turbo-capitalism or a second modernity, because this is an era that demands a reworking of subjectivity in all areas of life. Queer catches the expectations and uncertainties of a certain moment.

Does sex make our identity?

What determines sexual identity? We can chart broad trends – the sexual outcomes of urbanisation, industrialisation, feminism, changes at work. Individuals come to identity within the structures that these movements make – so we have a larger or smaller number of partners, more or less leisure and disposable income, different ideas of entitlement and fulfilment. But, again, how does this shift the detail of acts – or shape the mysterious trail from act to identity?

Mainly, these are accounts of changing opportunities – there is little account of the active agency of desire. Perhaps leisure culture and feminism suggest that sex should form one of life's central pleasures for everyone – and that suggestion may change people's choices and expectations. Although this is not quite a theory of determination, because one shift does not demand the other, it seems possible that as one set of social rewards and pleasures slips away, there may be more time and interest for the compensations of previously derided arenas of life.

This leads us back to the idea that sexuality has its own history – and the task is to chart this dynamic against other factors. A major theme in much recent debate in many areas is the idea of flexibility. This term famously describes the experience of the contemporary workplace, while also implying that a certain and perhaps pleasurable flexibility has crept into all other arenas of life. Ulrich Beck outlines the cruel joke contained within this promise (Beck 2000). Flexibility, of course, is life enhancing and enjoyable only for the privileged. For most of those experiencing this shift to exciting suppleness, there is no sense of empowerment or possibility. Instead, flexibility at work is regarded as a thinly veiled code for loss of security, erosion of workplace pay and conditions, and an escalating sense of desperation among ordinary people who must work to live (Sennett 1998).

Although these major changes in the nature and role of work in the Western life-course do reveal the cracks and inconsistencies in the always unfulfilled promise of orderly modernity, it is difficult to imagine this form of innovation as an escape from conformity into freedom. Too many of our expectations around social participation and entitlement revolve around the fiction of valued work for all, for any easy move into the ludic pleasures of a post-work society (Mercer 1998).

However, in other areas of life, flexibility seems to herald a new beginning of personal fulfilment. If the progress and security of modernity required absolute order and conformity, then the loss of this particular juggernaut of history opens the possibility of lives not characterised by their orderliness or their conformism. For those who do not remember the extreme poverty of those who have fallen out of the bargain of modernity, the chance to cut free and just express ourselves seems too sweet to miss (Baudrillard 1988).

This, of course, is where sexual expression comes into its own. If the construction of a separate sphere of sexuality served as a compensation for the rigidity of a public world ordered around the imperative to work and obey, then dismantling the imperative allows the tasty compensation of sex to seep into previously unfamiliar areas. Now, freed at last from the boring requirement to make ends meet, individual desire can take advantage of the accumulated material comforts of modernity and devote energy to fulfilment, not need.

The most exciting aspects of queer and its aligned calls for sexual variety and freedom seem to promise this escape from mundane constraints. Although much of the work mounts a highly politicised critique of the continuing power and violence of heteronormativity, the overpowering implication is that nobody needs to live in this way any more. Something has happened to free us all from the mistakes of our ancestors. If recent history has silenced sexual diversity, then this is only one more indication of the unwarranted suffering caused by constraining sexuality. Although many may remain disgusted by the sexual habits and choices of others, who does not demand absolute autonomy in their own sexual desire? Somehow we have all become queered in this demand for a non-instrumental sexual life.

This is something like the liberating flexibility promised by economic restructuring. In the free fall from post-industrialism, it seems that all social structures and identities become negotiable. There are many costs of this process: social institutions and employers retreat from their responsibilities towards individuals, individuals question or forget their interdependence on each other, the fiction of a shared social contract seems less and less sustainable. However, there is also a sense of immense possibility. While the orderly hierarchy of work-centred society demanded that most individual desires be deferred, now the infrastructure for some kinds of fulfilment seem open to everyone. If the preordained life-course of workerly obedience appeared to require certain forms of sexual conformity, then new structures of life and work offer new possibilities of sex and freedom. Perhaps this is the age of affluence we have all been waiting for? Without the immediate concern of staying alive, maybe the extension of personal experimentation is a democratising of decadence.

I realise as I look back over this work that the actual practice of sex forms all too little of the discussion. Despite my wish to avoid accounts that make sex abstract, theoretical or so far from everyday experience as to be unrecognisable, in the end I seem to have fallen into a different mode of abstraction. Although the account of sexual life developed here works hard to integrate different facets of everyday life, most importantly the material constraints and enablers that surround sexuality, the business of sexual interaction itself is hard to represent.

In part, this continued mystery also forms the celebration of fragmented possibility in sexual life. Unlike the core promises of modernity, in which fulfilment was predefined along with duty, the resistance to representation allows sex to signify a whole new way of being. For all the hype about freedom of expression, no-one wants their mode of expression determined by someone else. Sex can signify new possibilities precisely because of the promise that each articulation will be a new innovation. At last, here is an arena in which we can all follow our own personal journeys – at least, this is the nature of the promise.

In this work I wish to keep hold of some of this optimism, not least because the material shifts in social relations seem real and we need to believe that other things are possible. Despite the economic pessimism of much of this account, I do think that sex retains a special aura. This specialness may not compensate for material hardship or political disenfranchisement, but that does not mean that sex has no importance or value to add to the quality of life.

The question remains: how does sex offer fresh modes of value and fulfilment in these uncertain times? The chapters that follow will go on to suggest that the codes of intimacy may offer a model for remaking social relations. Whether this is another trick of capitalism or another indication of human resilience remains to be decided.

Although technological development displaces many previous forms of waged work, the relation to everyday technology also remakes the relation to the body. Although shifts in working patterns disrupt the lives of many, others learn new ways to pleasure and love through this disruption. Although global capitalism displaces human value into an abstract notion of the consumer, the practices of lifestyle shopping teach everyone new forms of identity and performance. However bad life gets, people reach for affection and excitement, use their bodies as an affirmation of their lives, and do their utmost to survive, whatever the circumstances.

Recent theorisations imply that all identities are in constant flux. Although the speed and depth of the flux may vary, it is hard to imagine any attribute of identification that remains static and known in the same way. Perhaps more than other identity traits, sexuality demonstrates the malleability of self-naming. Even when people feel assured of some constancy in their choice of sexual object, few admit absolute constancy in their style of sexual engagement, experience of sensation, enthusiasm and energy, tenderness and affection. Across the life-course, sexual behaviour, investment and experience vary considerably, even for those who remain gay or straight throughout. In our culture of intensive self-training, time allows us to learn to polish our inhabitation of intimacy. We learn to pace and be patient, to relax and to enjoy – and perhaps also to manipulate, play-act, force, take, overcome. None of it stays quite the same, however much we try to grow into our own desires – endlessly perfecting the ideal script of our dreams. Given this, sex may be our best chance of learning to live with the uncertainties of flexibility, because this is the place where we are allowed to try out new styles of being.

5   The exotic

Position of the chapter – objectification

In this position we arrange our bodies in order to imagine an uncertain new terrain as a static moment of hierarchy. Forgetting the limp vanilla pleasures of equality and reciprocality in intimate life, here we concoct a theatre of power imbalance in order to heighten the sexual hit. Learning the more worldly pleasures of the body requires recognition that social equity may not feel sexy. So, here, we learn instead that power relations can be solidified for erotic ends. When the world around us seems to be changing so rapidly, the erotic fantasy of an absolute object can provide consolation for other uncertainties.

This chapter examines the particular sexual heat that has accompanied some forms of power imbalance. The chapter is centred on the term 'exotic' and, therefore, much of the discussion focuses on ideas of foreignness and racialised difference, in keeping with the histories and connotations of this term. Here, I argue that the era of globalisation has unsettled the previous certainties of Western ascendancy, at least in the minds of Westerners. This reshaping of the world order shifts the framework of exoticist imagination. The chapter ends with the suggestion that an examination of new cultures of exoticism can illuminate the power struggles and uncertainties of a still emerging global order (for more on exoticism, see Said 1978; Kabbani 1986; Mercer 1994; Young 1995).

The adventure of sex is imagined as a far-from-home experience, away from the cosy familiarities of home. Think of the stock icons of eroticism – a stranger's glance, an unfamiliar place, an escape from norm and convention, the rush into hair, skin, breath, sweat, loss of self and the touch of another. Within all this, the role of the other – whether with the weight of psychoanalysis or only the contextual marker of difference – makes the story (Benjamin 1998). The thrill of sexual contact, in narratives of erotic fulfilment if not in boring reality, demands a brush with the edges of selfhood. Where is the excitement without the threat of dissolution? Who can undo the boundaries of selfhood more successfully than another alternative formation of being – a living proof that this is not the only way?

Of course, to the self everything else is other – the world is split into me and not me. So every sexualised encounter must include this brush with otherness, a flirtation with the boundary of self and a gamble on the ability to withstand disintegration through surrender to another. Is sex not always about this balance between confirming self and relinquishing self, some mixture of conquest and surrender? Perhaps the figure of the alien is always present in some way (see Kristeva 1994). Even now, when the world seems smaller, more interconnected, linked through the parallel commodifications of global sameness and local particulars, the fantasy of redemption through sex requires some markers of the foreign. Although the content of this exotic fantasy may vary, the structure of exoticism remains, even in the era of globalisation. This chapter explores the dynamic of the exotic in previous times and in this new time.

The history of the modern world quickly reveals itself as a story of the West's rise to global domination (De Landa 2000). Any attempt to reinstate sex in its proper and central role as a core dynamic in social relations bumps up against this realisation. If the task is to rewrite and adapt the insistently economic accounts of our turbo-charged and globalising world, in order to reinsert the less outcome-oriented confusions of something like sex, then the longer histories of global relations loom conspicuously.

The coming to globality of European ascendance, unlike turbo-globalisation, has been revealed as a more than rational and instrumental process already. Despite the very real and extensive material benefits of this long and various process, the extra-rational impetus of sexual longing is apparent in a number of processes and locations. The relation of master race to subject peoples has shown itself to be more than purely instrumental. Alongside the practicalities of wielding power, other less disciplined drives complicate the role of the powerful (on sexual drives that at once confound and confirm racial ideologies, see Ware 1992; McClintock 1995).

The *Oxford English Dictionary* tells us that the exotic refers to '… plants, words, fashions … introduced from abroad' or to the 'strange or bizarre'. The term links the foreign to the strange, so that what is from elsewhere slips into being what is unorthodox. In relation to sexuality, we can consider the idea of the exotic to refer to the strangeness of foreign sex – and the additional heat and attraction that comes from this heady mix of the strange and foreign in one. More generally, this chapter considers the sexual aura that arises from power disparity, because the myths of foreignness that inform the exotic come from the history that saw Europe come to dominate the world. For our purposes, the point is not to suggest that a fixed relation of power and sexualisation has endured through all time. Instead, I want to think about the role of exoticised power differentials in contemporary social relations. After all, the lesson is not that some people carry an extra titillation in their essential person, but that there is something about being socially disadvantaged, or even degraded, that makes for exoticisation. My suggestion is that this is a process that emerges in the interaction of the never quite complete project of Western subject formation and the resilient otherness of the rest of the world.

There is an implicit question in this discussion about the sexuality of the Western subject. Inasmuch as white subjectivity is an outcome of European ascendancy, because there is no consciousness of whiteness as the mark of racialised privilege without this, whiteness is created as an absence of sexuality (Dyer 1997). This is a central contention of the chapter – that the construction of the Western subject relies on processes of sex as well as processes of military and economic expansion. However, while claiming sole ownership of such valued attributes as reason, whiteness as the shorthand marker of Western subjecthood has been excised of sexuality. Sex has no role in the subjectivity of global dominance, apparently. I will go on to discuss some of the consequences of this desexualising construction of whiteness.

However, despite this mythology, the Western subject clearly has had, and does have, sex, and privilege can serve to increase sexual possibility – perhaps more than imagination or inclination. The varied histories of Europeans abroad reveal the many ways in which this opportunity has been taken (Kabbani 1986; Gill 1995). Far from exemplifying a heightened human existence, freed from the encumbrance of sexuality, white subjects have used every opportunity to grab a variety of sexual adventures. For every imperial fantasy of pale, virginal boys civilising the globe with maps, administration and Christianity, there is a parallel document of exotic titillation that promises journeys away from the stifling constraints of civilisation. And it is the case that certain Western subjects, often those given the task of standing in as exemplars of their race, have been granted the capacity to exercise sexual power and a free chance to abuse (Hyam 1991). A wider literature regards that Western subject as a creature defined precisely in opposition to myths of otherness, with sexual otherness high on the list of fears (Young 1995). The traits of the despised otherness come to be embodied by the rest of the world:

> [W]e in the West are heirs of a Christian tradition which tended to see in sex a focus for moral anguish and conflict, producing an enduring dualism between the spirit and the flesh, the mind and the body. It has produced a culture which simultaneously disavows the body while being obsessively preoccupied with it.
> (Weeks 2000: 131)

This discussion has had a long history – any examination of the present falls back to this concentration on the development of a capitalism that sprung up from Europe and came to creep across the whole world. For this reason many of the key terms of modernity appear as European inventions – modernity itself can be regarded as a name for the long era of European ascendancy. But even those other big metanarrative words, capital, reason, the self, are touched with the expansion of European influence (Bhattacharyya 1998):

The problem is that whites may not be very good at it, and precisely because of the qualities of 'spirit' that make us white. Our minds control our bodies and therefore both our sexual impulses and our forward planning of children. The very thing that makes us white endangers the reproduction of our whiteness.

(Dyer 1997: 27)

The culture of white supremacy that marks the world as inevitably and thankfully under the sway of Europeans claims human progress as an insistently white affair. The unspoken message of supremacist discourse, from law and order anxiety to the white man's burden of global policing, is that it is better for everyone if we, superior beings, take charge. This is based on the belief that human development occurs through a progressive shift away from the animal bodily calls of physicality to the higher planes of reason and the mind. Life gets better when we stop being pulled this way and that by the arbitrary and unreasonable wants of the body and instead form complex social structures which defer physical calls in favour of the more lengthy projects of technology and social order. Through this process, humanity conquers nature and takes control of its own destiny. All of which is well and good, except for the hidden sting in the tail – the exercise of reason belongs, handily, to white people. Everyone else is tied hopelessly to the body, and with it backwardness and primitive culture. We need the interventions of white folks to make it in the world.

Across centuries, apologists for white privilege have spun out a version of this story. However, the same structures can be seen in the more covert interventions of recent times – structural adjustment, global policing and market imperialism. The nasty ways of the powerful are legitimated still through an idea that the rest are distracted – if everyone else is too busy trying to keep up with the endless hungry demands of the body, then strategic thinking is left, necessarily, to the more far-sighted.

However, as we enter this fresh phase of capitalist expansion, intensification, speeding up and reshaping, the Western subject has a far less certain place in the power structures of the world. The location and identity of the supplementary other is less certain than ever. If exoticism echoes a real-world power differential, perhaps the Japanese desire for European lovers is an exoticist fetish rather than an Asian inferiority complex. Perhaps the continuing British fantasy about Scandinavian women is a displaced wish for better living standards, in the manner of Thai women's inexplicable desire for ageing British men. Although some trace of historical powers informs the self-conception of certain nations, charting the comparative status of all nations in an ever-changing global order is an impossible task. And without at least a momentary fiction of power and privilege, exoticism is hard to sustain.

All of this assumes that exoticism reflects some other, more basic, reality – so the titillated gaze is enabled by material power and privilege, and the vulnerability to becoming the object of that titillating gaze comes from a lack of material power and privilege. However, it also assumes that the exercise of that exoticising gaze fulfils some need for the powerful. Of course, some exoticising gazes misjudge the power relation – or use racist structures as a consolation for economic and political impotence (Hage 1998). However, I want to hold on to the idea that exoticism entails an assumption of power on the part of the exoticist – that is the extra kick that makes this structure of feeling.

Whether or not the exoticist wields real-world power, making someone your exotic object demands a fantasy of power. Therefore, I also want to suggest that exoticism transfers the contradictions of certain power structures into the realm of the sexual in order to rework discomfort. Sex promises to allow room for terror and desire and to conciliate the two. In this telling, exoticism performs a certain therapeutic function for the powerful – reworks cruelty and unfounded privilege as the more ambivalent position of desire, as if all this conflicted emotion was a product of psychic contradictions as opposed to class contradictions.

Of course, no parallel consolation occurs for the less powerful – destined to become the object of intrusive fantasies without ever accruing the prizes of the loved one. So the point here is not that sex represents a parallel to the public world, a space in which social contradictions may be worked on and resolved. Rather sex, or imagined sex, stands in here as an opportunity for the powerful to make the exercise of power more acceptable and appealing to themselves. Perhaps this need is for a space to acknowledge the contradictions of the position of power – so the mythologies of any exoticism rework key components of the myths of privilege, revealing the anxieties within the assumption of power. If this is the case, then the structures of exoticism offer a key to understanding the workings of power – if only in an account of points of ambivalence.

First, let us pretend that all systems of power must make their own exotic others – and if they do not exist, then they must be invented.

What are the factors in contemporary cultures of exoticism?

The concept of the exotic assumes a static model of global power. This is a version of the erotic that takes its meaning and frisson from the larger relations of power that surround the small-time adventures of sexuality. It is worth taking a moment to consider this construction. Rather than rapidly retreating into the privatised realms of apolitical desire, the exotic is an intensely and openly worldly articulation of sexuality. In the exotic, sexual excitement comes precisely from this echo of larger social structures. More than everyday versions of desire, the exotic relies upon an explicit and comprehensible power disparity. Without the sense that the object of desire is lesser, dangerous and forbidden – alluringly other and beyond any everyday social contact – there is no exoticist dynamic.

In its most well-known incarnations, this dynamic has centred around fantasies of foreignness and the particular heat of the myth of race. As we have discussed above, European expansion enables new cultural myths with fresh embellishments on older stories of the abominations beyond Christendom (Jordan 1974). In its many incarnations, the exotic lives in the social relations of these trading and military endeavours. Although an explicitly sexual cultural form, the exotic inhabits the power relations of other spheres. In this, the exotic functions as an alternative access to the workings of power. So, while the explicit accounts of European contact with the non-Christian world speak of depravity and souls to be saved, the exotic fixated upon the fascinations of non-Christian sexuality and its libidinous excess; while slavery stripped Africans of humanity, the exotic revealed a twisted hunger for African bodies; and, while the public world of economy and politics struggles to maintain a unitary narrative and practice of domination, the exotic shows the excesses not contained in this instrumental account.

The point here is not to suggest that somehow the cruelties of material oppression are undercut by the ambiguities of desire – the exotic may offer an alternative understanding of power relations, but it does not disrupt the workings of that power. If anything, the exotic must consolidate the power relations that it inhabits – because if the relation slips, the thrill is gone. Instead the point is to reveal that the exercise of power may always be more than purely instrumental. In a variety of locations, the exotic has served not to alleviate the excesses of the abuse of power, but instead to exacerbate and sexualise that abuse (Stannard 1992; Gill 1995; Wiegman 1995). Desire adds cruelty beyond any instrumental end.

This extra-rational element in the sexualisation of power relations both serves and confounds instrumental ends. The addition of sexual pleasure can add enthusiasm to the participation of powerful subjects – the fantasy of the exotic may allow the formation of a self-image that feels agreeably flattering or engagingly titillating. However, the deviation from purely instrumental ends can make the exercise of power messy and unpredictable – excessive pleasure in the rituals of power may detract from achieving its aims. This doubleness echoes other aspects of sexual life – and this is another recurrent theme in the book, the idea that sexual life is made by larger forces yet manifests this construction in unpredictable ways that knock back against other social relations unexpectedly. The exoticism of more absolute power relations has spun out into uncontrolled violence – and although this may work as a macabre functionalism, surely a sustainable power requires a sense of control?

When we examine the cultural products of exoticism, each instance comes from a very tangible set of political relations. Although the stories are dressed up in fantasy, it is not difficult to see the geopolitics that informs the desire. In exoticism the desired object is your slave, your enemy, your absolute other – the desire may fixate on the anticipation of danger or the pleasure of dominating the weak or the adventure of an alien and forbidden experience, but each scenario demands that the object has less agency and access to mainstream power than the one who desires.

For this fantasy to work, it must assume a relatively static and transparent model of power relations. Characters must know their place and boundaries between groups must be conspicuous and well policed. The archetypal framework of exoticist relations is the repertoire learned from colonialism. Here, there is a model of boundary-marking which uses both spatial location and physical features to identify the place of the other, while combining the myths of different races of human being with limited occasions for intimate contact between groups (Jackson 1989; Sibley 1995). The residues of race science ensure that the colonial model teaches the exoticist that the other is a conspicuously different order of being. Even when the boundaries are not those of race, the components of this mythology teach a method of racialising other objects of exoticist desire. This can be seen in the colonising and biologising impulses apparent in nineteenth-century scrutiny of the working classes. These endeavours that mark the birth of social science examine the living habits of working people in unseemly detail, intruding into every intimate crevice of daily life, in order to demonstrate that these people are of a different order of being, a race apart within the nation (Mayhew 1968; Walkowitz 1992). Equally, we can see the work of racialisation in the confusion between discourses of the foreign and of the perverse, so that one form of stigmatisation can provide the material for another mythology of race and vice versa (Bleys 1995).

However, for this portable model to work, there must be some sense of safety for those at the centre. The others may be interchangeable – all racialised categories of difference to a lascivious exoticising eye – but the power to look, categorise, fantasise and want must reside in the place of privilege. The exotic relies on some solidity of power relations – people need to know where they stand and feel secure about their position for its special frisson to be available.

Of course, as this work, among others, has stressed, this position of security is not available for many these days. The rapid changes of recent years, be they due to globalisation, turbo-capitalism or something else, have altered the terrain of the Western subject. Although there are still rich and poor worlds, with these terms revealing a pretty clear relation to the positioning of those at the centre and those at the periphery, the dynamic of the relation between these zones is far more opaque. Even when the inhabitants of the West reap the benefits of neocolonialism, they do not recognise the position of privilege. Instead, they experience their comparative wealth and unfair advantages – as witnessed by the World Trade Organization, the General Agreement on Tariffs and Trade and the business of multinational companies – as impoverishment and attack. This has become painfully apparent in the desperate struggles to retain a semblance of legitimacy for international bodies that protect the interests of the rich world. In this framework, the role of the exotic other becomes mixed up with other far less pleasurable myths of the foreign. Sex may fall out of the articulation altogether (see Bhattacharyya *et al.* 2001). Yet somehow, despite the many national anxieties caused by globalisation, the ephemera of everyday exoticism still flutter around Western lives.

The ephemera of everyday exoticism

An example of such ephemera: public telephone boxes in London (and a few other British cities, sometimes seaside resorts) have come to house a particular brand of advertising. Calling cards advertising sexual services clutter up the phone boxes of various parts of London – around major railway stations, close to tourist attractions, all kinds of places where large numbers of transient people might be. The cards take the logic of the public hoarding into the fleeting privacy of the booth, making use of the brief moment of private space that allows the telephone enquiry. The cards change rapidly – although a certain format is retained. A promising catch-phrase to encapsulate the service offered, an image of the pleasures to come and the number to call. Ten years ago the pictures were poor quality photocopies – my favourites were the 1950s-style cartoons of cruel mistresses and bullied men, each drawing calling up a history of fetish culture and its self-ridiculing iconography. Recently, cheap technology has enabled the use of digital photography, so that instead of line drawings the punter can see glossy magazine-style reproductions of girls in poses suited to the cards' captions. Sadly, this has put paid to the more theatrical depictions, and retro cartoons are hard to find nowadays. Instead, the focus has shifted to recall the older iconography of the bordello – women presented as an array of ideal types. Whereas previously these types were limited – hardly more diverse than blonde schoolgirl, busty brunette and black mistress – the expansion of representational capability has coincided with an increase in the range and depiction of types. Now phone sex cards resemble Fu Manchu's underground cavern, with perfect examples of beautiful women from all nations.

What is interesting is how quickly this shift has taken place. Whereas, only a matter of years ago, British sex work advertised itself as varieties of unmarked whiteness, with black women pictured in the role of dominatrix or wet-nurse if they were pictured at all, now sexual services, as sold through phone cards, are presented as a highly ethnicised affair (for more on the politics of race in sex work, but in a US context, see Nagle 1997). The rhetoric of exoticism has been extended and refined. Some have argued that this has taken place within a framework that continues to privilege whiteness:

> Even with the heightened exoticization of the sexuality of third world women and men, they are positioned within the global sex industry second to white women. White sex workers invariably work in safer, higher paid and more comfortable environments.
>
> (Kempadoo and Doezema 1999: 11)

It is beyond the scope of this discussion to consider the working conditions of different groups of sex workers in any detail here (see Scambler and Scambler 1997). However, the central suggestion is of interest. Perhaps even the proliferation and diversification of exotic types can serve to rebuild and consolidate the position of anxious white subjects in the era of globalisation.

I want to use the above example of phone sex cards to unpack some assumptions about the exotic.

First, exoticism describes an eroticisation of a power relation – and the exotic has come to mean the sexual hit of racialised power relations. This implies that the exotic object gains erotic status through association with a more mundane lack of status – exoticism reworks existing power relations. Although we could identify common structures and themes across different instances of exoticism, each manifestation is historically specific and combines components relevant to the particular history of that location. In terms of racialised exoticisms, this could suggest that while 'Africa' comes to stand in as the other of the West and therefore as archetypal exotic other, an erotic fixation with veiled women is linked to a more localised history of engagement with an Islamic world on the borders of Europe.

It is hard to imagine an exoticist fantasy that does not feed on an idea of lived social relations, however phantasmic. Racialised fantasies rarely extend to regions of the world that have had no historical relation with the homeland of the fantasiser – therefore inhabitants of the United States are unlikely to harbour exotic fantasies about the Burmese people, for example, whereas Indians from the Eastern states of West Bengal and Orissa may. In the past, I have believed that the familiarity that breeds racialised exoticism stems from colonial relations, either proper or neo-, and that the erotic hit is a result of the obvious and enforced power disparity between groups. The proliferation of racialised types from all over the world in the phone card end of the sex industry confounds my expectations of what is saleable and why.

Second, exoticism assumes some partial knowledge on the part of the fantasist – without at least some obvious tropes to construct the narrative, there is no fantasy to be had. Complete ignorance of the idealised type leaves no room for the particular pleasures of exoticism, because this requires a reworking of social boundaries and a breaking of taboos. However, recent phone sex cards show very diverse ethnic tagging – and although some tags can be traced to the outcomes of recent global shifts and crises, others remain fairly opaque in a British context. Third, exoticist mythologies take on a life of their own. Once demeaned groups have gained alternative acclaim in the sexual arena, that exoticist suggestion infuses their social character and becomes part of their racialised identity. However, it is hard to see the knock-on effects of commodified exoticism on, say, Argentinians.

The new exoticism of the digitalised cards confounds the idea that the exotic is only making strange the most mundane social relations. Instead, this new exoticism reveals its global ambitions and presents sex workers as highly differentiated and ethnically specific. Whereas previously such unfamiliar and unknown versions of foreignness appeared to be unsaleable to a British sexual imaginary with very public racial taboos and very formalised criteria of desirability, now commodified sex is presented as a global smorgasbord, tasty access to an array of authentic and unfamiliar treats.

I have some hunches about elements of this process – particularly in relation to certain nationalities and their emergence into the iconography of phone sex cards. The break-up of the Soviet Union and the disarray of the former Eastern bloc created large-scale economic hardship and desperate forms of population movement – and has included, famously, a sizeable influx of Eastern European women into the sex work markets of the richer West, as well as the more respectable flurry of Internet-bride websites. Despite the media scares around these processes, somehow economic neediness has succeeded in re-creating Eastern European women as exotic because they are seen as vulnerable and desperate objects. Of course, whiteness plays its part here in the construction of more valuable versions of femininity.

The great increase in cards advertising South-East Asian women of various nationalities may well be connected to the success and spread of sex tourism in this region (see Truong 1990; Bishop and Robinson 1998; Law 2000). It is hard to call up a British mythology of Thai or Filipina women – these places have not played an explicit role in Britain's recent imagination of itself. Yet the cards offer many varieties of South-East Asian women – and create a more explicit mythology in the process. Surely greater awareness of the possibilities of sex tourism informs the new myths around these unfamiliar racialised types.

However, other cards seem more mysterious. What is the extra saleability gained from declaring oneself Columbian? Although US cultural hegemony teaches the world that Latin means hot, is Britain not too ill-educated to understand this association easily? In 1992 my favourite card promised 'Naughty boys bow down before my dusky highness' – and I loved in particular the audacious reworking of political blackness and old-style coloured to make this inclusive and ambiguous identity of dusky. Now the terms are far more differentiated and, more than racial type, we are sold access to a national identity – 'Taiwanese Tiger Lily', 'Beautiful Young Indian Model', 'Japanese Special Massage', 'Oral Fantasy Brazilian', 'New from Madagascar – Your Black Fantasy, Wet, Juicy and Waiting'. The national and regional names slip in and out of older exotic types.

The orthodoxy of globalisation talk would have it that everything changes, rapidly and beyond recognition. Of course, this account has some resonance with how people feel about change and their lives and the attention to this process in both academic and popular arenas plays on these anxieties. At its most excessive, globalisation talk would have it that there are no uneven economic relations to speak of in the world, because these relations shift so quickly and without any logic of a centre that everyone has become part of the periphery. I do not want to detract from the real and ongoing suffering of the West's encounter with the new world economy – however, I do want to suggest that things are not equally bad for everyone, whatever the popular accounts may say. To return to an earlier point, I want to suggest that, once again, exoticism can offer an alternative access to the workings of power in our time.

The exoticist cultures that emerged in the heyday of empire mirrored the neurotic work of the imperial family – the construction of the domestic and the construction of the exotic went hand in hand (Haraway 1989; McClintock 1995). The implication of these more recent commentaries is that exoticism performed some necessary function in the construction of the nation as a domestic drama. As well as the handy disciplining of empire, this highly staged ambivalence enabled a restructuring of the home – and played a part in the birth of a whole new way of thinking of family, obedience and belonging. Without the alternative and complementary narrative of an excessive elsewhere, the linking chain between private home and national family was hard to sustain (Hall *et al.* 2000).

Perhaps the new exoticism of multiple peripheries and shifting centres echoes some aspects of this earlier model. Sex and intimacy still play their part in the imagination of the nation – and although the chain of belonging and obedience changes, the logic of linkage, from immediate affective bonds to larger kinds of allegiance, remains. The exoticism of ethnic fascination reveals the struggles around racial status and the state of the nation. Many of the themes and tropes of commodified exoticism continue a longer history of troubled whiteness as the pinnacle of world power. So adverts sell old myths of tropical idyll, carefree natives, sun, sand and sex – and sell this myth globally as a substitute and consolation for the real pleasures of imperial white power, for buyers of all colours. However, alongside this familiar and long-standing style of public exoticism, other more local negotiations occur. For a Britain struggling to escape the constraints of the nation as it was, while retaining the powers of the national family, the exotic becomes more necessary and exciting than ever.

If we read global crisis talk as an indication that the white Western subjects feel that the certainty of their privilege is being eroded, perhaps globalisation is remaking the Western subject by force. For an anxious Britain, this may offer an opportunity to remember bawdiness and relinquish the sexless status of whiteness (for a very British example of bawdiness, see Howell 1977). However, equally, this may open the door to new exoticisms, concocted to preserve the last traces of white privilege. Against the background of proliferating ethnicities in the advertised market for sex, signs of a new media panic begin to emerge. The erratic forces of the new world order have displaced and pauperised huge swathes of people – making grudging migrants of all too many, from many regions (United Nations 2000). As the boundaries and influence of nations come into question, fears of population movement take on a new urgency and virulence (Bhattacharyya *et al.* 2001). When globalisation is figured as an attack on the West, a corroding force that creeps in uninvited, contaminating the affluent with the diseases of the poor world, the contamination is all too often linked to the flows of migration. The debate about foreign sex workers echoes these mythologies:

> More than 1,000 women may be trapped into sexual slavery in Britain each year amid a boom in the illegal trafficking of women from eastern Europe …

… Women from the Balkan states and the former Soviet blocs, as well as south-east Asia and Africa, are charged thousands of pounds by criminal middlemen for visas or a smuggling arrangement to enter the country, often on the promise that they can pay off the balance of the fee in arrears by working for a few months in the sex industry or the 'entertainment business'…

('Sex slaves trafficked to UK', *Guardian*, 30 May 2000: 1)

The story asserts that up to 80 per cent of girls working in the sex trade in London are foreign nationals – they are tricked and deceived into coming to Britain, only to be trapped in an endless cycle of modern-day urban debt bondage:

She is just one part of a worrying facet that has changed the sexual landscape of the flats, massage parlours and call services that offer sex in the capital. Today, many women are advertised as 'young and fresh', 'brand new', and 'new in town' – all code words implying that the prostitute is foreign.

('Prostitutes imported into slavery', *Guardian*, 30 May 2000: 4)

In the manner of earlier Orientalist tracts, the piece expresses the most extreme concerns for the women involved. They occupy that age-old role of both scheming temptress and hapless victim. It would be easy for the reader to mistake the whole account as another episode in the history of titillating social investigation. The article ends with a quotation from Inspector Paul Holmes, and here the larger fears which underpin contemporary exoticism come into view again:

We have not yet reached saturation point but we will. There is nothing to indicate that we are not going to get the violence that has gone with the spread of the trade across Europe.

(*Guardian*, 30 May 2000: 4)

The panic narrative echoes some of the components of my guesswork analysis – the economic meltdown of the new world order, financial crises and brand new forms of colonial dependency all create fresh crops of vulnerable and needy people. The same forces remake the terrain of global crime, so that after defeating the old enemy of communism, the West is endangered by the uninhibited networks of organised crime mutating from the debris of various disintegrating societies (Castells 1998). The fear of a new traffic in women echoes the larger fears of new movements of populations:

The trade in human beings is an outcrop of international labour migration, and cannot be separated from it. Millions of people seek to migrate temporarily to work in richer countries in order to improve their economic standing at home. For men, in spite of the closing of borders in Europe and North America, opportunities still exist. For women migrants, apart from domestic labour (itself often subject to conditions of virtual captivity), prostitution is one of the few options. The traffickers, with their extensive networks, move in on the voluntary movement of women, and divert them into forced labour.

(Skrobanek *et al*. 1997: 98)

The concerns about the traffic in women are contained within a larger narrative that fears all population movement. Although one version views population movement as dangerously uncontrollable and therefore contaminating, and another views immigration control as dangerously exploitable and therefore contaminating, in both versions foreign people bring foreign practices which bring crime, disorder and uncertainty (Hage 1998; Fetzer 2000). In part, the anxiety here is that whiteness disguises a variety of types and roles – and that these women who pass as Italian or Greek in fact hide much more threatening national origins. In the age of rapidly changing identities, the distinction between exotic object and Western subject, between what is dangerously foreign and what safely belongs, threatens to collapse altogether.

As with other horror stories that link the hot topics of crime, sex, ethnicity and danger, the narrative fluctuates around a central ambivalence. The exotic represents extreme dangers to social order – but that danger is what makes the excitement. The detour through sexuality manages threat by making it pleasurable – which does not lessen the threat but provides an alternative strategy through which to encounter it. The machinery of exoticist fantasy imagines the new and shifting terrain of globalised networks as a static moment of knowable hierarchy. If exoticism solidifies power relations for erotic ends, perhaps the fiction of an exotic object consoles for other uncertainties and losses.

Although accounts of the exotic can take on an old-world style – as if the colonial postcards of another era are the last example we have – that structure of making power differentials erotic, not through any sub–dom role-play but through an appeal to the real world beyond sexual connection, continues. In order to refine our understanding of contemporary exoticism, let us review some key themes in the culture.

First, there is the continuing fascination with the foreign. Despite the changes in the global terrain, skin retains a special place in this mythology. Despite the decentring of the Western subject and the complications around any straightforward access to white power, dark skin still arouses plenty of exoticist excitement in 'white' nations, not least through the glamour of global commodity culture. Fantasies of fulfilment through consumer practices reveal a desire for the experience of darker skins, however disprivileged the lives of darker skinned peoples (Dent 1992; Klein 2000). Skin continues to work as the most obvious of fetishes – a covering that occludes the creature beneath, so that the exoticist eye sees only the gleam, the contrast, the downy texture of the scrutinised surface. Although ethnicity can be signalled in other ways and exoticist pleasure is being taken in other manifestations of ethnic difference, skin occupies a particular role in our visually addicted culture (see Ten.8 1992; Mercer 1994; Dyer 1997). The relearning of exoticist attitudes through consumer culture presents skin as the totem of certain experiences. Dark skin, and in particular African skin, appears endlessly – a marker for all kinds of pleasurable commodity. This is a continuation of the exoticist mythology that suggests that these lesser peoples have retained some valuable physicality that has become lost to the scrutinising subject of modernity proper.

However, as shown by the earlier discussion, global restructuring creates some new fetishes of foreignness. Eastern Europe emerges as the phantasmic other of the West, awash with shadowy dangers and contaminations. As part of this fantasy, the former Soviet bloc enters the pornographic imagination of the West as a source of endless and desperate flesh, all the more attractive for being white and admitting, belatedly, that the spoils of Western living are desirable and even necessary (Finckenauer 1998).

Contemporary exoticisms of the foreign are cut through with everyday experiences of commodification. The awareness of commodification inflects the exoticist gaze. On the one hand, authentic ethnic cultures, as opposed to commodified ones, are seen to retain higher and more spiritual values and an ability to resist the contagion of the market. This is an echo of very old mythologies in which landscape and people melt together to become a blur of sexual possibility. This is a story about self-realisation for the powerful subject, enabled by the warm weather and relaxed morality/spiritual culture/alternative value system of the new others of the tourist gaze (for more on consumer practices that seek to escape the failings of modernity, see Lau 2000). On the other hand, commodified ethnic cultures, as opposed to so-called authenticity, also elicit their own sexual heat of the not-quite-foreign. This is a tricky moment in exoticist dynamics. Rather than maintain the boundary between self and other, this is a process of incorporation, decorating the privileged self with fragments and trophies of otherness, all sold neatly packaged through international corporations. The role of the exoticised other in the form of any actual person is relegated here – and perhaps the accumulation of commodities replaces the need for any actual contact with the desired other. Of course, wearing the bought accessories of exoticism is pleasurable only for those certain of their position of relative power. As the frameworks of social status and power shift, dragging up as the fetishised other may become more dangerous.

These reworkings of myths of the foreign exist alongside other styles of exoticism. The intensive sexualisation of children is one such long-standing theme – despite the mob violence surrounding the sexual abuse of children, children continue to be sexualised through mainstream culture, precisely through their vulnerability. Like other fantasy natives, children represent a more innocent version of the desiring subject, a better, less formed and more vulnerable version of your self. In this we can see a continuum between national and global cultures of child sexualisation –

here children's lack of social status and power renders them vulnerable to becoming other, as if childhood is a race apart from adult humanity (see Clift and Carter 1999).

It is this recurring idea of the race apart that links the diverse themes of contemporary exoticism. In the main, we can see in each theme the residue of an older exoticist form. However, in relation to ideas of class the terms of desire have reshaped significantly. This is an older and almost lost exoticism, the desire of the powerful for the earthy and debased delights of worker's flesh. In a time when class has been so remade and reframed through such complex cultural traits, it can be hard to spot the resilient survival of this mythology. But look closer, and the perverse desire for downward mobility is apparent in the sexual aspirations of new lad and ladette cultures, in the rebirth of bawdiness as the English version of sexiness, in the anti-glamour and cockiness of having a laugh. Some eroticisations of a phantasmic working-class culture value the sense of looking back to another time:

> My suspicion is that skinheads hold an erotic fascination for gay male subculture precisely *because* they represent and preserve all these conservative notions of masculinity.
>
> (Healy 1996: 14)

Even if it is fictional, exoticism can make the categories and structures of our complicated social world seem more solid and knowable. Different objects address different points of insecurity. A nostalgic exoticisation of working-class cultures and identities can offer an illusion of security in a time of rapid economic restructuring. Remaking the mythologies of the foreign might produce a way of managing the status shifts of the global order. Relegating children to the role of absolute and vulnerable other may reassure anxious adults that they are, in fact, in control. More interestingly, the notion of the exotic as a moveable target reveals the possibility that this process is a characteristic of the powerful. Although the insight that the exoticist gaze sees what it wants to see regardless of the reality of the gazed upon is familiar and banal, a more useful idea is that studying the processes of exoticism may illuminate the workings of the powerful.

Again, this stretches back to our earlier search for a model of inter-relation between different spheres of human activity. All of our mixed-up and contradictory stories of sex and love and desire must somehow impact upon the self-conception of the powerful. The sensations of affirmation and anxiety seep across different arenas and carry the connotations of other homes – how can they not?

Does social disadvantage enhance sexual attraction?

The discussion so far has focused on ideas of foreignness and mythologies of race in the marking of power disparity. However, some theorists of heterosexuality have suggested that, even within the white nation, this most normative of sexual styles is based around an eroticisation of power differentials. The critiques of heterosexuality seem to imply that this has been the background of straight relations – that women are attractive to men because of weakness, that the privilege of active desire accrues to men and that what they are drawn to is the marks of disprivilege, all those conspicuous traits of femininity (Dworkin 1987). This whole dynamic is strong in many popular depictions of straight culture – from the manly desire to protect your little woman to the womanly wisdom that understands that, after all, he's just a man. Despite the various rhetorics of equality, heterosexuality is more often sold as a contract of complementarity than similarity. The power differential is part of the erotic charge – so that men can dominate or relent, women can resist or negotiate, all within the exciting role-play of heterosexual relations:

> It has been a main element of much feminist writing that heterosexuality is about the eroticisation of power difference. On the one hand, it is argued that it demonstrates a real problem of masculinity that men get aroused by women's vulnerability; on the other, it is argued that this eroticisation both disguises and naturalises social inequalities.
>
> (Smart 1996)

This form of heterosexuality survives through a myth of complementarity – the two halves fit together even if they are not exact mirrors of each other. Most other forms of explicit power differential must be denied in order to enable sexual contact – if not denied, presented as insignificant. However, the most normative of sexual cultures forms around a narrative of necessary power differential. This is the power differential under such consistent attack by the assorted processes of gender shift and global change. In the chapters that follow, I suggest that this may force a renegotiation of the styles and roles of intimate life for all, not least because so many people feel that globalisation represents a desperate attack on their well-being and sense of self. No love story tells desire as a process that demeans the loved one. However implicated in other, perhaps wider, sets of relations, love (if not sex) still represents the best hopes of many.

For the powerful, their sexual interest and even their sexual favours (although many would question who was doing the favour) can be presented as a valuable gift. Franz Fanon develops his analysis of the psychology of colonialism, for both coloniser and colonised, as a means of retrieving the debased humanity of both (Fanon 1986). Yet when he writes about the neurosis of seeking affirmation from the desire of the racially privileged, another sickness for the minds of the colonised, he forgets to include the other side. For the racially privileged, desire for the lesser can be an intended affirmation. If we can just get beyond violence, control, damaging contradiction and unresolved aggression, slightly calmer versions of exoticist desire can be presented as patronage. Occasionally, this can take the form of patronage proper, with sexual contact also initiating an entry and passport into another, more bountiful, world.

Although it seems unlikely that love can change the world – the small weapons of affection are ill-prepared for the more resilient forces of capitalism, state and other worldly forces – perhaps it is not decided that love must fall into the structures of the powerful.

Reworking the power relations of the global arena alters the availability of exotic objects. Although residues of the old exoticist histories leave marks in the popular imagination and in the structure of geopolitical relations, the position of the Western desiring subject is severely shaken by the uncertainties of globalisation. Whereas once exoticism provided a framework to enact the anxieties and desires of almost unassailable power, now that position of absolute objectifying desire has become far less sustainable. Perhaps there can be moments when the Western subject can regain the pleasures of the past – through travel to the poor world to confirm the economic power of developed economies and the availability of impoverished flesh, or through the displaced pleasures of consuming exotic commodities. However, the texture of everyday life under globalisation only occasionally offers such certain pleasurable confirmations of superiority.

Most of the time, the various shifts of global changes reveal the declining influence of the West. Or, at least, that is what is feared by the inhabitants of the West (Luttwak 1998). Whereas once the accelerated economic development that, along with its assorted free goods and labour, is the prize of imperialist expansion constructed imperial subjects who surveyed the world as their property and birthright, now Western subjects feel anything but omnipotent. The dangerous terrain of economic restructuring and the various national declines of the West dismantle the edifices of Western subjectivity. Without the reassuring rhythm of endless expansion, machine-like militarisation, absolute order in home and nation, the pleasures of exoticism become uncertain and threatening. After all, even at the height of imperial power, exoticism revealed a frisson of anxiety, a clue that the current order was not the only possibility. The security of material privilege allowed Westerners and other imperialists to toy with this fear in the pursuit of sexual pleasure. Without the safety of unassailable power, the exoticist imaginary opens other frightening possibilities. If the ability to objectify and take sexual conquests through force and coercion is a perk of economic ascendancy, perhaps the new economy will make new exoticists and new objects? Economic decline may signify the first step to becoming the abused sexual objects of some other occupier – and this anticipated loss of honour and gender propriety haunts the restructuring West. If Western man becomes a sexual object, he gives up the role of non-bodily reason, invisible subject, masculine controller. If Western women are no longer protected by the brutal machinery of empire, then they become as vulnerable to sexual terrorism as the women of the rest of the world. Without the cover of racialised economic privilege, the Westerners fear that it is their destiny to become no more than another form of native and to suffer the horrors of natives.

If the new world order demands a rollback of the long militarisation of the West, or at least its reinvention in another form, then the threat of new unknown armed forces brings with it a fear of sexual intrusion. In previous chapters I have discussed the widespread changes in the domestic and intimate lives of developed economies. Men and women painfully begin to relearn their roles and relations to each other. The relation between individual home and national economy is reworked to fit new circumstances. Emotional and sexual sustenance proliferate into a variety of forms in an echo of the flexibility demanded of all other spheres of life. The exoticist culture that typifies the moment of high imperialism relies on a chain of mutual definition – family to home, home to nation, nation to empire, empire to family of man. Changes in the relation between family and home within the white nation jeopardise the entire chain – without that component, the others cease to make the same sense. The whole complex bundle that we can tag 'the crisis of (white) masculinity' – ranging from the impact of feminism to deindustrialisation and partial demilitarisation, from male grooming to popular celebrations of a variety of styles of intimacy – articulates a fear that loss of power means becoming someone else's exotic object.

As well as the cultural shift away from fictions of an imperial centre, globalisation brings its own geography of power and influence. This may not be as starkly divided as previous geopolitical maps, but there are plenty of indications of neocolonial power imbalance. Whatever the components of this new imperialism, it seems certain that new cultural contortions will emerge. How closely these fresh myths of sex and power echo the structures of exoticism proper depends on the material context of their imagining. Will this new world retain the certainty of such binary roles as coloniser and colonised or, even, centre and periphery?

Although the crisis talk around globalisation assumes that the whole world has become vulnerable to this almost natural disaster, in fact, for much of the world the intervention of the global feels pretty much like old-style Western domination. However unsettled and disempowered Westerners may feel, the rest of the world continues to view our relative privilege with envy. When the signs of a globalising presence appear – be it in the form of branded goods, changing employment practices, foreign tourists or military – the global appears to inhabit Western styles and manners of being. The new order of dispersed and shifting power may have no actual centre – and certainly no proper imperial capital from which legitimation and cultural coding emanates – but the assumption of a nebulous, but certainly Western, centre pervades its lived culture (Latouche 1996).

Therefore, when we attempt to examine the construction of any new exoticism, this assumption of Western power and influence must play a role. Importantly, when the inhabitants of the poor world imagine an escape from the terror of global forces, they still imagine this as a journey to the metropolis of the West. Paradoxically, the jaded inhabitants of the West travel to the world of the poor in order to feel alive, escape the rat race, discover their spirits and their bodies and overcome the intense alienation of post-industrial decline. It is in this context that the phenomenon of sex tourism emerges and blossoms. Although the history of contact between richer and poorer communities has often included sexual exploitation as an add-on privilege of wealth, the emergence of an open and largely non-criminalised industry that organises this activity across national boundaries is relatively recent (Truong 1990; Bishop and Robinson 1998; Law 2000).

Some commentators have placed this event within a wider history of leisure and travel. It is this intensification of the leisure industry coupled with developments in international travel that has spawned the sex tourist (Truong 1990). Whereas previously travellers may have associated trips abroad with the possibility of sexual adventure, and fervently hoped to engage in some exotic and illicit activity, their success depended upon their own attempts. Now with such an open sales pitch to the fantasies of frustrated tourists, nothing need be left to chance. This industry acknowledges the desires of its customers. Once sex tourism becomes an open and explicit objective of the wider leisure industry, travellers need no longer rely on their own initiative to satisfy the desire for sexual adventure on their holidays. If anything, once certain poor economies realise the potential of mixing tourism with the sex trade, marketing flesh becomes almost official (Bishop and Robinson 1998). Despite the local costs, sex tourism brings much needed revenue to poor regions of the world. Predictably, this consideration has ameliorated the most ardent moral objection to the trade.

Commentaries on the growth of sex tourism economies and the related trafficking in sex workers have suggested that these events come out of larger disturbances in the global economy. Certainly, economic restructuring in many regions has given rise to large numbers of people desperate for work of any kind. The same forces that create pools of cheap and disposable labour for capitalism wherever it wishes to alight also increase the numbers of people entering sex work, for whatever period. However, there is a far longer history of sexual service from poor to rich nations – and the history of a militarised world order has included the necessary lubrication of tolerated prostitution. Cynthia Enloe argues that the public arena of militarised relations between nations and regions has always implied a parallel politics of gender:

> The militarism that was legitimated when mutual superpower hostilities were at their fiercest had to be fed by enormous infusions of public funds, distorting whole economies in both large countries and small. But even then, militarism couldn't live on money and weaponry alone. It depended upon policies to ensure certain sorts of sexual relations: male bonding that stopped short of sexuality; men's sexual liaisons with foreign women that stopped short of the affection that might reduce militarized racism; misogyny that stopped short of a domestic violence that might undermine discipline and morale; wives' and lovers' sexual fidelity that stopped short of their having any sense of entitlement.
>
> (Enloe 1993: 253)

Important within this project is the idea that gendered relations must be organised to sustain and reproduce the valued object of the male soldier. Enloe writes that this sustenance has often included provision for so-called sexual comfort. While militarised culture requires certain feminine behaviour at home, most obviously in the form of doting and patriotic mothers and patient waiting wives, there is also a need for access to flesh for military men (for more on the impact of military cultures on women's lives, see Enloe 1983). Enloe focuses on the official tolerance and enablement of sexual servicing of military bases – and in this implies that the participants are local women. No doubt this is most often the case, however the important relation is that of service, irrespective of gender. It is the occupying power of the military, even when only in training, that elicits this cost-effective service. When the military power of richer nations is based in docile and dependent regions of the poor world, the presence of soldiers with earning power itself transforms the local economy. This is an explicit benefit of hosting such bases, not only the declaration of allegiance to a greater power but also the trickle-down effect of military wages far from home comforts (for critiques of this suggestion, see Moon 1997; Kirk 1999).

Since the end of the Cold War, this long-standing arrangement of patronage has been disrupted. Economies that had learned to mimic home comforts for boys stationed overseas have now found themselves competing for more transient occupation by amateur travellers. The framework for global sex work was determined during the Cold War era – this was the period in which global sexual servicing adopted the style of an Americanised commodity culture. With the end of Cold War certainties and payoffs, sex tourism sells a momentary pretence of this imperial omnipresence. In the moment of buying sexual services abroad, every tourist can imagine themselves as a GI, embodying the epitome of military power and popular culture cool. Exoticism is as much about these fantasies of becoming a powerful subject as it is about access to the subjugated body of the other. Even without the accompanying machinery of empire, sex tourism echoes these older exotic structures.

Because the structure of this internationalised sex trade is a response to the buying power and movement of those who travel, other forms of market behaviour come into play. Sex as a competitive service, particularly when poor regions compete desperately for this custom, must be constantly represented as a new and exciting form of consumer hit. Just as the commodification of sexuality within rich nations gives rise to market segmentation and niche marketing, as well as a variety of product innovation, so also the sexual service economies of the poor world must learn to refine and repackage their products. Enloe discusses the pressures on Asian sex workers to learn new tricks and tolerate strange practices in order to retain the attention of their American clientele. She argues that the infamous debauchery and exotic perversions of the sex trade in these regions, in fact, has been concocted and performed to meet the limited attention span of foreign buyers. Exotic objects must learn to remain exotic by never becoming familiar or too much like the mundane stuff of back home:

Thai women working in prostitution … had to earn new sexual skills in the 1980s that they hadn't needed in the 1960s because by the 1980s their male customers, now mainly local and foreign civilians, had acquired new tastes, new insecurities, and new grounds for competing with other men. Similarly, around the US Navy base at Subic Bay in the late 1980s, bar owners, still dependent on military customers, introduced 'foxy boxing'. These entrepreneurs believed that having women wrestle and box each other on stage would make the American sailors in the audience more eager for sex with the Filipina employees. Women, in turn, learned that they would be paid for their performance only if at the end of a bout they could show bruises or had drawn blood. At about the same time, women in the bars were instructed by their employers to learn how to pick up coins with their vaginas. This, too, was designed as a new way to arouse the American customers.

(Enloe 1993: 156)

The economy of international exoticism itself creates new forms of subject. Just as the poor world scrabbles to become a source of cheap and hyper-disciplined labour in order to participate in the global market, cultures of exoticist consumption teach people to perform the identities that pay. In another painful instance of Orientalist distortion, the rest of the world tries to embody the fantasies of the West, because these are the terms of global participation. After the explicit militarisation of the Cold War, the more covert military presences of the not-so-new world order continue to enable the business of global sex:

We often think that increasing numbers of women are pressed into prostitution because of militarization. But there are forms of demilitarization – such as in Russia or Vietnam – that can bring rising prostitution, as men look for new enterprises and as women are displaced from other forms of livelihood.

(Enloe 1993: 27)

Although the turbulence of the shape-changing global order opens the possibility that the power and influence of the West may be in decline, there is no corresponding increase in the power of the rest of the world. Whatever we may wish, this is not payback time – at least, not yet. Instead, it is the unhappy experience of the poor world that becomes globalised, spreading its corrosive tentacles to previously more secure locations. The plight of the poor world is not improved by having more people join its unhappy state. The chances are that the times to come will bring more internationalised forms of commodified sex – more desperate, more disparate, with fresh styles of service emerging to answer the increasing anxieties of the relatively powerful, whoever they turn out to be. The new exoticism takes on the transnational and mobile structure of other institutions of our time:

Sex tourism has become a new industry. Recruitment agencies and impresarios link the local sites and sex industries in various parts of the world, indicating a parallel with transnational corporations in the formal global economy.

(Kempadoo and Doezema 1999: 16)

More than just another global industry, internationalised sex cultures inform and lubricate the contours of what the global is becoming. If exoticist cultures stage the discomforts and tensions of the powerful, new incarnations of these mythologies can reveal the character and constitution of new global powers. The structure of the transnational sex industry can reveal not only the shadowy flows of the illicit global economy, but also the fantasies that animate the subject formation of the globally powerful, new and old. This is the promise and the fear of the many mainstream attempts to relearn and harness the habits of intimacy, as discussed in Chapters 1 and 3. In the era of globalisation, the West feels its position threatened in many regards – from national sovereignty to economic security, from moral superiority to the ability to make others into objects. In the discussion to come I will suggest that, despite these anxieties, a more practised approach to intimacy may help us all to survive the unknown times ahead.

6 Representing sexuality

Position of the chapter – representation

In this position we learn how uncertain the boundary between showing and doing has become. This is a point on our educational journey at which we can at last begin to appreciate the pleasures of learning. Here we look, watch, wait, learning to pause. This lesson convinces us that carefully learned technique promises far greater satisfaction than the thin fictions of nature, that the artifice of culture is more fun than the imperatives of biology. In the process, representation becomes an end in itself, and we find that showing has its own pleasures.

This chapter examines some recent debates about the representation of sexuality – particularly representations that are intended to educate or to arouse. Ideas about the role and benefit of sex education are reviewed and the overlap between these issues and the debate about pornography is considered. It is argued that sex education cannot fulfil its social function if sex is imagined as either a purely biological or a purely technical affair. The chapter ends by suggesting that the worldly manipulation of Machiavelli should be combined with the educational journey of the *Kama Sutra* in order to imagine a sex education that prepares us for the intimate citizenship required in a globalised age (for more on the various debates about sex education, pornography and other forms of sexual representation, see Wolpe 1988; Segal and McIntosh 1992; Preston 1993; Thompson 1994b; Kipnis 1996).

This chapter puts forward the argument that the representation of sex is an essential component of learning to be a citizen in our time. In this, it follows a larger discussion about the centrality of representations in the construction of modern consciousness. The debate around representation continues to hurtle around popular culture – do representations change reality? Does culture matter? The discussion of sexual representation is implicated in this wider debate – will what people see affect what they do? But the heat around representations of sex comes from a far longer battle about the role of representation.

First, it is important to remember that representation becomes a hot topic at a certain moment. Much of the recent debate around issues of representation assumes that the contemporary world is distinguished by the excess of images and information available. The suggestion is that representations not only reflect another reality, they have become so omnipresent that representation is itself that reality. (For more on saturation by representations, see Baudrillard 1994. For more on the constitutive role of representations in making social meanings, see James and Ley 1993.)

In the realm of sex, this would suggest that sexual experience, despite all its tasty organic and spontaneous promises, is itself discursively constructed and, therefore, discursively experienced. This is Foucault's all too well-known point – that there is nothing natural about it and that the practices of sexuality are as tightly disciplined and coded as the rules of the Elizabethan court. We have already discussed these issues in previous chapters. The point here is the suggestion that sexuality is learned and made through representation. Once we accept this, the quality and nature of available representations becomes far more important – because this is what determines the nature and quality of lived sex.

How do we learn about sex and acknowledge desire?

The *Kama Sutra* persuades us that learning sex is a highly technical and highly philosophical endeavour. The knowledge that we seek to acquire combines physiological familiarity with spiritual contemplation, while tempering both these endeavours with an ongoing attention to instrumental ends. When examining the processes by which sex is learned through representation, it is helpful to remember the different aspects of this programme.

Sex education must address anatomical detail in some manner, because the competent lover must be prepared to navigate the range of human bodies. However, as numerous contemporary critiques insist, sex is also an emotional event. Without an acknowledgement of this, physical adventure can become unpredictable and potentially hurtful. The sex education of the *Kama Sutra* attempts to link an education in physiology with an understanding of social context and relations. For this reason, this educational project stretches from the arts of courtship and entertainment through the navigation of varied anatomies to the political consequences of intimate life.

Sex education could be seen as one component of the competencies required by contemporary citizenship. This volume has depicted an era of rapid change and suggested that even the safety of intimacy has been shaken by new kinds of social relation. Crisis talk about the effects of global economic shift also focuses on the dangerous instability of affective bonds. Refiguring interpersonal relationships through different combinations of training, punishment and incentive is a goal that appears in all kinds of visions of the future. Reconsidering the role and approach of sex education could be part of this project.

So, the heat around sex education is a recognition that how people learn sex has an impact on how society maintains itself. Despite continuing secrecy around sexual practice, there is some social investment in a public contract of shared understanding. In part, sex education through the school system attempts to foster this shared contract – this is the bottom line of contemporary practice and mores. Participate in the suggested manner and you too can live a life of fulfilment and useful contribution. Stray into other ways of being and seeking pleasure and you know yourself to be outside this contract of the norm. None of this necessitates an allegiance to heterosexuality – and although much discussion of same-sex contact has been disallowed in schools, popular culture ensures that awareness of that possibility is high (for more on banning discussion of gay lifestyles, see Smith 1994).

Perhaps for us the normative shared understanding is to imagine sex as genital contact between two people with an investment in the meaningfulness of this ritual. The meaning may vary from romance and commitment to fun and excitement – but the overall agreement that sex is this kind of action, with discrete beginnings and ends, and with a due recognition of significance, pervades most public discussions of sex. Sex education – in focused and formal incarnation as well as in the more diffuse lessons of other parts of education – works to teach this as one aspect of entry into society. In this, schooling in matters of sex echoes larger beliefs about the processes of education. This is a residue of the belief that schooling transforms the young into human beings – so that education is as much about adapting behaviour and adopting styles of being as it is about imparting knowledge (Bowles and Gintis 1976; Centre for Contemporary Cultural Studies 1981).

The varied public discourses of sex – from sex education to porn – seek to delimit the boundaries of sexual contracts. But there is still a huge investment in the potential benefits of articulation – talking about it, being open, educating the young about emotions, choices, diversity. Despite Foucault's warning that representation may not be all it promises to be because more talk means more constraint, not more freedom, all sorts of well-meaning people put their faith in the power of representation to alter social behaviour. If we could just learn to say and show the right thing at the right time, a better life could be available for all.

From this belief in the power of representation, sex education is based on the premise that both knowledge and technique can be imparted through the machinery of mainstream education. There is a strictly informational moment in this – the approach that teaches the most biologistic account of reproduction through line drawings of body segments. In an era which has seen greater and more virulent appeals to morality in mainstream politics, with a corresponding anxiety about any public representation of sex that does not constitute a prohibition, it is this disembodied information that has survived as the heart of sex education.

This is an account that presents heterosexual sex as an inevitable outcome of the imperative to reproduce. In this account, straight sex of the baby-making variety is presented as a 'fact' of nature – and the education consists in no more than a description of what is. By inserting sex education into this model of education –

'this is what happens in the natural world, I tell you the facts of it and values do not complicate the process' – everyone attempts to side-step the far trickier questions of morality (for a recent alternative and critique of this approach, see Harrison 1999). Accounts of young people's reactions to this form of schooling reveal a variety of resistances. However early the induction, they always know all this already – there is no point at which the biological account of sex can be taught as interesting non-social mechanics, the whiff of the social is always hanging around. Equally, the strange depictions of sex education seem to bear no relation to young people's experience or self-narratives. As a result, what is taught has little impact on how people choose to behave (for an indication of the confusions of formal sex education, see Blume 1996).

Before we assume that this confusion is inevitable given the contemporary ambivalence towards issues of sexuality, it is worth remembering that all views in the debates about sex education are deeply shaped by the belief that schooling makes morality and that this is the proper business of the school. This belief may be at odds with the beliefs of those receiving the education – and this resistance to moralising is a long-standing aspect of the history of popular schooling (Centre for Contemporary Cultural Studies 1981; Donald 1992). This resistance is not acknowledged by arguments for outlawing sex education from the school curriculum that assume that sexual representation will make useable sexual knowledge and therefore encourage sexual activity. Rather than suggesting that schools are beyond moral questions, this is an argument which says that schools must discourage sexual activity by silencing discussion and dissemination of sexual knowledge. In some versions, this silencing is to be augmented by an active discussion and dissemination of real non-sexual moral issues. The proper moral business of schooling in this model is the containment of sexuality.

For all the mud-slinging about dangerous permissiveness, the various positions advocating more detailed and socially grounded sex education are themselves highly moralistic. For advocates of more information, both of the range of bodily possibilities and of the emotional and social relations around these practices, schooling can adapt behaviour and inculcate different moral values. Here the moral agenda is less likely to be abstinence than responsibility – but even if this more permissive approach favours greater information and accepts a certain level of sexual activity within the framework of a moral life, the idea that schools will create and preserve a moral contract for the social good is strong within this sense of permission. Sex education raises these questions about knowledge, behaviour and moral life. And our knowledge about how some education affects behaviour is highly incomplete.

There is a question here about the nature of knowledge itself. Sex education combines a number of genres of understanding – biology in its non-deterministic version has a role here, as does some discussion of the emotional experiences that surround sex and the wider social relations which impact on our cultures of sex. Many commentators also advocate that teaching about diversity should address and diffuse fears, and therefore encourage tolerance. In a more directly instrumental vein, moral panics around teenage pregnancy and sexually transmitted diseases (STDs) demand a certain style of informational scare story. The difficulties of combining these modes of information and manners of learning into one coherent and useable understanding of the (sexual) world are not addressed.

In the end, we are left with the same old conundrum. Sexual knowledge demands an understanding of the body and its various irrational imperatives, with all their uncertain intersections between the biological and the cultural. But it also requires a far more complex form of understanding in order to place these strange drives in some comprehensible social context. Combining both forms of knowledge stretches the framework of existing forms of education almost beyond their limits:

> These essential requirements of good sex education include such basics as realizing that sex is not simply a physical act. It takes place within a framework of cultural, social, and emotional forces and must be dealt with as much more than simple plumbing. Sex is a magnificent, mighty force in our lives and must be seen as an element in the whole of who we are.
>
> (Preston 1993: 164)

The best and most sustained efforts to imagine this form of sexual learning come from gay thinkers and activists. The crisis of HIV and AIDS forces a widespread reappraisal of the processes and effectivity of sex education. In part, this has been a defensive response to a scary healthcare problem. But, alongside the very real and urgent need to understand sexual learning in order to enable safe behaviour, there has been a parallel and equally honourable wish to relearn and sustain the energy of eroticism.

For all the concerned talk about feelings and emotions, and the whole messy human context of sex, nothing can be learned without fostering some level of anatomical confidence. The feelings do not happen on some other plain, far from the dirty deed itself. Learning to negotiate pleasurable sexual encounters requires both kinds of knowledge, as well as an understanding of the ongoing tussle between mind and body, emotion and desire:

> But that is not to denigrate the importance of the treatment of the physical realities of sex. It is critical that an understanding of its physical workings must be given to any audience trying to understand its role in their lives. To do so, there are certain canons that must be recognized. The fundamentals include not assuming that one's audience knows everything. A sex educator must begin at the beginning and work from there.
>
> (Preston 1993: 164)

The *Kama Sutra* presents another model of learning sex through representation.

Here the assumption of full citizenship requires an understanding of these aspects of life. Unlike the pornographic take-up of this text in the West, the promise is not that every student will become an expert lover. Instead, much of the work concentrates on the more modest aim of recognising the role of sex in wider social rituals. The technical aspects advise the lover to adapt to the variations of the loved one's body – to learn sex as a constant improvisation in response to a particular human form. Unlike more recent and popular forms of sexual learning, there is no promise here to stay hard for hours or give her the best sex she has ever had – technical attention is encouraged, but is not fail-safe.

Unlike the model of education that promises positive knowledge and an insurance against uncertainty, the *Kama Sutra* offers a method of learning about the vagaries and changeability of sex. In this regard this famously pornographic text refuses the transfixed and transfixing spectacle of a representation of sex, in favour of a narrative about process. The experience and practice of desire, however, remain unspoken – there is little sense of a desiring agent here. If anything, this is a lesson that assumes sexuality to be insistent, irrational, one of those uncontrollable drives that will get you into trouble. All we can do is learn to pursue our pleasures and anticipate the possible social consequences. Representation provides the space in which we practice the route to satisfaction, however constrained.

Are dirty pictures bad for us?

There is a long tradition of thought which views dirty pictures as demeaning and damaging because they represent a distortion of healthy sex. This is an approach that attempts to be pro-sex and anti-porn – because sex is valuable and beautiful and spiritual and porn is degraded, commodified and dehumanised. Although I am caricaturing the argument, the central tenet of this position is hard to escape. Representation does miss that special something about sexual experience – the more obviously commodified the representation, the more obvious the gap between sublime escape and the depiction.

> Pornography does 'dirt on sex' by stripping it of its mystery, allure, and joyousness, and displaying it as tawdry, ludicrous, undignified, and sometimes hate-filled.
>
> (Grey 1993: 88)

Of course, the most familiar argument in our time is that sexual representations are degrading to women, and, perhaps, to children. This argument has been rehearsed many times, and remains powerful in its appeal to many (for a key text in this tradition, see MacKinnon and Dworkin 1997). At the root of the critique of pornography is the accusation that pornography fosters a fantasy of sexual power in which the ability to satisfy personal desire without regard for the consent or pleasure of the sexual object itself becomes the erotic moment. Pornographic representation teaches a way of being sexual that dehumanises the desired object – sex becomes an exercise of power upon the subjugated flesh of women, and those with no more status than women. As a set of representations, porn matters because of this painful effect in the world.

Alongside this argument that pornography teaches men to exercise violence through sex, and therefore the representation of sex should be censored, there is also another distinct version of the critique of pornography, one more often heard from within the anti-censorship camp. This is the accusation that mainstream pornography operates by eroticising things as they are (see the contributions in Segal and McIntosh 1992). This is also a concern that the sexual representations of pornography will shape lived sexual cultures, but here the concern is the homogeneity and normative pressure. Rather than providing a point of critique for contemporary sexual relations, porn perpetuates a damaging status quo – not only confirming that this is all there could be, but also making what there is seem sexy. For those who feel that the politics of sexual relations need to be changed and adapted, not least due to the unsatisfactory and sometimes damaging effects of male power and privilege, pornography as it is, and has been, operates as a block to change.

Without any room for alternatives, this erotic aesthetic limits our sexual imaginations. While the interaction of human bodies can take many forms and rhythms, public representations can become normative injunctions. Instead of freeing a realm of greater sexual diversity and possibility, commodified sexual representations show and sell the most mainstream of sexual choices and actors – when other kinds of people appear, it is as freak-show titillation for majority audiences. (See the use of 'dwarves' or obese women in porn. For another view on this, see Kipnis 1993.) And although porn may concoct a number of set scenarios for our erotic imaginations and give us the options of sex with a stranger, a lesbian try-out or group experimentation, the overall effect is to limit sexual adventure to a series of stock tropes. The surprises of real live sex never get on screen, because that element of surprise is not easily represented and packaged for sale.

The anti-porn critique argues far more than this. Not only is the charge that porn distorts and limits sexual innovation and possibility – in fact little tends to be said about the positive qualities of any form of sexual life – the main allegation is that porn presents abuse as the norm. This is the view that regards all porn as the eroticisation of power differentials, no more than a way of making attacks on the weak sexually exciting. In this account, porn not only limits the range of sexual possibility, it presents abuse as the only sexy option and distorts the sexual imaginations of a whole society. Instead of the diffuse and surprising adventures of real live sex, porn defines sexiness in terms of force, violence, conquest and aggressive exertion. Once people begin to learn their sexual repertoire through pornographic means, real live sex starts to become pretty violent and aggressive too. The anti-porn lobby argues that some, maybe many, men learn bad sexual habits through their addiction to porn – and the result is violence against women and children and a debasement of all human relationships. Andrea Dworkin argues that this becomes a human rights violation, as women face living with the consequences of a pornographic culture:

> We learn – still now, despite the gains of feminism – not to call attention to ourselves, only to the signets of our conformity: the sexualized conventions of grooming. We cover over being the victims of sexual abuse, because otherwise we are exposed in poses and positions and with bruises that excite some men or many men or nearly all men or the next man. Each abuser makes his cut, adds his mark, his smell, his ejaculate, his contempt, his destruction, to the social identity of a woman exposed. She is in the male mind – the minds of men – as the spread-out thing, or the bruised and brazen thing, or the serially fucked thing. She's rarely more than a picture in his mind anyway: spread ejaculate on her and she's a dirtier picture.
>
> (MacKinnon and Dworkin 1997: 31)

The argument is that pornography not only shapes the possibilities and practice of sexual behaviour, but also that these representations of sex come to infect everyday consciousness. The unfortunate dynamics of porn come to shape all social relations – and for women, this becomes the framework of all social experience. In order to reclaim access to full social participation, the incitement to violence and degradation of pornography must be policed and silenced. While pornography circulates, women become reduced to echoes of these images. Only censorship will allow us to see beyond the confines of the representation. In this telling, pornography grows to become the evil of our time – the rot at the root of all other social ills. Although the connection to economic relations tends not to be developed in this literature, there are indications that pornography is regarded as the very embodiment of corporate power:

> Every day the pornography industry gets bigger and penetrates more deeply and broadly into social life, conditioning mass sexual responses to make fortunes for men and to end lives and life chances for women and children.
>
> (MacKinnon and Dworkin 1997: 23)

The problem is that the commodification of sex, like other forms of commodification, sets up a chain of endless longing and unachievable goals. The process of commodification sells us products to sate our desires – but instead lures us into a never-ending quest for satiation through consumption. If any of us ever get the perfect product to satisfy our wants, the market is dead. Each moment of consumption must inculcate the buyer into a habit – each promising product must make another raft of consumption indispensable. Of course, this is all theoretical –

the term consumption encompasses a large range of buying habits, from buying bread or rice and oil in many locations because we all must eat to purchasing the accessories of particular leisure choices because this act promises to transform the kind of person we are. Not all buying rushes into the realms of commodity frenzy – and most of the world is not economically equipped to take part in this practice anyway. However, a version of anti-materialist critique of consumption lurks in the rhetoric of some anti-porn writing. There is a disgust that men can buy so many indistinguishable products – interchangable breasts and beaver shots, the same pictures and narratives in every publication. The similarity between pornographic products increases the sense that this consumption is compulsive and addictive – a neurotic repetition which robs men of agency and self-control.

This process of endless buying colonises erotic experience, so that the longing for the perfect product invades intimate relations and distorts people's relation to each other. With porn as the model of ideal interaction, real live sex can become a poor shadow of what is desired. In the manner of other commodified reworkings of everyday experience, porn sets up unrealistic expectations – and as a result, real life seems frustrating and limited.

Representation and liberation

So much harm is done in the name of sexuality – including terrible violence and pervasive abuse – that it is hard to resist the arguments against sexual representation. In a frenzied and undisciplined world, pornographic representation seems to present another incitement to the weak-willed – another bad lesson in how demeaned and limited human relations can become. Perhaps it is better to say and show nothing and hope that the return of self-teaching will bring better forms of living and loving.

However, our discussions so far have stressed again and again that sex straddles physical need and social convention – and that, whatever the role of the mysterious instinct, sex must be learned like any other social behaviour. However much we wish for magic and mystery, sex is already in the realm of the social and of representation, however coded and indirect that representation may be. The quality of sexual life can be improved only through improving the process of learning sex – there can be no return to an untouched natural sexual experience, free from the ugliness of modern society.

To return to the injunction to learn sexuality, rather than assume some innate or passively attained expertise, we must return to the role of representations in learning. We are back again to the mysterious relation between seeing and doing, between comprehension, understanding and activity. The baseline assumption for sexual education has been that experiencing sexuality through representation will lead to a replication of that experience through behaviour. First you see it then you do it. This assumption is based on a particular and simplistic model of learning that regards the untutored subject as empty and passive, waiting to soak up the representation of learning without mediation of any sort. Images and suggestions enter the consciousness of the student as discrete fragments, unrelated to other forms of knowing – what is learned serves as a manual of activity and the student becomes a sexual actor by recreating the representation (for related discussions of the role of the audience, see Ang 1991). Accounts of sexual life stories suggest that no-one processes representations in such a mechanical fashion – whatever the influence of seeing and hearing things, it is never a case of straightforward replication. Even if people intend to replicate, real live sex is not so standardised or predictable (see Plummer 1995):

> For all of us, writing those books was a means of investigation. We weren't promulgating a political position; on the contrary, we were playing with politics to find out just what was going on in our minds and our fantasies and, for some of us, our lives.
>
> (Preston 1993: 17)

Representation offers an opportunity to try out possibilities and to represent what could be as much as what is. Although pictures can play a part in this exercise, the representations that are imagined use a wider repertoire of communication to suggest the life that could be. Sex education may include this learning of possibility – through the varied suggestions of narrative and fragment, not only the copy-me diagrams of convention. Constructing our sexual selves may be a much more active process of readership, collection and creativity – because even the quest for pleasure is connected to other realms of social meaning and experience (see Bartlett 1988). When John Preston reflects on the response of gay men to early public warnings about the threat of HIV/AIDS, he suggests that, for those who had come out around the so-called sexual revolution, sex had been a political gesture as well as a bodily endeavour. He argues that the intensity of the sexual energy that characterises the early years of gay liberation and gay public cultures in the West was also an expression of the pent-up energy of selves that had been surviving in constrained circumstances. When the mouthpieces of still gay-hating authorities attempt to limit that sexual expression, it does not matter that this is done in the name of health concerns. To those listening, it sounds like the same old homophobic campaign with a new rhetoric. Any sexual lesson that exists is lost in the distrust of this history (Preston 1993: 163).

The wish to educate never comes free from its social context – and those receiving the boon of education know this as well as the educators. In relation to sex, there is already a popular suspicion that authority always wants to spoil everyone else's fun and that schooling is just another outreach of authority. This suspicion is more strongly verified in relation to gay sex. Sometimes the attempts at curtailing certain activities act as an advert to make them more appealing than ever. Given these complications, there is little point in designing alternative representations as positive images to be learned and repeated. The range of representation may enhance the range of sexual imagination and tolerance, but no image can guarantee a matching action in response. Instead, the benefits of sexual representation must be thought of in another way, not dependent on mimicry. Once again, the *Kama Sutra* emerges as an alternative model of teaching representation, in part because of its status as manual.

The fixed stances of porn or the frozen moments of sex education both present sexual interaction as a completed accomplishment – satisfaction or safety depend upon the replication of this finished moment, the recreation of a similar snapshot in time. Visual representation teaches sex as a series of poses. Even the most adventurous accounts can appear to be little more than mechanical – if you can contort your body into this position then this resulting ecstasy will occur. Despite its infamous status as a collection of sexual positions, the *Kama Sutra* outlines some guidance on the processes of sex. Although this is not the demanded emotional aspect of sex, with its irksome revelling in feelings and the dangerous risk of being broken-hearted, this is an account of sex as an interaction, a dialogue, a journey, something still in movement, not frozen in time.

Can representations be educational and erotic?

Of course, there is always a tension between the do-gooding of education and the turn-ons of people's choice. Even representations that succeed in being hot and trashy lose their appeal at the first whiff of educational value. The education that suggests restraint, or which hints at any restriction of sexual possibility, surely must scupper its erotic potential. Although useful information and even practical suggestions may be imparted, the element of warning caution probably dispels the dreamy excesses of eroticism. People want all kinds of things – but being told what it is acceptable to want is unlikely to be a turn-on for anyone.

However, the education that promises to instruct in the pursuit of more and greater pleasures occupies a different place in the Western sexual imagination. Although educational, this material presents its pedagogic project as amoral and purely practical. Pleasure is something that is taught and learned outside the framework of education proper, in either the guise of schooling or health guidance. The public good is not served by the pursuit of individual pleasure and so the public purse will not be wasted on training people to reach this goal. Instead, this has been an education under cover – in part learned through the revelations of others, in part through the non-respectable tracts of 'teach yourself eroticism' (for an example of diaries, see Walter 1995; for an infamous example of popular sexual training, see *A Lover's Guide*).

Sadly, the institutionalised versions of sex education do not concentrate on producing the best possible lovers for the health of society. Quality of sexual life is not an explicit concern at all, unless introduced in later life through some therapeutic or recuperative process. Instead, official sex education, as meted out through schools and public health campaigns, focuses on the technical without technique and the risky without adventure.

The aura of pornography, on the other hand, as a commodified and debased representation of sex for pleasure alone hides all trace of its educational project. In part, this is because these products are designed for sale, not edification – consumption comes into its own here, because it is not good for you or sanctioned by some higher purpose. The resistance to learning evaporates with the promise that you are buying some sought after and precious pleasure – instead of indifference, the suggestions of pleasure manuals can create the most diligent of students. Attempts to teach sex are torn between these two poles of telling people what is good for them and showing them how to get what they want. The rest of this chapter explores some other forms of instruction and tries to imagine a sexual education that can combine these two goals:

> The contracepted Westerners of today have many alternatives before them. It is surprising, now that love is more highly valued than ever, that schools do not teach its history, its battles, the rise and fall of its dominions, its diplomatic methods and rhetoric, and the hypocrisy of its economics. Perhaps sex education will prove to be the first lesson of a much longer syllabus.
>
> (Zeldin 1995: 76)

Much of this work has been concerned to retrieve sexual knowledge from the confinement of the private and to suggest, instead, that it forms a central strand of the worldly knowledges of our time. The problem is only to see this. Here I want to explore the idea that sex education may begin a longer syllabus – that description and talk of technique may lead to more sophisticated versions of education, and that this extended sex education may inform other arenas of thought and knowledge. To this end, let us resume our earlier discussion of sex and politics and their strange and troubled relationship.

Sexuality and statecraft

> The estrangement of the erotic from the domain of everyday life, so fundamental a legacy of the modern Western tradition, made the erotic a domain where the abstractions of moral discipline could find concrete and persistent illustrations and tests.
>
> (Simon 1996: 49)

The *Kama Sutra* acknowledges the role of intimate life in politics – sexuality cements and disrupts the public contracts of money and power and wily lovers can use this knowledge to their own benefit. However, equally, sex has its own impetus and may not be contained by the instrumental constraints of the public world – a clever politician or merchant may still be undone by the ways of love.

In this regard, the *Kama Sutra* suggests a way of thinking about sex and state – by imagining the key players of state as always sexualised in another arena it is possible to configure the mutual impacts that sex and politics exert on each other. Admittedly, this is the most simplified model of state, with wealth and power accruing through the overlapping endeavours of war, commerce and politics, all valued in the public arena of a courtly circle. However, this model is not so different from the examples that inform the great works of Western statecraft – in terms of political practice, ancient India and Renaissance Italy seem very close indeed.

I am taking the idea of Machiavelli's *The Prince* as the archetype of masculine statecraft – whether we value the prince himself or the adviser who makes this politics, this is a public world made by men and its politics is as military as its warfare. In more recent times this approach to power-broking has been reclaimed as a more general pattern for living – a management approach that spreads out to become an all-round life-skill and a particularly effective personal style. This is testosterone of the intellect, whereby manly accomplishment is measured not by brawn or brain alone, but by the ability to employ judgement and guile to achieve worldly ends.

In this, of course, the prince is very much the antithesis of a sexualised negotiator. Unlike the teachings of the *Kama Sutra*, which advocate wise but accepting manners of inhabiting both sexuality and state, without relinquishing hold of either, *The Prince* acknowledges no impact from the private world. Instead, here the political world is sufficient in itself, and although affections have their role in its workings, particularly the changeable affections of the people, there is no sense that the parallel world of sexuality has a bearing on the public world of statecraft.

I want to focus here on the various lessons that advise on how to elicit affection for political ends. Much of the role of the prince depends on this performative role – how to manage power in a manner that endears without inviting disdain, that maintains authority without inciting terror. Although the arena is the highly public business of state, the advice constructs politics as a series of affective relations:

> The subjects are satisfied because they have direct recourse to the prince; and so they have more reason to love him, if they want to be good, and to fear him, if they want to be otherwise.

(Machiavelli 1961: 8)

The first and central lesson in the exercise of power is to learn that the relations of power are experienced through reference to affective relations. However distant and fantastical the relation between prince and subjects, the mutual illusion that this political relation is, in fact, an emotive connection allows the political process to take place. Rather than explain the responses of subjects as a rational reading of the dangers and rewards which may come from the powerful, this is an account of political power as a sexualised relation to the populace. From our twenty-first century vantage point it can be hard to conceive of government as anything other than an emotional appeal for unquestioning love. However, it is worth remembering that Machiavelli emerges as scary master strategist of modernity partly because of this introduction of the personal address to the governed. The anticipation that the exercise of power may come to be experienced as a personalised and intimate relation leaps ahead through the next five centuries of political thought (on personality politics, see Oborne 1999; Plissner 1999):

> A prince, therefore, must have no other object or thought, nor acquire skill in anything, except war, its organization, and its discipline. The art of war is all that is expected of a ruler; and it is so useful that besides enabling hereditary princes to maintain their rule it frequently enables ordinary citizens to become rulers. On the other hand, we find that princes who have thought more of their pleasures than of arms have lost their states. The first way to lose your state is to neglect the art of war; the first way to win a state is to be skilled in the art of war.
>
> (Machiavelli 1961: 47)

This is the insight that Machiavelli is known for – the philosophy that has caused so much excitement and disapproval across the years. Politics is always a state of war, either overt or covert. Rulers who fail to prepare for this reality will not rule for long. But equally those not born to rule can become rulers by learning this lesson about the art of war (on the relation between war and politics in Machiavelli, see Garver 1987: 75–80). The other part of the lesson has been less discussed – that princes may be distracted from the public pursuits of warfare by the private concerns of pleasure. The retreat into luxury and personal satisfaction is a dangerous emasculation here – as we have all heard before – because it will leave you unprepared to meet your enemies. However, although the art of war is a constant requirement for any ruler, governance also requires the prince to deploy the rhetoric of intimacy. Abandon all knowledge of private pleasures, and no amount of expertise in war will gain the love of the population. In part, this is because the prince must elicit the allegiance of the people through strategic displays of strength and weakness, power and emotion:

> You must realize this: that a prince, and especially a new prince, cannot observe all those things which give men a reputation for virtue, because in order to maintain his state he is often forced to act in defiance of good faith, of charity, of kindness, of religion. And so he should have a flexible disposition, varying as fortune and circumstances dictate. As I said above, he should not deviate from what is good, if that is possible, but he should know how to do evil, if that is necessary.
>
> (Machiavelli 1961: 57)

The art of war demands the most worldly of rulers – rather than assuming a role of absolute virtue, successful government depends upon the ability to read and adapt to circumstances. The prince must become a flexible citizen long before the more recent demands of global flexibility. And, in the manner of more recent calls for flexibility, the prince must reveal an ability to collapse the boundaries between personal and political, between the affective and the governmental. Getting away with the moral expedience necessary for government demands an appeal to both heart and mind – because to elicit fear alone brings its own dangers.

The take-up of Machiavelli as a blueprint for modern management has itself given rise to critiques of this proposed masculinist style. (For more on the popular take-up of Machiavelli, see Harris *et al.* 2000. For critiques and reservations, see Fisher *et al.* 1994; Rubin 1998.) In one of the many populist take-ups of Machiavelli, Harriet Rubin suggests that women must strive to become princessas – because the public style of the prince relies upon a caricature of masculine power, and women can achieve more through other means. What the philosophy of *The Princessa* suggests is that women have already learned the successful use of intimacy in the public sphere. Rather than the enthrallment with power prescribed by the art of war, princessas use more affective strategies in order to 'best' their opponents – and in the process turn them into allies. The idea is that making enemies always has a cost, so instead, the smart operator uses her proficiency in the private-sphere skills of emotion and feelings in order to transform potential rivals into co-conspirators. In this, the book echoes other management/self-help tracts that promise women an alternative route to worldly success – as the book jacket of *The Princessa* puts it, 'to become powerful without becoming a man'. And the key argument is that women's greater proficiency in the language and texture of intimacy somehow makes a more effective preparation for the new demands of globalised public life. Wearing the costume of intimacy for effect has become one of the most valued strategies of power (Cooper and Sawaf 1997).

Against this, *The Prince* is a fantasy transposed to the present-day – another example of everyday stresses being re-imagined as battles of wit and strategy. Success in public life, however modestly public, seems to require this attention to military strategy and political manipulation – as if these were the people skills that bring everyday influence. Becoming princely has been presented as a self-aggrandising narrative adopted to negotiate power. In the mythology of *The Prince*, the public man shuts off the dangerous vulnerability of sexuality and instead concentrates his attention on the gratifyingly knowable world of political intrigue.

The modern-day critiques of self-deluding princehood, on the other hand, invite us to inhabit sexuality and emotion as a positive strategy for encountering everyday power struggles. Much of this is linked to a conscious attempt to feminise public strategy – if boys learn combat, girls learn compromise through affective strategies, and the implication is that more can be gained through the second approach. However, *The Princessa* critique is also an acknowledgement that women cannot assume the role of unsexed manipulator easily – even as women attempt to unsex themselves in the public world, the eyes of their social interlocutors make them into sexual beings once more, and perhaps not in a manner they would choose. The guides to success for women advocate a negotiation with lived social relations – so that strategies make room for an awareness of sexualisation, subordination and the longer-term punishments of success. *The Prince* is also an exhortation to anticipate the effects of power, yet the softer styles of negotiation are downplayed in favour of the war-state model of activity.

But given the shifts in public life (see Chapter 4), could a modern-day Machiavelli begin with a lesson in sex education?

The uncertainty of the present is caused, in part, by the collapsing of public and private worlds through a variety of forces. Many of the more recent strategic documents that have been reviewed here attempt to plan for some greater integration between intimacy and political intrigue, between the realm of affective connection and the realm of instrumental strategy (see Chapter 3). Whatever the ill-considered slogans of emotional reason, feminised work practices and work-life balance, the underlying message remains – success in public life requires some lubrication from the language and style of intimacy. Now any effective prince must acknowledge these demands when constructing a strategy for worldly engagement. My suggestion is that the lessons of Machiavelli can be combined with the guidance of the *Kama Sutra* to construct a sex education that begins the longer syllabus of relearning citizenship.

The *Kama Sutra* presents induction into sexual practice as one aspect of a more general induction into civilised life. *The Prince* presents political life as an induction into self-presentation and strategic use of personal connections. Both treatises assume that the complicated business of human interaction and affective allegiance must be studied and learned – nothing at all comes naturally in either document.

This volume has attempted to reveal the extent of the changes impacting on global sexual cultures. As we have discussed in earlier chapters, the expression of sexuality takes place in relation to other forms of social expression. Although there may be no absolutely determining factor in this relation, sexual culture adapts to wider contextual forces – and the new expectations that have emerged in this time of change have pushed many to become students of intimacy again. It is in this context that sexual education becomes open to debate and reform. Previous discussions have been split into the opposition between increasing information and encouraging abstinence, preferably through ignorance – and this chapter has reviewed some of the pitfalls in this either/or debate. Increasingly, however, there have been signs that sexuality cannot be learned as either natural impulse or as a series of cautionary health bulletins. Neither one prepares the young, or anyone else, for the lives that they will lead. Perhaps instead some combination of the insights of the *Kama Sutra* and Machiavelli could inform a more effective programme of sexual education for shifting globalised times?

Let us review the requirements of any such programme – what knowledge is needed for happy sexual citizenship?

1   Mechanical knowledge cannot be avoided. However, these mechanics must be placed in the context of social relations.
2   Individuals need to negotiate social norms that are in the process of change and may change further, in unpredictable ways, within a single lifetime.
3   Sexual education needs to expand its parameters to balance sexual pleasure and safety – and to suggest methods of managing the balance between the two.

At the heart of these suggestions is the assumption that the arena of sex exemplifies many of contemporary society's most valued attributes and experiences. The conception of sex grounds other forms of intimacy and closeness. Learning to be sexually confident and secure becomes indistinguishable from the ability to be generous and supportive in non-sexual or less obviously sexual arenas. Even if these ill-supported claims are never made openly, the excessive weight placed upon the largely mechanical sex education of compulsory schooling reveals a greater anxiety. If we cannot teach young people an effective manner of combining and negotiating physicality, affection and emotion, then other social relations may crumble. As discussed in Chapter 1, the crisis talk around heterosexuality assumes that if this foundational sexual arrangement flounders, the rest of society will fall. This is why sex education should be informed by both the *Kama Sutra* and Machiavelli – one approach that links the spirit with pleasure, the other that places the destiny of individuals in their interaction with the group. Sexual citizenship must reach an equilibrium between these two calls – and perhaps it always has.

Let us review once more the key lessons of the Machiavellian education that promises to prepare us for the shifting terrain of contemporary life. First of all, getting what you want is always a process of negotiation. However powerful, whatever your resources, instrumental ends are gained in the terrain of the social, and so the social effects are part of the outcomes that must be anticipated. Second, the social terrain is one of extreme and constant danger. No-one can maintain absolute fortification at all times, so staying safe depends upon maintaining contracts of mutual benefit. Third, and related to the second lesson, maximising individual benefit depends upon maintaining contracts of mutual benefit. The exercise of power is tested by the ability to form bonds of identification with your associates at all levels. Personal interest can be pursued most successfully through an anticipation and accommodation of the context of the social.

Most of all, and this may be the heart of the whole lesson, a well-orchestrated plan can make everyone happy. In *The Mandrake Root*, Machiavelli (1979) turns his (heavy) hand to comedy and constructs a play in which everyone wins in the highly instrumental pursuit of love. Here a young man desires a great beauty – but she is married and pious. Fortunately, her foolish husband wishes to gain an heir – and is persuaded to surrender his wife's honour to a stranger so that he, the husband, may be saved from the poison of the fertility drug, the mandrake root. Through a convoluted plan that involves the collusion of a corrupt priest and a debauched mother, the young man strikes up an affair with the beauty and the cuckold can look forward to his future offspring. In the end, everyone gets what he or she wants.

Learning sexuality from Machiavelli appears as the most post-romantic of cynical jokes. How can the double-dealing of statecraft be reconciled with the selfless passion of love? How can the irrational calls of the body be contained in the instrumental plans of princely ascendance? In part, Machiavelli is apt because the joke about calculated deployment of sexuality reveals a key lesson. The joke is the form that makes the lesson comprehensible (see Zizek 1997). Whereas the endless battle between liberal informationalism and censored restriction in sex education assumes that the kernel of sex is there, waiting to be formed by the intervention of public discourse, the nod to Machiavelli reminds us that the pursuit of sex is only one aspect of the self-interested quest for self-realisation.

The quality of sexual life will be affected by the ability to effectively negotiate the wider social terrain around any encounter. Mechanics alone cannot guarantee pleasure – in either immediate or more enduring varieties. For this reason, the lessons of the *Kama Sutra* appear to be more suited to the endeavour of sexual education – after all, this tract sets outs to achieve precisely this aim. However, as we have discussed, the context and conception of sexual life in this work is far from the spiritually uncertain sexual cultures of the unevenly de-industrialising and/or post-industrial spaces of globalisation, formerly known as the West. So, to refocus and to contrast with our other key text *The Prince*, let us return to the lessons of the *Kama Sutra*.

First, the attainment of sexual skill requires due diligence – and cannot be achieved in isolation from other essential aspects of education. Second, sexual skill is not only a way of learning how to give pleasure – it is also a training in experiencing pleasure. Neither part of the bargain can come without learning.

Although the *Kama Sutra* has taken on its own joke quality through the exoticisation of Western translations, I have tried to argue that its injunction that the route to citizenship requires an attention to the business of sex – an injunction that is both serious and funny – has lessons for our time. In this, it offers a complement to the insights of a Machiavelli reworked for the era of globalisation. By combining the call to serious study that retains a sense of the ridiculous and the call to hard-headed social negotiation that remembers the frailty of the individual, perhaps we can imagine a new framework for sexual learning.

Imagine the points of resonance when we combine the two sets of lessons. Getting what you want is always a process of negotiation – and learning to give and get pleasure are mutually dependent. Of course, there is a mechanical moment in this lesson – a suggestion that it takes some time and patience to experiment with the machinery of more than one body and the interaction of those bodies. However, there is also a larger lesson about instrumentality and the pursuit of individual interest.

Most immediately there is a need to think again about how anyone learns to explore, exercise and enjoy their sexuality. As we have discussed, this must entail both mechanical information, emotional, extroverted explanation, and some clues about negotiating the unpredictable minefield of contemporary social and sexual relations. However, the impetus behind bringing together the *Kama Sutra* and *The Prince* comes from a belief that the core lessons of sexual education can and must find a life beyond the purely sexual. In the instance of the *Kama Sutra*, this extension is contained in the original text. This is the informing belief structure of the work – that an induction into responsible and responsive sexuality is an essential aspect of any schooling in citizenship. In the worldview depicted in the *Kama Sutra*, this is important not only because society requires good lovers but also because the qualities of the tutored lover bring benefits to other arenas of social interaction. The skills of the bedroom have a life beyond the moment of sexual union.

Inasmuch as this larger lesson has been acknowledged by Western admirers and translators, there has been an assumption that the benefit is of a purely personal nature. This is the much vaunted payoff of Eastern practices. With this instruction, the formerly alienated Westerner can learn to reunite body and spirit, pleasure and morality, physicality and peace of mind. Here the pursuit of sexual enlightenment and pleasure promises to deliver a greater ease and satisfaction in all other areas of life. If there is a larger social benefit from this process, it comes as a by-product of this individual endeavour. The world becomes calmer because individuals learn a greater ease.

The introduction of Machiavellian approaches to the arena of sexuality sits less easily with mythologies of love and romance. Whereas the *Kama Sutra* at least focused on the legitimate pleasures of sex, albeit within a hedonistic and commitment-shy framework, Machiavelli makes little mention of the softer world of sexuality. Instead, his works present a highly calculated approach to public social interaction. This is the world of skulduggery and intrigue – not in the pursuit of romantic conquest or even momentary sexual pleasure, but with far more sinister and far-reaching goals in mind. This is the philosophy that promises to teach the most ruthless pursuit of self-interest. For this reason, it seems uncomfortable to suggest that this approach could lend itself to sexual education. The ruthless pursuit of self-interest would seem to be a major cause of harm and pain in contemporary sexual culture. A sexual education that taught individuals how to pursue these self-interested goals more effectively would only exacerbate existing problems.

This misapprehension has been at the heart of most discussions of sex education. Successful sex education purports to create better citizens – people who exemplify the moral standards of their time. Although this morality may take the form of abstinence or of honest affection, there is an expectation that effective learning will persuade people to look beyond their own individual wants. Otherwise the world threatens to become a scary place in which selfish goals overtake any communal good.

The introduction of Machiavelli is a response to this fear. Although the model of statecraft proposed appears to favour the pursuit of individual power and influence, this is a highly social account of networks of power. If anything, the individual is revealed to be in thrall to the group – even, and perhaps most especially, when that individual is a prince. Worldly power is shown to be subject to a social contract that is in a process of constant renegotiation. Maintaining personal power requires individuals to make a nuanced reading of their surroundings and to adapt their behaviour to these constraints.

This is the lesson that could be usefully transferred to sexual understanding. First of all, there is the possibility of re-imagining selfish goals as a negotiation with social forces. Second, learning to pursue these selfish goals effectively may teach people to be better citizens, precisely because individual goals cannot be achieved without a dynamic process of social negotiation. Placing an instrumental and goal-based model of social relations at the centre of this most intensely social of activities may encourage everyone to think of their individual interest in relation to the group.

Of course, this account of the benefits of learning citizenship as an ongoing process of negotiated constraint sits more easily with ideas of public life. In the public realm, it is expected that each will pursue individual goals yet adapt to social constraints and expectations. There is even some celebration of the dynamism that self-interest can bring to social formations. Think of the cult of the entrepreneur or the quest to build community leaders; these endeavours portray selfish energy as a force that contributes to wider social well-being despite itself. The goal may not be social benefit, but the quest to achieve personal goals drags along the rest of society. This is an account of the social that assumes that some people must be leaders and doers, while others will never progress without the injection of someone else's personal ambition. More recently, the apparatchiks of the new centre-left who have come to occupy the centre ground of so much policy and political debate, have shown some discomfort with such a self-centred and individualistic account of social progress. Surely human well-being depends on more cooperative and caring kinds of social relation. It is this critique of new right accounts of economic vanguardism that informs the return to communitarian ways of thinking. Now we are all supposed to understand that well-being must entail more than the simply economic. Social and affective ties also determine quality of life. Naked ambition cannot sustain any society. The *Kama Sutra* and *The Prince* together offer a route to negotiate this recent realisation.

This is not a call to return to a rhetoric of social Darwinism or to suggest that non-instrumental social interactions have no value. Instead, this is a suggestion that we recognise how far most people are from realising their personal goals, in the realm of sexuality or anywhere else. The cult of entrepreneurial self-interest has largely impressed upon people how ill-equipped they are to pursue or achieve the things they most desire. Far from expanding the empire of the selfish individual, for most people the years of the new right only confirmed that their destiny was to be led – always dragged behind in the wake of some more enterprising person's selfish dream. This is no model of sex education – although many have learned that even their desire is not their own. Instead, Machiavelli proposes that everyone can negotiate the social to take power. What more empowering or inclusive story of learning could there be? In this, the sexual stands in as the archetypal practice ground for learning morality and self-interest.

Taught in this manner, perhaps sex education could become the first lesson in a wider education? It could be an access route to the opaque demands of citizenship that draws us in by our own weak and human desire for love and physical pleasure. If we are in the business of learning new modes of the social, intimacy may be a better place to start than many:

> A cultural tradition that advertised the dangers of the sexual made of the sexual, a road map where other dimensions of self that were to be excluded from the everyday self or were denied full expression could rally, enriching the erotic and being enriched by the erotic, which is then to be experienced as having a domain, an elaboration of discourses, a license of its own.
>
> (Simon 1996: 49)

The separation of spheres from which sexuality emerges grants a paradoxical power to the most private realms of the self. This is the space of licence, where new modes of being can be considered and tested, where we invent our best selves and keep them safe from the harms of the public world. If we are to learn new ways of being, then that moment of innovation must play its part. The next and final chapter argues that these new ways of being are emerging and that a reworking of the terms of sexual propriety may teach us to see the possibilities for human survival in dehumanising times.

7   Spaces of sexuality

Position of the chapter – open secrecy

This is more an attitude or a style than a position. Here the knowledge of
the outside world, with all its strange dangers and possibilities, enhances
the heightened moment of intimacy. Although the secret moment may not
be strictly private, or strictly public, the sensation of occupying another
space suffuses the experience. This is not quite a spatial sensation, yet the
particularity of this doubleness can be best understood through reference
to the metaphors of spatiality – the special frisson of being somewhere
between inside and out, between hidden and revealed, partly expansive and
partly enclosed. This is the pleasure of the socially sanctioned secret.

This chapter reviews some ongoing themes of the work and relates this previous
discussion to the debate about the nature of public and private spheres of life. This
includes a discussion of myths of the city as the space of sex, and the threats and
promises contained in this mythology. Ideas of sexual propriety and the spatial
implications of these ideas are examined, in order to suggest that shifts in the terrain
of everyday life demand corresponding shifts in concepts of propriety (Hallam 1993;
Califia 1994; Bell and Valentine 1995).

Sexuality has been described as a land apart – foreign in the best sense of freeing
possibility, but also strange and requiring translation and mediation. In Orientalist
imagination, the *Kama Sutra* typifies this myth of foreignness. Coming from one of
those overwritten lands apart that have come to constitute the formation of the
West, the work enters Western imagination through the task of translation. The
escape to another place that is already right here needs the mediation of some other
language or register. My suggestion in this chapter is that perhaps sex is this kind of
secret? Perhaps this most close-to-home of matters, this endeavour and arena that
touches our most intimate places, requires the fictional excursion to another realm
in order to become visible and comprehensible. If this is the case then the language
of closeness and of distance offers the necessary diversion for an understanding of
sex – the journey into these fictional spaces allows the translation of the much too
close. In the telling, sex comes to belong to the otherness of distant places.

In part this myth of foreignness stems from an era of exploration – not only out into an uncharted world, but also inwards into an unknown body. The expectations and style of contemporary understanding retain the traces of the scientific revolution that accompanied Europe's realisation that it could own and rule the world (see Jardine 1999). This is a manner of scrutiny and exploration that wishes for mastery and wonderment – the belief in humanity's ability to experiment, measure, chart, dissect and ultimately demonstrate the constitution and workings of the world is accompanied by a desire to find the elsewhere beyond human conception (see Fausett 1993). With dissection and anatomical science based on these observations, the medical echo of adventure travel, the body as instrument becomes increasingly known. Anatomy constructs the body as a series of functional machines – each with its own purpose and interdependence. In this process of bodily mapping, creation becomes both more and less wondrous – infinitely complex, but no longer the magical, 'made in seven days project' of an absolute god (see Sawday 1995).

The birth of science did not herald the immediate death of God. In fact, as the twenty-first century returns to very tired spiritual questions, the announcement of the death of God may prove to have been somewhat premature altogether. However, the ascendance of science has heralded a new chapter in the long tussle between faith and learning – a more bloody continuation of the tradition that executed philosophers because they had the temerity to think.

However, the curiosity of the anatomists who laid the path for modern medicine was not fuelled by a desire to overturn the rule of God – or at least not explicitly. Instead, their pursuits were legitimated by the more modest goal of better knowledge – a quest of obsessive detail rather than an alternative account of all creation. In the manner of many other dedicated and pragmatic researchers, these men of science presented their findings as proofs of the greatness of God. Science wishes to complement and supplement religion, not overturn it. Anatomy may have unpacked the workings of the material body, but the soul has remained unchartable and beyond scientific knowledge (Barker 1984).

This developing contract between religion and humanism, the arena of faith and the arena of knowledge, has given rise to new conceptions of the body. Science has claimed the instrumental features of the body – and describes its machine workings as a knowable and rational system. However, in an appeasement to faith, science acknowledges the limits of this functionality – the body as machine cannot account for the many non-instrumental aspects of human existence. Into the catch-all of the non-instrumental fall the various enigmas of the soul, consciousness, sexuality and physical pleasure – the characteristics that distinguish humanity from beasts and make us all more than flesh alone.

Although commentaries have focused more often upon the mysteries of consciousness and the soul and have taken these as limits to materialism, sex as a more than instrumental process also falls into this discussion. Within the framework of knowing through looking and a sense of exploration as pushing forward frontiers of knowledge, the mystery of sex, soul and consciousness is figured as just over the horizon. Although there are some suggestions that soul and consciousness are intrinsically unknowable because divinely ordained, sex, as an altogether more human mystery, always promises to be on the brink of discovery.

In fact, the endeavours of anatomists have made some headway in describing the physiognomy of sex. Of course, the processes of reproduction are among the first adventures of dissection. But more than this, there are attempts to uncover the bodily make-up of sexuality's mysterious excesses. However, the exciting secret of reproduction, and by implication the even more mysterious realm of sex and pleasure, remains somewhat distant from the central activity of anatomy (Laqueur 1987). The normative model for the divine creation of the human body remains male. Women's bodies enter the frame as the conduit through which this wondrous creation can be reproduced, but the larger secrets of the human body are seen to reside in the forms of men (Sawday 1995).

Of course, there is an elision in this account of the interface between divine creation and human knowledge. Whereas the male body could serve as a model of the whole complex machinery of the living being, only the secrets of the female body could reveal the moment when humanity becomes a necessary partner in the project of divine creation. Reproduction is relegated to the sidelines of mainstream anatomy, because women's reproductive organs represent a deviation from the norm of the male body. Yet the most central secrets of the anatomical project, how the mortal body can replicate the divine prerogative of creating life, can only be understood through the anomaly of the female form. Sex becomes the domain of that other country, women, an association that enhances the adventure of secrecy but also confirms the division from public life:

> Cultural license was granted to contemplate the sexual, but in an isolation that actually reinforced the continuing exile of the sexual from the rest of social life. The experience of sexual conduct was necessarily viewed as translatable into the facts of sexual behaviour – the idea that the establishing of the physical geography of the sexual orgasm could become the foundation of sexual science at its most transcendent. The naturalization of the sexual required a view of the sexual that was increasingly ahistorical.
>
> (Simon 1996: 21)

In the manner of other educational journeys, this work ends with a return to the concepts of mapping. Although much of the previous discussion has shown how hard it is to find the place of sex, sexual life is still framed and constrained through the importance of placing. This last chapter attempts to chart the contemporary effects of that deep uncertainty about anatomy and geography, the ongoing mystery of the proper place of sex.

The dirty places of sex

> And we cannot overlook the past and future impact of deviant individuals with
> unusual amounts of insight or resources who attempt to alter the boundaries of
> the city, an anatomy which most people accept as if it were the map of their
> own bodies.
>
> (Califia 1994: 213)

In our attempts to rediscover sexuality as a project of education, the concept of
navigation takes on a heightened importance. When Califia compares the map of
the city with the map of the body she reveals the interdependent resonance between
these different scales of geography. Her point, in this celebration of outlaw innovation,
is that for most people the navigation of the places of sex appears to be preordained,
without room for individual exploration or alternative routes. Without unusual
amounts of insight or resources, we are unequipped to discover the hidden
possibilities of bodies or cities.

Sexuality appears as another country, comprehended through the translations of
travellers – or as another space, distinct from the orderly conduct of everyday life.
The spatial imaginary of exploration informs the discussion of sexuality – certainly
at the moment when anatomy attempts to render the body transparent, and still
now when sexuality does so much work as the space apart from the tedium of the
everyday. The discussion that follows focuses, in part, on the lived geographies of
sexuality, because these are the spatial relations that constrain and enable sexual life.
But more than this, this chapter explores the idea that sex is made through spatial
concepts – as a journey or an elsewhere, as private and public, as a terrain to be
mastered.

Commentators have increasingly placed space and place at the centre of debates
about social meaning and relations. This comes in part from the academic trend-
chasing of geography fanciers – another moment that seems already past. More
substantially, attempts to theorise the nature of the newness in this allegedly new era
– of postmodernism, globalisation, new world order or end of history – have taken
spatial relations as a key indicator of shift (for an overview of these debates, see Soja
2000).

Alongside that body of work, another more populist set of accounts has emerged
which presents a world of dramatic change as a professional challenge – a new maze
for entrepreneurs and policy-makers, full of fresh puzzles to solve. Although many
of the readers of these works may have no role in these earth-shattering events, the
manner of presentation encourages the happy pretence that these are changes that
can be understood and capitalised upon by those in the know. That work also stresses
the importance of spatial understanding in this new world (Kennedy 1994; Luttwak
1998; Soros 1998).

Alongside these developments, academic interest in sex has grown a branch of
sexual geography – not the promising charting of the body, but an awareness that

sex occurs on a terrain of spaces. That work has developed accounts of the sexualised mythologies that surround particular places and zones (see Bell and Valentine 1995). In keeping with the discussion of this volume, it reveals the role of territory and individual navigation in the performance of identity, perhaps most of all in the identities of sexuality that emerge in the moment of performance:

> Disalienation in the traditional city, then, involves the practical reconquest of a sense of place and the construction or reconstruction of an articulated ensemble which can be retained in memory and which the individual subject can map and remap along the moments of mobile, alternative trajectories.
>
> (Jameson 1991: 51)

The flexible, performative subject of globalisation, that person who is in a constant process of remaking themselves anew, traverses space idiosyncratically to construct a map of personal meaning. The articulation of sexuality is part of this mapping – one of the ways to be embodied in space. Attempts to understand the role of spatial experience in the construction of our sense of self, including our sexual selves, range around these various journeys.

One aspect of this has been the interest in community formation around sexual identities (Bell and Valentine 1995; D'Emilio and Freedman 1988). Another has been the creation of sexual zones and maps. This is an old mythology of the city, as old as Sodom. Somewhere, among various signs of urban decadence and wilful pursuit of pleasure, there are cities that live for sin. And, however much the story is told as a warning, it always contains a promise as well. In the commentary and anthology, *The Book of Sodom*, Paul Hallam describes the strange dynamics of this mythology:

> I want neither bricks nor brimstone. No return to the fears of the fifties, the closed-curtain clubs. It's just that I miss Satyricon Sodom. Sodom circuit-walks should take in alleyways, dark passages, stone steps down. I'm wary of the clean and pure, and all that is done in their name. Leave a few corners dark, not designer dark, but plain.
>
> (Hallam 1993: 45)

Hallam charts the mythic reverberations of Sodom – a city destroyed because of its sexual excess, giving its name to the pleasure-seeking non-instrumentality of anal intercourse. Of course, the story of Sodom is a warning – lewdness leads to destruction, depravity spreads until a city cannot even rely on ten righteous men among its population. At the same time, there is a promise of this possibility – a city overtaken by the demands of sexual fulfilment, endless opportunity for sexual experimentation and diversity, a whole society organised around the pursuit of pleasure. However elaborate the warnings, the tale cannot help but advertise the temptations and pleasures of this depraved existence – only the most intense and distracting of pleasures could call for such absolute punishment. Even God gives up the battle for these souls – they cannot be won back from their wicked ways, only destruction can reassert the rule of morality.

Although frightening, the story of Sodom is a poor argument for sexual restraint. Presented with the image of a city of people so intent upon the pursuit of physical pleasure that they cannot even save their own lives, who does not envy that fixed concentration on sensation? As Hallam suggests, the danger of telling horror stories about depraved places is that some listeners will choose the path of depravity and try to find this place of kindred spirits. If it does not exist, the story shows its possibilities – and people use the warnings as a blueprint for creating their own society. If the scare stories try to decry existing places of sexual tolerance, the story becomes a route-map for those eager to reach this other possibility. For every tabloid, muck-raking story, someone catches the bus, train, plane away from home to the land of this perverse promise (Weston 1998).

Perhaps this is no accident. Stories are so hard to control – warnings become fantasies, tragedies become romances, you can never be sure what the audience will hear or what will touch their innermost places. Perhaps even the goriest of warnings is also an acknowledgement that there are other ways to live.

In all these warnings, the big, bad city holds a special allure. If sexual freedom and experimentation is available anywhere, this is where it is. There are some obvious benefits to city living in this regard – enough people, enough movement, enough diversity of interest, enough venues, public places and nooks and crannies in which to meet. Most of all, the city promises anonymity and the chance to reinvent yourself on the hoof – perhaps choosing to be different things at different times or for different audiences. Smaller and more static populations make this role-play harder to sustain.

Historians of the gay community have argued that the city is the enabling factor – urbanisation is the process that allows the formation of explicitly gay communities, with their own patterns of residence and leisure, their own special routes across the city (D'Emilio 1999). In this account, it is the city itself that enables the creation of Sodom. Alongside the instrumental call of industry and the complex economy that arises with a concentrated population of waged labour, with all the accompanying demands for provision of food and family and leisure pursuits, the space of perversion appears as a by-product of these economic imperatives. Sex and the city, pleasure and industry – interdependent moments in the organisation of modern spaces. Sexuality becomes a story worth telling, it seems, only as part of this spatialised account of human history – the dirty spaces become possible only as a by-product of some other larger process.

The uncomfortable space of propriety

More than this, however, understanding sexual cultures requires an account of space and propriety. Recently, old debates about public and private have reappeared in more dynamic and undecided form. All the talk about turbo-capitalism and globalisation that has suffused this volume refers at root to a shift in spatial relations. This unsettling encroachment includes the most intimate spaces of life – and much of the political anxiety about the outcomes of these changes has fixated on the consequences for everyday life. I want to suggest here that this anxiety could be seen as a concern about propriety – that most old-fashioned of sexual concerns.

Alongside the celebratory myths of the city as a place of experimentation and liberation, there is another set of stories. In part, this account overlaps with the stories of Sodom – but without the hint of pleasurable promise. These are the stories that depict the city as nasty and dangerous – not because you may be tempted to try something new, but because this space belongs to someone else who wishes you harm.

Versions of this cautionary tale can be seen in a number of quarters – warnings to small girls and other wayward women, the anxiety about crime of the respectable and monied, the survival strategies of persecuted minorities and the bedtime horror tales of innocents everywhere. Each version shows public space as highly policed in the most repressive of manners. Accounts of sexualised violence attempt to explain the process by which ambiguous powers are maintained and fragile hierarchies are upheld. For all the talk about safety, violence against women, children and sexual minorities – especially that violence that tries to erase the victim's humanity through sexual degradation – reveals nothing so much as how difficult it is to feel safe. Attackers show their deep fear of difference, change, their own inadequacies, perhaps suggested unknowingly by the hapless victim of their rage – and they show that although they have the physical strength and social privilege to attack, they do not feel safe:

> Zealots of the system, men transfixed by some masculine ideal, feel called upon to punish the less zealous. Sometimes their rod falls on the 'unmanly' men who embrace ambivalence, but the primary objects of punishment are the women whose paradigmatic role it is to embody ambivalence. A woman may be judged to deserve punishment whenever she steps beyond her paradigmatic position; her role as an embodiment is protected from injury by doing injury to her body. A woman may come to deserve such punishment either by affirming whatever features of femininity are stigmatized in her particular milieu or by unmasking the condition of stigma-free masculinity there as an illusion. Sometimes, however, she may seem to do one of these things merely by being alive.
>
> (Kramer 1997: 2)

The mythologies of freedom and adventure in the city depend on the privileges of relatively free movement. If anything, it is this free movement across highly varied terrain that embodies the celebratory version of city living – it is this collected free movement of many individuals that creates the possibility of Sodom. This other story of the city, as a place of unpredictable dangers and anxiously defended privileges, reveals the limits there may be to movement:

> The city may be a positive choice for minorities or it may be the only place where a sufficient size of group exists to permit a social and cultural life. At the extreme there is no choice, as in the ghetto … Whilst the city offers diversity there have been many victims of those who use force to reduce diversity and to reassert their own dominance.
>
> (Darke 1996: 98)

The ongoing battle is not only about ownership – although the turf war between the more and less powerful remains a major dynamic across public and private spaces. This battle is also about the terms of propriety – because this contract of propriety provides the framework for the exercise of power.

> The private/public distinction is then, a sexualised notion: it has a different meaning depending on whether one is applying it to a heterosexual or homosexual context. For lesbians and gays the private has been institutionalised as the border of social tolerance, as the place where you are ' allowed' to live relatively safely as long as one does not attempt to occupy the public.
>
> (Richardson 1996: 15)

This revelation shifts the whole discussion. Far from being no more than a trivial elsewhere, not to be spoken of in polite company, sex emerges as the defining limit of the political. Without the sexualised boundary between public and private, the arena of propriety cannot be formed – no secret world of sex, no public world of proper and socially valued business. For those marked as endlessly visible and conspicuous by their sexual practice, the public world of the political is barred. Yet, equally, no place is sufficiently secret to maintain the high levels of privacy demanded of sexual minorities. Whatever the fictions of propriety, the public arena is always threatened by the imminent approach of the most inappropriate signs of the private.

The magic of the elsewhere of sex depends, of course, like other magical elsewheres, on a host of spatial mythologies. In relation to sex this means that the abandonment, possibility and danger is always going on somewhere else. Over here is safe, constrained and bound by propriety – because everything else is consigned to another space of controlled permission.

However, the geography of sexuality reveals not a place apart, but a parallel universe. Respectability and debauchery inhabit the same spaces – perhaps at other times, or at a different rhythm, or simultaneously in another manner. Within this sense of parallel universes other myths of the city emerge. As suggested above, the urban comes to be coded as the realm of sexual possibility, in part because the urban is the space of many other social possibilities. The urban at its most romantic offers a whole mythology of the crowd that begs to be reworked for sexual fantasy. In the crowd, everyone becomes anonymous, stripped of history and background. Instead, we emerge as self-inventions, conspicuous displays of the cultivation of the self (Berman 1982). The ability to invent yourself also opens the possibility of reinventing your relation to others, including the sexualised fantasy figure of the stranger. In this fantasy, the most desirable outcomes of urbanisation become adjuncts to the sexual fantasy. Variety, anonymity, possibility – the excitement of high modernity is presented as the exhilaration of sexual potential. Yet it is precisely this potential adventure that can signal danger:

> Common interpretations of women's safety, which are often reinforced by both the media and in policy development, place an emphasis on 'stranger danger'.
>
> (Morrell 1996: 100)

The investment in the city as a site of sexual fantasy is linked to far wider mythologies. The city enters as a location that transforms human life. From the moment of the urban, there is access to leisure, even if this leisure is stolen in snatches within the working day and the compensatory night. Despite lack of income, the rise of consumer living pervades the articulation of self. Fulfilment becomes another proof of the skill of your personal choice.

Again, this doubleness emerges as a recurrent theme in modernity. While order makes progress and the public is reconstructed as an arena of reason, progress and orderly interaction between public individuals, disorder is always bubbling away somewhere. The machinery of modernity constructs order as a response and constraint to various sources of disorder – so criminality lives alongside wage-slavery, decay seeps up through the cracks of hygiene, the vagaries of the organic kick against the strictures of the social. The respectable world of daytime geographies lies alongside the dreamtime fantasy world of the night. After all that intensive fantasising about the elsewhere that permits sexuality, it turns out that sex has been right here on our doorstep all along. Like all the best exotic depravities and threats to civilisation, the fantasy of foreign sex arises from the peculiar disciplines of civilisation at home.

Finding the secret maps of sex

For those struggling to resist the norms of respectable society, the promise that an alternative life is right here, to be found by whoever cares to look, holds a special glamour. This is a chance to pursue self-discovery through another form of journeying – another supplementing voyage for the Western subject. Rather than search for self in other lands or other classes as such, this is an after-dark exploration – consider the favoured cultural products of crisis moments, Jekyll and Hyde, murder stories, after-hours fantasies about the closeness of depravity.

This exploration is related to the fantasies of exoticism – but here the excessive otherness of alternative sexuality resides in the heart of the Western subjects themselves. Other less privileged beings may serve as accessories to this discovery, but the revelation is the secret at the heart of the civilised subject. As everyone relearns their own selves in relation to an ever-expanding global framework, the exotic fantasy of the elsewhere of sex is transformed for these new circumstances. Recent attempts to refashion the boundaries of public and private life, to re-imagine the terms of propriety and to agree the proper place of sex, could all be regarded as responses to larger social changes:

> The sex zone does not have an independent existence; no area of the city is dedicated solely to this use. It is usually superimposed upon another area: a deteriorating neighbourhood where poor people, especially those who have recently arrived in the city, must live; an area that has very few residents because it is designed to manufacture or transport goods; or one of those offerings to eco-guilt, a city park.
>
> (Califia 1994: 205)

Even the most liberal and permissive view of sexuality tends to agree that sex is a private affair – no-one's business but your own, as long as you keep it that way. Once sexuality strays into the public realm, the sex police rush out in force.

Or do they?

As discussed in Chapter 3, sex is policed as a matter of location as much as a matter of activity. The idea that the public interest demands protection from exposure to the depraved sexual behaviour of other, less private individuals continues to underpin much popular debate and actual law enforcement. Inasmuch as sexual freedoms are tolerated, they are tolerated as a strictly private affair. Any whiff of merely tolerated sexuality in the proper realm of the public is a breach of trust and proof that zealous policing is no more than necessary (see the various discussions in Leap 1999).

But elsewhere it is apparent that sex is anything but private. Chat and banter, scandal and glamour – schooling, entertainment and service provision – all show sex as a constantly public affair (Dangerous Bedfellows 1996). Without this continuous publicity how would norms be established and maintained? Even with this bombardment, sexuality remains resistant to regulation. There is always the danger that too much privacy will just give people a space to do as they please.

In his account of the legal construction of the homosexual as the limit of articulable sexuality, Leslie Moran describes the ambiguous role of silence in policing the sexual. Moran argues that legal constructions have used silence as the boundary of prohibition and propriety. The implication that unspeakable acts have been committed allows a concept of unspecified depravity to create criminals without reference to the deeds themselves. However, this attempt to both criminalise and silence in one sweep itself opens other possibilities:

The law's injunction to silence does not mark the absolute limit of imagining the male genital body in male genital relations outside the law.

(Moran 1996: 44)

Although Moran describes a legal construction that attempts to silence the frightening prospect and possibility of sex between men, there are other ways to imagine and articulate men's sexual experiences with each other. The tricks of the law force other innovations:

Examples can be found in the popular comfort of the eighteenth century that describe sodomy trials at the Old Bailey. They provide examples of marginal dialect generated by and for men who had genital relations with other men whereby the unnameable might be named without the experience of violence. These examples are also of interest in another way. They provide an opportunity to consider the relationship between the official lexicon of representation and the marginal vernacular of certain genital practices.

(Moran 1996: 44)

The silence, meaning violence, of men's sexual relations in law forces open another space, the space of innovation and alternative articulation. By not saying what is meant, the law enables others to say and decide the meaning of male sex. As long as the law shies away from describing the detail of sex in order to render some sex as violence, the amateur dialect of lived sex can escape criminality. The prissy ordering of the official public makes the permissive experimentation of the secret world:

The silence of the law does not in the first instance produce an absolute prohibition but gives rise to a certain proliferation of speech about these genital relations by way of a multiplicity of euphemisms.

(Moran 1996: 45)

Not saying does not erase other ways of life; it only produces other ways of saying. This is where we come to learn that sex is for ourselves alone – myself and those I love – a chance to get lost in our private world and forget everything else. This is the appeal and consolation of the public, the ripples of other potentials that flicker around its edges.

So far this volume has discussed the manner in which the processes of global capitalism have de-territorialised private life. Economy remakes the texture of everyday life, even if this is not a one-way process of absolute determination. Relationships change, identities shift, we all learn to be new things in new ways for new times. Underneath this discussion of change in both public and private spheres, there is another narrative about changing landscapes, and, of course, this includes the landscape of sex:

> The end of 'privacy' in all the sex-and-violence senses, the prodigious
> enlargement of what we can still call a public sphere, if we really mean all the
> senses of 'public' by it, also results in an enormous enlargement of the idea of
> rationality itself, in what we are willing to 'understand' (but not endorse), as
> what we can no longer have removed from the visible record as 'irrational' or
> incomprehensible, unmotivated, insane or sick.
>
> (Jameson 1991: 354)

The terrain on which we live encompasses a number of stories – as well as the
material landscape of built and non-built environments, our social terrain includes
interactions with others and the imagined spaces of life. Previous accounts and
commentaries link the rise of self-identified gay communities to the processes of
urbanisation and industrialisation. These big historical shifts inadvertently make
new kinds of space – and these new spaces allow people the possibility of these new
innovations. This is not quite a model of determination – one event does not make
the other happen – but it is an account of how some events facilitate others,
accidentally, as an unexpected side effect.

Both city and industry have come to mean quite different things since the broad
descriptions of urbanisation and industrialisation. Everyday landscapes have reshaped
to different imperatives – no longer concentrating population as accessible labour
for capital. This chapter attempts to describe the unexpected side effects of more
recent landscaping. A wide array of literature already asserts that globalisation remakes
urban spaces – to form the multi-speed city, or the information network city, or a
cosmopolis, or a technopolis, or a carceral city, or a global city, or some other name
that indicates a new version of the urban (see Soja 2000). This literature, in various
ways, suggests that social identities are transformed in new urban spaces through
activity, different levels and forms of affiliation and different arenas of display and
recognition.

Although these debates question the extent and reality of post-industrialism in
the city, there is some agreement that the shell formed by the industrial city of high
modernity comes to be inhabited by more recent parasites such as the leisure and
finance industries. The industrial proper may still shape the city and region, but
alongside this activity other forces develop a service economy of infamous flexibility
and post-Fordist organisation. Unpalatable as it may be, it is hard to deny that both
these forms of organisation persist in the cities of the affluent world, and that the
shift towards services, even if not total, calls more women and young people into
the workplaces of the urban (Walby 1997; Sassen 1998). Overall, the discussion
about the changing profile of urban landscapes echoes other debates about the
structures that make social actors. In part, previous chapters have outlined key aspects
of this new landscape, in both its material and imagined incarnations.

The changing character of heterosexuality reveals some of the impacts of the
internationalised economy on the West and on the links between jobs and the shape

of households. The most popular accounts of crisis in the traditional family point to the changing role of women in the workplace and the decline of many areas of traditionally masculine work. This, combined with a growth in jobs for the young and workplace obsolescence for older men, unbalances the purported power structures of the patriarchal family. Although men continue to accrue all sorts of social privilege, patriarchy does not seem the most apt title for this process any more. Economic restructuring strips fatherhood of many powers and entitlements – the hierarchy of the family is less certainly supplemented by the imperatives of the economy.

Overall, the family has shifted from a conception of productive unit to one of welfare unit. New forms of work hail various family members as individuals rather than components of a larger family unit – and this kind of work rarely acknowledges the larger work of the family, unlike the earlier experiments of Fordism or Cadburyism. Instead, as shown in the earlier discussion of Chapter 1, the family is conceived as providing a parallel set of values in the form of welfare, affection, social bonds and belonging (Wilkinson 2000). Heterosexuality comes to be celebrated as the model of sex that can ensure this parallel process. Instead of a previous rhetoric of national wealth and health being linked in the sanctity of the heterosexual family, now heterosexuality is valued as the best possible supplement for uncertain economic times. Family units are not conceived as economic units – rather, various actors carry out a variety of economic activity, and these various actors combine in a variety of domestic arrangements – but families are imagined as the force that can offset the worst social effects of global economy.

Sexually, the outcome is a culture that celebrates sexual pleasure in itself – but continues to market heterosexual coupling as a particularly rewarding life goal. Women accrue greater influence in this new heterosexuality – and as a result, leave it more often, in search of experiences that match the promises. The explicit cultures of heterosexuality indicate more room for experimentation, innovation, play – and there are all sorts of attempts to expand what can be included in the normativity of heterosexual coupling. Whereas the earlier discussion of changes in heterosexual cultures suggested that small adaptations served to consolidate a continuing normative power, here I want to consider the extent to which heterosexuality is forced to adapt by changes in the landscape.

One set of social trends makes us all serial monogamists, choosing to live alone for greater portions of our lives while young and while old, shaped by the changeable call of our own desires far more than by the scrutinising don't-do-that of family networks. Yet another parallel and related set of trends makes this wish for individuation impossible to fulfil. Housing stock has been accumulated painfully and through struggle to accommodate a population of family units working for industry – and even this family housing remains in short supply. The idea that people might choose to live alone as adults has no echo in available housing. The increasing desire to live in different formations at different points in life is even more alien to housing providers (see Williams 1997). One result of this is the increase in young single people living in the family home – stretching out their dependence on parents into their twenties and even their thirties. This, of course, is one aspect of the desired welfare function of the family – to ameliorate the effects of a fragmenting social infrastructure. However, not all the homeless young can be absorbed by welcoming and nurturing family homes – in part, due to the increasing geographical mobility in an era of multiple job shifts.

All of this has its impact on sexual behaviour – and perhaps most of all on conceptions of heterosexuality. As the world of adulthood becomes less and less hospitable, with little trace of the brief promise of an affluent youth boom, young men are increasingly loath to leave the warmth of the family home. Young women, on the other hand, are loath to enter dependency or to give up their autonomy. Without the sanctions of old-style domesticity, with its mixture of economic imperative, social approval and housing infrastructure, sex seems destined to become increasingly public, in-between, caught as leisure rather than family life. The changing conception of commodification and sexual experience reveals a different relation between buying and being in certain places – if not an absolute rewriting of where and how the economic makes the social, at least a significantly new emphasis.

Alongside this, the rise and fall of government interest in sexual matters tells us something about the role of rationed or sanctioned sexual pleasures in maintaining public order and obedient citizenship. How this strategic permission is granted depends upon a reading of the changing social terrain – sex is a means of adapting subjectivity, both an indicator and an enabler of different ways of feeling.

In the chapters concerning fragmenting identities and exotic remnants it is argued that individuals relearn identity in relation to new circumstances and that one of these circumstances is the downsizing of certain national identities in a global network. Unexpectedly, all kinds of people feel a loss of privilege in their sexual lives – because the previous markers of propriety are more elusive for everyone. The larger argument of this book is that the amalgam of these social changes remake the terms of sexuality – but are inadvertently remade through sex themselves. The unexpected possibilities enabled by larger social processes, in the manner of the gay communities enabled by urbanisation, may have a disproportionate impact on the ways we live.

The old ideas of sex and the city took high modernity as a context for narrating self in urban settings. And in these famous accounts, the city is indubitably where modernity happens and where selfhood is learned. More recent debates suggest that the old European model of the city of high modernity is undergoing some significant changes – and, again, the culprits are postmodernity, the international economy, eco-horror and transnationalism in all spheres of life. Overall, the impact of economic restructuring through international forces on city spaces queers far more types of sexual behaviour. In a variety of manners, the possibility of privacy and respectability becomes less available to many city inhabitants and visitors. Who retains the privileges of privacy in this economically uncertain and boundary-shifting world? Of course, affluence plays its usual differentiating role – offering play to some and criminality to others. Yet the boundaries of public life change for everyone, and that means that privacy is a far more uncertain state. That sense of an expanded public sphere of stretched moral vision, of there being no place of our own any more, of the extension of the public right into our most intimate places and the expansion of the private out into every place of public display – all of this signals a shift in contemporary cultures of intimacy. Now that intimacy has become a central register of public life, so the old-style privileges of privacy are difficult to maintain.

Throughout this volume, sex has been revealed as highly historicised, deeply social, always contextual – and as a result, always vulnerable to reworking by other shifts in the terrain of the social. However timeless and natural it may feel, sexual expression must bear the impressions of other determinations – otherwise how could we make sense of it? Previous chapters have argued that we are witnessing an era of unprecedented realignment. This paradigm shift has been identified by commentators in a number of areas – economic analysis, the international relations debate, cultural matters and financial strategy, as well as ecological catastrophists, Internet visionaries and media moguls and critics. Of course, the linking theme through all accounts is the idea that global networks have intensified and now affect all human life. Somehow or another, the spatial relations of human life are being rearranged.

The well-known commentaries focus on this spatial change at a geopolitical level – the emergence of a local–global nexus that threatens to dethrone the sovereignty of the nation-state, the fractious rise of regional alliances that attempt to navigate and make peace with the global, the reach of the branded corporation versus older and more traditional forms of political power (Ohmae 1995; Sassen 1998; Klein 2000). But does this new era not bring a change in spatial consciousness? Is it not possible that even the more figurative conceptions of spatiality could be affected and altered by the irresistible hype of globalisation? Is not part of the impact on conceptions of the public and the private and their inter-relation?

So far we have examined the processes by which larger realignments adapt more mundane experiences such as family and romance, or restructure the compensatory pleasures of sexual adventure and the performance of identity. All of these are an indication of the shifting boundary between public and private spheres and the changing determination of what constitutes each arena. Of course, this shift has a particular impact on cultures of sex. The division between public and private has represented one of the most resilient markers of propriety. The empire of sex may expand and diversify – but public expression remains a momentary incursion into another territory. The private, however elastic this concept has become, remains the legitimate and legitimated realm of sex, intimacy and emotional expression. If the boundaries shift, then new processes of legitimation must be learned.

In the UK, there has been some recognition of this boundary change, and its implications, from that most official of bodies, the Home Office. For those unfamiliar with the domestic designation of this branch of national government, 'home' here signifies a variety of ordering issues within the nation, from the boundary-marking of immigration policy to the internal ordering of policing. If there is a government department that defines the terms of legitimacy within the fast disintegrating nation-state of the United Kingdom, it is the Home Office.

On 26 July 2000, the Home Office published a consultative paper entitled *Setting the Boundaries*. This long-awaited document promised to review the antiquated legislation around sexual offences. Through a process of consultation with government officials, legal experts and church and community groups, the avowed plan was to develop a legal framework more fitting to the practices and beliefs of modern times. Although there was an almost immediate indication that the recommendations would not be acted upon – at least not before a general election – the key points reveal some areas of renegotiation and disquiet in contemporary sexual life.

Proposed changes to British law reveal more widespread anxieties about sexual and moral codes. Although these recommendations are the amalgamated thoughts of various interest groups, the push towards legislative change in still morally conservative Britain is an indication of the impact of wider forces. The consultative document makes little mention of these other larger motors of social change, but we can speculate on the relation between globalisation and reviews of the laws around sexual offences. Previous discussions have revealed the not always obvious relation between the detail of sexual policing and practice and the more mysterious and unpredictable forces that shape social relations. For these reasons, I want to take the detail of the particular debate around definitions of privacy and consent in British law as an indication of how global forces might remake the boundaries of the private in many locations. Of course, this remains largely speculative – but as guesswork goes, this is at least relatively informed.

The document states that one reason for the consultation is the shift in social values. There is a welcome recognition that much of the legislation around sexual offences is out of date, if not positively archaic. Some key aspects have retained a framing from the nineteenth century. Others assume levels of social intolerance that no longer apply. Most of all, there is the criticism that the law continues to protect the socially privileged and relatively powerful at the expense of truly vulnerable groups of people. The attempt to address these criticisms and problems reveals a shift in thinking around sexual agency and rights. The Home Office document refers again and again to the provisions and implications of the Human Rights Act. Although there has been some local resistance to the imposition of this European framework, for legal practitioners it has provided a much needed opportunity to revisit the nature of rights and law.

The emergence of a human rights discourse that extends to interventions within the rich world as well as the objectified poor world could be regarded as another manifestation of global forces. Although this appears to be a benign extension of basic rights to all, this purported extension runs in parallel with the more troubling intensification of globalisation. If the development of a previous era of capitalism created the dynamic of uneven development and its close cousin the cult of domesticity as a marker of privilege, then the emerging spatial dynamic of intensified global expansion may well rework previous patterns.

The discourse of human rights attempts to reinvigorate the enlightenment promise of rights, reason and citizenship. Whereas the long-running critiques of modernity have revealed the many limitations and failures of this project, not least the inability to include most of the world's population, the deep wish to imagine and judge freedom by the standards of the enlightenment continues to haunt contemporary dreams of progress. Although we know better than to believe in rights, there is no alternative conception of empowerment that can take its place, either in terms of political recognition or emotional punch (on the emergence of talk of human rights as a strategy for managing the political and moral crises of our times, see Klug 2000).

Human rights assume some similarity between actors in all locations. Unlike the implied logic of uneven development, which constructs the inhabitants of different locations as dissimilar agents, constructed by the imperatives of their locale, this is an old-style universal discourse. If previous phases of development could not deliver the promise of freedom and citizenship for all, this is globalisation's contribution to human dignity. While global forces may appear to reduce humanity to its lowest rung, reminding even the relatively affluent that they are replaceable by the more desperate and impoverished of other locations, human rights talk reassures us that humanity has a basic and non-negotiable worth.

It is this double-think that makes the human rights initiatives of the West vulnerable to criticism, if not outright ridicule. In fact, critics from the poor, only-just-now-getting-rich world have questioned the impetus behind the global push towards human rights as the criterion of participation on this score (see China's resistance to US moralism in Shanor and Shanor 1995). However, because this volume wishes to identify and celebrate sexual possibility, let us concentrate on the effect of human rights talk on British discussions of sexual offences.

The authors of *Setting the Boundaries* outline their agenda in the following manner:

> Our other key guiding principle was that the criminal law should not intrude unnecessarily into the private life of adults. Applying the principle of harm means that most consensual activity between adults in private should be their own affair, and not that of the criminal law. But the criminal law has a vital role to play where sexual activity is not consensual, or where society decides that children and other very vulnerable people require protection and should not be able to consent. It is quite proper to argue in such situations that an adult's right to exercise sexual autonomy in their private life is not absolute, and society may properly apply standards through the criminal law which are intended to protect the family as an institution as well as individuals from abuse. In addition

to this, the ECHR [European Charter for Human Rights] ensures that the state must uphold its responsibility to provide a remedy in law so that a complainant can seek justice.

(Home Office 2000: 0.7)

The discussion begins from an assumption that individual rights are tempered only by circumstances of harm to others. There is still an area of interpretation, of course – not only the definition of consent, but also who is to be designated as very vulnerable – but there is a grudging admission that adults may have a right to sexual autonomy, if only in the problematic space of their private lives. This account attempts to hold on to the leeway of a moveable boundary of the private, but still enshrines the need to attend to individual rights:

We also thought it was vital that the law was clear and well understood, particularly in this field of sexual behaviour where there is much debate about the ground-rules. There is no Highway Code for sexual relations to give a clear indication of what society expects or will tolerate. The law should ensure respect for an individual's own decisions about withholding sexual activity and protect every person from sexual coercion and violence.

(Home Office 2000: 0.8)

The report admits the uncertainty about the terms of propriety that characterise our time. This is a confusing terrain with no code of agreed behaviour and etiquette. Changes in the law must re-establish some sustainable social contract for sexual behaviour, because we all need to relearn what is tolerable when sexual cultures change and the private becomes indistinguishable from the public.

Alongside this, there is at last an attempt to excise the explicitly discriminatory aspects from sex law. This becomes possible through the appeal to individual rights – because now sexual minorities also have rights to be protected:

We looked at the way the law treats gender issues and those of differing sexual orientation. We thought that the law should offer protection to men and women, boys and girls and recommend:

The criminal law should offer protection from all non-consensual sexual activity.
It should not treat people differently on the basis of their sexual orientation. Consensual sexual activity between adults in private that causes no harm to themselves or others should not be criminal.

We therefore felt that the law did not need to make particular provision for any same sex behaviour and recommend that:

the offences of gross indecency and buggery should be repealed; those aspects of the offences providing protection for children, vulnerable people and animals would be replaced by our other proposals.

(Home Office 2000: 0.19)

The universalising discourse of human rights has opened a new opportunity for campaigners for civil liberty. Although these campaigns adopt a knowing and sceptical attitude to concepts such as equality and citizenship, the discussion around what basic rights should be available to all allows a legitimate arena to speak of individual freedoms. Before this, it has proved difficult to persuade the public that sexuality is a matter of rights. Sex is your own business, something private. If you need recourse to your rights in this area it means you have already transgressed the rules – if you were not doing something wrong, pushing your business in other people's faces, then your rights would not be at issue. Nice people do not need to assert their rights to their sexuality, because it is no-one's business but their own.

The introduction of human rights talk to the political agenda, albeit through another route, allows a less threatening discussion of what might be anyone's business. Precisely because we are experiencing dramatic social changes, this debate begins to include and engage far wider numbers of people. Many now seek some definition and assurance of what they are entitled to – without previous markers of status and belonging, what is a human being worth? The parameters and values of sex play a central role in these redefinitions. As we have already discussed, the private has been marked as the space of permission, where we can be ourselves:

> The 'public' is a realm of the law's full presence. It is a space of order and decency through the law. It is also a place where the citizen is protected from what is offensive or injurious. It is presented as a place free from the exploitation and corruption of others, particularly for those who are young, or weak in body or mind, the inexperienced and those in a state of special physical, official or economic dependence. This 'public' suggests an alternative place where the law is absent, the 'private'.
>
> (Moran 1996: 56)

The public is the place of legal intervention and the private is its mirror, where the law does not enter. Although Moran is poking fun when he suggests that the public is the space beyond exploitation, the larger point has been made throughout this work – the private is exciting and dangerous because relations are so much more disorderly there, and innovation makes things unpredictable. The public, sadly, has been the place where very little adventure is possible:

> This 'public' cannot be reduced to a geographical or spatial phenomenon. 'Public' refers to an embodied place, to the body in general as public, and in this context the genital body as a site of the full presence of the law. No matter where the

spatial location, the (male genital) body as youth, as weakness, as inexperience and dependence is always a public body, always the site of law's full presence, and as such this body is the impossibility of the 'private'. At the same time, in this scheme of things the 'private' is also a question of the body.

(Moran 1996: 56)

This assumption of the constant and necessarily public status of some bodies underlies the logic and practice of British law. This is the overall argument being made by Moran, that the apparently neutral adoption of the terms of public and private as the framework of legal propriety with regard to sexual behaviour in fact creates the conspicuously and inevitably public figure of the deviant, most often in the form of the criminalised male homosexual. However, as this volume has discussed, that scrutiny has extended to include other groups of people, including those who may have considered themselves to be respectable in other times. Yet equally, the expansion of the private into the realm of the rational and comprehensible increases the expectation that we have a right of sexual expression. The uncertain boundaries of propriety in our time reveal how moveable the line between public and private has become:

The very idea of 'private' and 'public' as separate spheres appears to be central to understandings of what sexuality is. Sexuality in turn helps to demarcate the private and the public as discrete and separate domains, through various instances in which it 'crosses over', ceasing to be merely a private act and becoming a matter of public concern.

(Harding 1998: 23)

Now that these spheres have become blurred, with both seeping into each other and not much discretion anywhere, once again it may be sexuality that can demarcate the boundaries of a new propriety. Sex may be our best hope of learning to navigate such new terrains.

After the long and endlessly ambitious expansion of Europe into every crevice of modern existence, with this colonisation becoming the very symbol of modernity, now the spaces of the West begin to implode. There is little sense any longer that there are wide-open spaces still to be explored and conquered. In this sense, in both the looking outwards to new lands and the looking inwards to new subjects, modernity feels the constraint of its limits. It is in this context that the spaces of modern identity are re-imagined. Many of the themes of this volume, the concern to both understand and ameliorate the forces of this new era of globality, return to the possibilities of this re-imagining. The wish to remake the arenas of the public and the private, in order to resurrect some previous conception of the relation between individuals and society, reveals the high anxiety attached to this project. In case we have not noticed, this is a crisis situation:

The city has been viewed as an arena for consumerism. Political and commercial expediency has shifted the emphasis of urban development from meeting the broad social needs of the community to meeting the circumscribed needs of individuals. The pursuit of this narrow of objective has sapped the city of its vitality. The complexity of 'community' has been untangled and public life has been dissected into individual components. Paradoxically, in this global age of rising democracy, cities are increasingly polarising society into segregated communities.

The result of this trend is the decline of the vitality of our urban spaces.

(Rogers and Gumuchdjian 1997: 9)

What is at stake here is the quality of affluent life in the time of fading modernity. The move to more privatised spaces makes cities feel dangerous – and the accompanying loss of a shared public arena cuts away previous strategies for negotiating social crisis. We are left with inter-cut spaces that are neither quite public nor quite private – neither socially sanctioned nor excitingly secret. Being a proper subject has become increasingly difficult, resulting in more adventure and more anxiety all round. The magical elsewhere of intimacy has more work to do than ever. The last chapter suggests some beginnings for this task.

8 All sexed out

The last lesson

A mark on the skin, a land, a nation: these are the metaphors of tribe and family. Queer is being used not just to connote and glorify differentness but to revise the criteria of membership in the family.

(Gamson 1998: 593)

The stretched out moment of queer, even for those who have not realised that they are taking part, remakes concepts of belonging. If everyone has become a performative innovator, because that is the only mode of being available in our time, we must all revise our queer relations to each other. As the terrain of the social shifts beneath our feet, more traditional bonds of allegiance become uncertain. Family life changes, life seems to demand an endless quest for intimacy, without any hope of the lazy complacency of old-style marriage. Whatever the shape and resilience of your intimate relationships, there is no alternative but to work at their quality. Otherwise, we learn painfully, we find that even when together we may be alone.

Fortunately, sex retains its magical promise. Sex can still save from loneliness, console in hardship, distract from boredom, elevate from the everyday – or, at least, it can if you are doing it correctly. Whatever the uncertainties of contemporary social relations, there is little indication that interest and investment is sex is on the wane. If anything, now everyone covets the witchcraft of pervert status:

The homosexual sodomite was a penetrator of males, unlike the larger class of sodomites, who may have committed any number of sexual and nonsexual 'crimes'. A synonym for bugger (derived from *boulgre* or *bougre*, apparently a Bulgarian), 'sodomite' was an extreme and opprobrious form of condemnation designating religious blasphemy, political sedition, and even satanic activities including demonism, shamanism, and witchcraft.

(Rousseau 1991: 7)

The machinery of earlier persecution begins to look more like a temptation than a prohibition. Sexual dissent may have brought extreme punishment – and may do still – but the pursuit of desire also promises an entry into an alternative universe. The magic of witchcraft and the spiritual elsewhere of the shaman both appear dangerously close through sex. For the troubled survivors of global shift, the suggestion of shape-changing magic offers fresh possibilities for self-articulation.

Weeks describes this as the sexual opportunity unleashed through globalisation – 'a real revolution in sexual possibilities. I will call these "detraditionalization", "individualization" and "identity creation".' (Weeks 2000: 239) Whatever is lost, some new possibility opens. The fragmentation of traditional social forms creates spaces in which new innovations of intimacy can appear. We lose many of our ties and contacts to each other, but this also allows more freedom to make ourselves as we wish, led by the promise of our own desires. Old identities may dissolve, but now everyone can have the identity that they long for, really be their own best work of art.

This work has attempted to overview debates in the study of sexuality in order to argue that understanding the sphere of intimacy may come to be among the most central political lessons of our time. In part, there is a nod here to the claims of self-help literatures – because it may turn out to be the case that we all need to do some work on the project of relearning intimacy (see Giddens 1992). More than this, however, this is an appeal to reconsider the assorted debates about contemporary crisis words such as globalisation. My argument is that these alarming shifts in the structure and speed of international economy and politics signal a need to develop new ways of being – because our ability to survive the turbulence of the new era will depend also on these strategies of subjectivity. Sex occupies a privileged role in this project because its status as the arena of secrets where the truth of the individual self is hidden creates a space where this renegotiation can be imagined. The performance of sexuality presents an opportunity to practise new ways of being.

This work began by reviewing debates about the nature and status of heterosexuality. Here, we considered the suggestion that sexual life is shaped through the ideological forces of heteronormativity. However, despite the weight of these injunctions, the first chapter ended by arguing that larger forces of change have affected the everyday cultures of heterosexual life in the West. Key components of the edifice of the heteronormative are undergoing rapid and irresistible change – what heterosexuality is and means must adapt accordingly. Chapter 2 picked up this idea of change and turned to the question of history and the conception of sexuality. This chapter considered the emergence of sexuality as a historical concept and our understanding of sexual activity in different periods and contexts – because this sense of change can help to make sense of the present.

The following chapters outlined the changes that we are living through. Chapter 3 reviewed ideas of state and economy and their relation to the realm of sexuality. It examined the suggestion that sexuality is determined by the instrumental demands of either economy or state. The chapter ended with a discussion of shifting political cultures in Britain and the role of sex in the articulation of any popular consensus.

Chapter 4 considered recent debates in the study of sexuality. Here, there is a discussion of ideas of fragmentation and instability in social life. The concept of 'queer' and other performative accounts of sexual identity are placed in this context of the emergence of flexible styles of being. As these changes take place under the pressures of the global, Chapter 5 relived the old internationalism of exoticist imagination and examined the place of power disparity in sexuality. By arguing that the restructuring of global relations has displaced the certainties of Western privilege, it was suggested that exoticism must change to fit new circumstances. An analysis of these new forms of exoticism promises to uncover the tensions and contradictions of new global powers.

Chapter 6 proposed a strategy for negotiating this era of change and returned to the issue of representing sex, this time in the context of sex education and pornography. This chapter revisited debates about the impact of sexual representation, in the realms of both education and entertainment, and argued that neither the calls for censorship nor the belief in free expression offer an adequate account of how sex is learned. Here, we imagined an alternative framework for sex education that combines the competing demands of technical competence and social awareness by linking the worldly instrumentalism of Machiavelli to the spiritual quest of the *Kama Sutra*.

Chapter 7 ends this work with a consideration of space and sexuality. It examines the myths of the city as the space of sex and the effect this mythology has had on recent sexual cultures. It is argued that ideas of sexual propriety have relied on spatial concepts for meaning, and therefore that shifts in spatial relations impact on the conception of propriety. How we imagine the proper business and location of sex could offer a first step in the process of developing sustainable and sustaining cultures of intimacy.

This is the final parting shot of this project. The attempt to understand the strange beast of sex, as a lived practice and cipher for larger social meanings, promises to illuminate some of the key shifts of our era. A critical understanding of sex may turn out to be the knowledge that enables an imagining of survival strategies in a turbulent time. While nostalgia for the old ways will never turn back the tide of turbo-capitalist change, because even a return to a more regulated market cannot reverse the social changes that have accompanied this period, a creative intimacy may offer a means of retaining some social value and sense of citizenship. This book does not pretend to offer a blueprint for this process – but it does argue that this will be the place to learn.

Everyday culture and international economy

Much of this work has been concerned with exploring the role of a study of the everyday in our understanding of larger social structures and events. In this discussion I have suggested that the uncertain project of studying the everyday may hold some clues to the link between the most mundane and the most earth-changing of experiences.

For most of this work, I have chosen, perhaps perversely, to focus on sex as the archetypal theme of cultural study – because sex has been constructed as the realm of the private and magical, sensuous and non-instrumental, individuated and chosen. Of course, what is obscured by this claim is the extent to which the well-known work in the study of everyday culture concentrates on other issues altogether. Youth sub-cultures, the formation and maintenance of community, the impact of media representations on social outcomes, performing identity and choosing leisure – if there is an area of study owned by this interest, most would assume it to be among these topics. Sex might pop up as another marker of subculture or a component in leisure and style choices, but its impact has been as peripheral here as in other approaches to social enquiry. So using the study of sex as my case-study example of practice and possibility is, as I admit, perverse. But the special promise of sex remains close to the heart of the sweetest and most wayward claims of studies of the everyday, because sex is the place of everyday hopes and dreams.

The endeavour to create an academic space for the study of the everyday, despite all the in-fighting and attempts to become professional, remains deeply permissive. Within its elastic remit, it is hard to think of many topics that would not be considered fit for study. In part, this permissive tendency comes from the formation of the discipline – itself a response to the arbitrary constraints and boundaries of single discipline enquiry. But more than this, the sense of permission comes from an organising belief that the business of everyday life is worthy of study. As no-one can tell where everyday life begins and ends, everything is permitted. Therefore, although sex has not been a major area of this work, the social role of sex allows it to become emblematic for the business of studying the everyday.

My argument has been that the emblem of the everyday provides a synecdoche for larger society. Although the study of the so-called ordinary culture celebrates and even fetishises the minutiae of everyday experience, there is always a promise of some larger relevance. No case-study is so particular that there are no transferable lessons to be learned – if that was the case then no learning could be done and the endeavour would be reduced to a series of unrelated commentaries which had no relation to each other. However much we may wish to champion the importance of empirical work and local particularity, no-one suggests that the particular has no relation to the general. The question, then, is how we conceptualise this relation between the everyday and the transglobal – what is the move from small to large?

Somewhere in the broad sweep introductions to globalisation and the musings and focus groups of the Third Way wallahs, there is an embryonic model of this relation. Somewhere in the idea that private individuals resist, negotiate and change global forces, there is an acknowledgement that the local and private and everyday has its own agency and effects. So this is the first important point – ordinary culture is not shapeless putty in the grip of the all-powerful forces of globality. Instead, this relation is always mutual and dynamic – different histories and factors work on each other in both directions, and the outcomes of this complex interaction then go on to have their own impacts.

This realisation of the complex mutuality of social relations leads to the second important point – attention to the detail of mundane aspects of everyday life may illuminate structures far larger than themselves. At its very best, an attention to everyday culture can help us to understand international finance, because the manner in which people become the subjects of their time determines the play of economic relations. I am extremely indebted to the work of Aihwa Ong for this point – and as I write I realise that she may not recognise herself in my peculiarly British account of cultural analysis. However, the move from an account of everyday meanings, albeit in a global context, through an analysis that encompasses a wide range of intellectual traditions and methods, to an explanation of the impact of these community behaviours on global economy smells of the irreverence and ambition of studies of the everyday with which I am familiar.

The cycle of knock-on impacts, from global economy to personal life choice and back out to national economic well-being and the construction of global players, is articulated from another viewpoint in the broad-brush accounts of global forces. When Luttwak describes the tendency of turbo-capitalism to create instability and social disharmony, he is acknowledging the agency of the everyday and personal aspects of life:

> Once the chain of repercussions is followed step by step from an economic system that achieves efficiency by imposing constant structural change, to the fragmentation of family life that is thereby caused, to the resulting psychological consequences, to the consumption habits they induce, and then to the impact of those habits on the economic system by way of low savings and baroque consumer preferences, it may be concluded that a more rigid but more stable economy could be even more efficient.
>
> (Luttwak 1998: 213–14)

While we all learn new habits of being in order to navigate new terrains, the imperatives of the global economy are themselves adapted by the impact of everyday strategies of survival. If the new global subject becomes so atomised that no value is given to social relations or financial planning, then even this flexible identity has become an economic liability. At every level of operation, from very big to small and fleeting, relearning the manner of our relation to each other is the only game in town.

In the past, when I have been diligently and perhaps evangelically (although I hope not too much of the latter) teaching my sex course, occasionally students have asked why we need to do this – understand, document and represent sexuality? Why does it matter if some things are unspoken and unexplained? And I have tried to answer by suggesting that the silence privileges the already privileged, making the norm normal and legitimating the persecution of everyone else. On a good day, I try to make more space to acknowledge their discomfort – by saying that Foucault agrees that all this talk is part of the policing – but I still end up saying that we make the choices in an imperfect setting, and saying more seems like a better option for now. On the whole, I believe my teacherly response – how can you be a teacher and not be invested in stretching for better understanding? But I know that I am ducking something in the question.

Although academic study endlessly attempts to give voice and attention to the ordinary world of everyday culture, many of the most valued areas of everyday culture become organised to resist the various incursions of commodification, objectification and policing through the public sphere. Instead of empowering other realms of cultural practice, study can feel like another version of exploitation – a new trick to steal people's experience for the delectation and surveillance of the more powerful and privileged. More than anything, the business of study can transform the most valued and exciting practices into another source of boredom – even sex seems pretty dull when viewed through piles of photocopies and bibliographic references.

What does study miss? Although one theme of this work has been an insistence on the educational importance of everyday activities, another has been the special role of the realms that resist easy understanding or narrating. Sex remains exciting and interesting because of its close relation to magic – and I want to argue that magic is necessary to healthy living. The tendency to dispel magic is one of the least attractive and engaging aspects of any educational project – the consolation that it is good for you does not compensate for the loss. When my students suggest that maybe some things are best left alone, I guess that, in part, they are making this point – all this scrutiny can make sex seem like a sad and overdetermined affair, with no space left to become human.

What does study change? The other submerged theme of this book has been the active role of study in remaking the world. When Soros makes this point in relation to economic theory, he is arguing that a conception of international economy that imagines economy to be akin to a natural force, always subject to eternal laws, fails to understand the shaping impact of economic theory on the key choices of economic actors, and, therefore, upon the world economy. The manner in which economy is theorised informs the behaviour of players – and this creates a different set of economic relations.

Sex is not subject to the same kinds of frenzied speculation. However, a range of popular theorisations of sexual behaviour impact upon sexual understanding in our time. Rather than assume that each account competes to describe a static sexuality that is determined by, say, human nature or biology, this work tries to identify the moments in which commentaries on sex shape sexual behaviour. This makes any account of the thing itself far more complicated, because the object of study is this dynamic interaction between many forces and influences. Partly for this reason, it avoids any attempt to chart real, live sex. Instead, the emphasis has been on acknowledging how mysterious real, live sex remains. We can learn lots of things, but that moment of magic remains mysterious. This volume has attempted to place the construction of sexual experience within a context of geopolitical and economic change. Whereas on the one hand there has been an extensive discussion of the many painful circumstances brought by recent changes, on the other it has stretched to retain a sense of the joy and excitement of sex, in spite of difficult circumstances.

It is this excitement that makes sex such a resilient and important social signifier. The history of Western culture, which develops a social world of separate spheres, accidentally creates the realm of sex as the most intoxicating escape from public constraints. Even when this stark division between private and public begins to crumble, the aura of that former separation hangs about the experience of sex. However public and commodified sexuality may become, that hint of the boudoir remains. And it is that imagined recollection of a space of sanctioned experimentation and protected weakness that pushes the idea of sex forward in any contemporary conception of fulfilment. This is not to suggest that sexual freedom is the only freedom, or even that the chance of sexual fulfilment can compensate for lack of fulfilment in other areas. It is, however, to suggest that the conception of satiation and satisfaction at living cannot help but take on a sexual tinge in this cultural moment. And given the paucity of other forms of recognition and fulfilment, we may all have cause to be thankful for our sex-centred culture.

This has been one half-spoken implication of Third Way thinking. Much of this celebrated new realism coupled with old compassion has revolved around repackaging an end to economic growth for electoral politics. The analysis that previous promises of social progress and improved living standards for each successive generation are no longer sustainable, if they ever were, appears to be admirably honest. However, this has meant that the political project of the Third Way in many locations has worked to lower electoral expectations. The hard lesson has been that there is a limit to the power and influence of any government – the cunning trick has been to repackage this cynicism as an honest realism that can enhance the party's image. For the first time a government can be elected on a ticket of limited influence; acknowledging how little it can do and how hard that little is to achieve is part of its charm.

These lowered expectations leave a gap in public consciousness. Even in an age of new realism, there must be some compensation for adhering to the social contract. This is where a rhetoric of intimacy comes into its own. The chance to remake our interpersonal relations compensates for larger and more immediate social goods. By calling upon the unfinished project of learning intimacy, there is a suggestion that the quality of globalised living depends upon all of our everyday efforts. The style of the *Kama Sutra* returns as a strategy of mainstream politics. In the end, this has been the core lesson of this work. Due diligence to the project of learning sexuality among other social skills may give us space to become the subjects we wish to be. This may not compensate for the uncertainties and deprivations of the global economy of turbo-capitalist second modernity, but it may equip us better for the larger battles of social change.

I want to end by acknowledging the place of love in this long and abstract story. Much of this work has spoken of sex as if desire has no relation to emotion and as if sexual longing is quite apart from the longing not to be alone. While writing this book, I listened often to Al Green – and, in particular, to a song that signals the unspeakable insights of sex and love in its title, *Sha la la*. This song suggests that there is something resilient about the human capacity to love, with an intensity that forgets the greedy boundaries of the self. Something close to the salvations of spirituality, something that can inspire reverie. I end with the hope that this capacity may prove to be the saving of us all.

Bibliography

Abelove, H., Barale, M. A. and Halperin, D. M. (1993) *The Lesbian and Gay Studies Reader*, London: Routledge.

Abercrombie, N., Hill, S. and Turner, B. S. (1986) *Sovereign Individuals of Capitalism*, London: Allen & Unwin.

Adams, M. L. (1997) *The Trouble with Normal: Postwar Youth and the Making of Heterosexuality*, Toronto: University of Toronto.

Adkins, L. (1995) *Gendered Work. Sexuality, Family and the Labour Market*, Buckingham: Open University Press.

Aggleton, P. (1999) *Men Who Sell Sex, International Perspectives on Male Prostitution and HIV/AIDS*, London: UCL Press.

Amin, A. (1994) *Post-Fordism*, Oxford: Blackwell.

Andahazi, F. (1998) *The Anatomist*, London: Transworld.

Anderson, P. (1998) *The Origins of Postmodernity*, London: Verso.

Ang, I. (1991) *Desperately Seeking the Audience*, London: Routledge.

Aries, P. (1962) *Centuries of Childhood: A Social History of Family Life*, New York: Vintage.

Aronowitz, S. (1996) *The Death and Rebirth of American Radicalism*, London: Routledge.

Aronson, T. (1994) *Prince Eddy and the Homosexual Underworld*, London, John Murray.

Assiter, A. and Carol, A. (1993) *Bad Girls and Dirty Pictures*, London: Pluto.

Baker, R.(1999) *Sex in the Future, Ancient Urges Meet Future Technology*, London: Macmillan.

Barker, F. (1984) *The Tremulous Private Body, Essays on Subjection*, London, Methuen.

Bartlett, N. (1988) *Who was that Man?* London: Serpent's Tail.

Baudrillard, J. (1988) *The Ecstacy of Communication* (trans. by B. Schutle and C. Schutle; ed. by S. Lotringer), New York: Autonomedia.

Baudrillard, J. (1994) *Simulacra and Simulation*, Ann Arbor, MI: University of Michigan Press.

Bauman, Z. (1997) *Postmodernity and its Discontents*, New York: New York University Press.

Beck, U. (2000) *The Future Worlds of Work*, Cambridge: Polity Press.

Beck, U. and Beck-Gernsheim, E. (1995) *Detraditionalization*, Oxford: Blackwell.

Bell, D. and Klein, R. (1996) *Radically Speaking: Feminism Reclaimed*, London: Zed.

Bell, D. and Valentine, G. (1995) *Mapping Desire*, London: Routledge.

Bell, S. (1994) *Reading, Writing and Rewriting the Prostitute Body*, Bloomington, IN: Indiana University Press.

Bendelow, G. and Williams, S. J. (1998) *Emotions in Social Life, Critical Themes and Contemporary Issues*, London: Routledge.

Benhabib, S. (1992) *Situating the Self: Gender, Community and Postmodernism in Contemporary Ethics*, Oxford: Polity Press.

Benjamin, J. (1998) *Shadow of the Other. Intersubjectivity and Gender in Psychoanalysis*, London: Routledge.

Bennett, O. (2001) *Cultural Pessimism*, Edinburgh: Edinburgh University Press.

Berman, M. (1982) *All that is Solid Melts into Air*, New York: Verso.

Betz, H.-G. (1994) *Radical Right-wing Populism in Western Europe*, New York: St Martin's Press.

Bhattacharyya, G. (1998) *Tales of Dark-skinned Women*, London: University College London.

Bhattacharyya, G., Gabriel, J. and Small, S. (2001) *Race and Power*, London: Routledge.

Bishop, R. and Robinson, L. S. (1998) *Night Market: Sexual Cultures and the Thai Economic Miracle*, New York: Routledge.

Blair, T. and Schroeder, G. (1999) *Europe – The Third Way – die Neue Mitte*, London: Labour Party and Sozial Demokratischen Partei Deutschlands.

Bland, L. and Mort, F. (1997) 'Thinking sex historically', in Segal, L. (ed.), *New Sexual Agendas*, London: Macmillan.

Bleys, R. (1995) *The Geography of Perversion/Desire*, New York: Continuum International Publishing.

Blume, J. (1996) *Letters to Judy*, London: Macmillan Children's Books.

Boffin, T. and Gupta, S. (1990) *Ecstatic Antibodies: Resisting the AIDS Mythology,* London: Rivers Oram Press.

Bondanella, P. and Musa, M. (1979) *The Portable Machiavelli*, London: Penguin.

Bongie, C. (1991) *Exotic Memories, Literature, Colonialism and the Fin-de-Siècle*, Stanford, CA: Stanford University Press.

Bonnell, V. E. and Hunt, L. (1999) *Beyond the Cultural Turn*, Berkeley, CA: University of California Press.

Booth, C., Darke, J. and Yeandle, S. (1996) *Changing Places, Women's Lives in the City*, London: Paul Chapman Publishing.

Bornstein, K. (1994) *Gender Outlaw*, London: Routledge.

Bornstein, K. (1998) *My Gender Workbook*, London: Routledge.

Bowlby, R. (2000) *Carried Away, the Invention of Modern Shopping*, London: Faber & Faber.

Bowles, S. and Gintis, H. (1976) *Schooling in Capitalist America, Educational Reform and the Contradictions of Economic Life*, London: Routledge and Kegan Paul.

Boyarin, D. (1997) *Unheroic Conduct. The Rise of Heterosexuality and the Invention of the Jewish Man*, Berkeley, CA: University of California.

Brah, A., Hickman, M. J. and Mac an Ghaill, M. (1999) *Global Futures, Migration, Environment and Globalization*, Basingstoke: Macmillan.

Bray, A. (1982) *Homosexuality in Renaissance England*, London: Gay Men's Press.

Bright, S. (1995) *Sexwise*, San Francisco: Cleis Press.

Bristow, J. (1997) *Sexuality,* London: Routledge.

Brooks, A. (1997) *Postfeminisms*, London: Routledge.

Bryden, I. and Floyd, J. (1999) *Domestic Space, Reading the Nineteenth Century Interior*, Manchester: Manchester University Press.

Burk, K. and Cairncross, A. (1992) *'Goodbye, Great Britain'. The 1976 IMF Crisis*, New Haven, CT: Yale University Press.

Burston, P. and Richardson, C. (1995) *A Queer Romance, Lesbians, Gay Men and Popular Culture*, London: Routledge.

Burton, R. and Arbuthnot, F. F. (1993) *The Kama Sutra*, London: Diamond Books.

Butler, J. (1990) *Gender Trouble, Feminism and the Subversion of Identity*, New York: Routledge.

Butler, J. (1993) *Bodies that Matter, on the Discursive Limits of 'Sex'*, London: Routledge.

Butler, J. (1997) *Excitable Speech, a Politics of the Performative*, London: Routledge.

Califia, P. (1994) *Public Sex, the Culture of Radical Sex*, San Francisco: Cleis Press.

Califia, P. (1997) *Sex Changes. The Politics of Transgenderism*, San Francisco: Cleis Press.

Calvino, I. (1997) *Invisible Cities*, London: Vintage.

Carlip, H. (1995) *Girl Power: Young Women Speak Out*, New York: Warner.

Carver, T. and Mottier, V. (1998) *Politics of Sexuality. Identity, Gender, Citizenship*, London: Routledge.

Cassirer, E. (1964) *The Individual and the Cosmos in Renaissance Philosophy*, New York: Harper & Row.

Castells, M. (1996) *The Rise of the Network Society*, Oxford: Blackwell.

Castells, M. (1997) *The Power of Identity*, Oxford: Blackwell.

Castells, M. (1998) *End of Millennium*, Oxford: Blackwell.

Centre for Contemporary Cultural Studies, Education Group (1981) *Unpopular Education, Schooling and Social Democracy in England since 1944*, London: Hutchinson.

Clarke, J. (1991) *New Times and Old Enemies*, London: HarperCollins Academic.

Clift, S. and Carter, S. (1999) *Tourism and Sex. Culture, Commerce and Coercion*, London: Pinter.

Collier, R. (1998) *Masculinities, Crime and Criminology*, London: Sage.

Cooper, D. (1994) *Sexing the City. Lesbian and Gay Politics within the Activist State*, London: Rivers Oram Press.

Cooper, R. and Sawaf, A. (1997) *Executive EQ, Emotional Intelligence in Business*, London: Orion Business Books.

Craib, I. (1998) *Experiencing Identity*, London: Sage.

Crary, J.(1990) *Techniques of the Observer: On Vision and Modernity in the Nineteenth Century*, Cambridge, MA: MIT Press.

Cray, E. (1992) *The Erotic Muse: American Bawdy Songs*, Urbana, IL: University of Illinois Press.

Dangerous Bedfellows (1996) *Policing Public Sex. Queer Politics and the Future of AIDS Activism*, Boston, MA: South End Press.

Danielou, A. (1994) *The Complete Kama Sutra*, Rochester, VT: Park Street Press.

Darke, S. (1996) 'The man-shaped city', in Booth, C., Darke, J. and Yeandle, S. (eds), *Changing Places, Women's Lives in the City*, London: Paul Chapman Publishing.

Davidoff, L., Doolittle, M., Fink, J. and Holden, K. (1998) *The Family Story*, London: Longman.

Davidson, R. (1999) 'The culture of compulsion: venereal disease, sexuality and the state in twentieth-century Scotland', in Eder, F. X., Hall, L. A. and Hekma, G. (eds), *Sexual Cultures in Europe. Themes in Sexuality*, Manchester: Manchester University Press.

Delacoste, F. and Alexander, P. (1988) *Sex Work*, London: Virago.

De Landa, M. (2000) *A Thousand Years of Nonlinear History*, New York: Swerve.

De Lauretis, T. (1994) *The Practice of Love. Lesbian Sexuality and Perverse Desire*, Bloomington, IN: Indiana University Press.

D'Emilio, J. (1983) *Sexual Politics, Sexual Communities. The Making of a Homosexual Minority in the United States 1940–1970*, Chicago: University of Chicago Press.

D'Emilio, J. (1999) 'Capitalism and gay identity', in Parker, R. and Aggleton, P. (eds), *Culture, Society and Sexuality, a Reader*, London: UCL Press.

D'Emilio, J. and Freedman, E. B. (1988) *Intimate Matters. A History of Sexuality in America*, New York: Harper & Row.

Dent, G. (1992) *Black Popular Culture*, Seattle: Bay Press.

Dews, P. (1987) *Logics of Disintegration: Post-structuralist Thought and the Claims of Critical Theory*, London: Verso.

Diamond, I. and Quinby, L. (1988) *Feminism and Foucault, Reflections on Resistance*, Boston: Northeastern University Press.

Diamond, E. and Silverman, R. (1995) *White House to your House. Media and Politics in Virtual America*, Cambridge, MA: MIT Press.

Docker, J. (1995) *Postmodernism and Popular Culture*, Cambridge: Cambridge University Press.

Donald, J. (1992) *Sentimental Education, Schooling, Popular Culture and the Regulation of Liberty*, London: Verso.

Duncombe, J. and Marsden, D. (1998) 'Doing emotional work, doing gender and "authenticity" in intimate heterosexual relationships', in Bendelow, G. and Williams, S. J. (eds), *Emotions in Social Life: Critical Themes and Contemporary Issues*, London: Routledge.

Dworkin, A. (1981) *Pornography: Men Possessing Women*, New York: Perigee.

Dworkin, A. (1987) *Intercourse*, New York: Free Press.

Dyer, R. (1997) *White*, London: Routledge.

Eagleton, T. (1991) *Ideology, an Introduction*, London: Verso.

Eder, F. X., Hall, L. A. and Hekma, G. (1999) *Sexual Cultures in Europe. Themes in Sexuality*, Manchester: Manchester University Press.

Eisenstein, Z. (1998) *Global Obscenities, Patriarchy, Capitalism, and the Lure of Cyberfantasy*, New York: New York University Press.

Ellis, K. (1988) *Caught Looking: Feminism, Pornography and Censorship*, Seattle: Real Comet Press.

Engels, F. (1972) *Origin of the Family, Private Property, and the State*, London: Lawrence & Wishart.

Enloe, C. (1983) *Does Khaki Become You? The Militarisation of Women's Lives*, London: Pluto.

Enloe, C. (1993) *The Morning After. Sexual Politics at the End of the Cold War*, Berkeley, CA: University of California Press.

Evans, D. (1993) *Sexual Citizenship: the Material Construction of Sexualities*, London: Routledge.

Evans, H. (1997) *Women and Sexuality in China. Dominant Discourses of Female Sexuality and Gender Since 1949*, Cambridge: Continuum.

Faludi, S. (1992) *Backlash. The Undeclared War against Women*, London: Vintage.

Fanon, F. (1986) *Black Skin, White Masks*, London: Pluto.

Fausett, D. (1993) *Writing the New World. Imaginary Voyages and Utopias of the Great Southern Land*, Syracuse, NY: Syracuse University Press.

Fausto-Sterling, A. (1999) *Sexing the Body: Gender Politics and the Construction of Sexuality*, New York: Basic Books.

Featherstone, M. (1990) *Consumer Culture and Postmodernism*, London: Sage.

Feminist Review (1994) *The New Politics of Sex and the State*, London: Routledge.

Fetzer, J. S. (2000) *Public Attitudes Toward Immigration in the United States, France, and Germany*, Cambridge: Cambridge University Press.

Finckenauer, J. O. and Waring, E. J. (1998) *Russian Mafia in America. Immigration, Culture and Crime*, Boston, Northeastern University Press.

Fisher, R., Kopelman, E. and Schneider, A. K. (1994) *Beyond Machiavelli: Tools for Coping with Conflict*, Cambridge, MA: Harvard University Press.

Fisher, T. (1995) *Scandal, The Sexual Politics of Late Victorian Britain*, Stroud: Alan Sutton Publishing.

Forgacs, D. (1986) *Rethinking Fascism. Capitalism, Populism and Culture*, London: Lawrence & Wishart.

Foucault, M. (1979a) *Discipline and Punish. The Birth of the Prison*, London: Penguin.

Foucault, M. (1979b) *The History of Sexuality,* Volume 1, *An Introduction*, London: Penguin.

Foucault, M. (1986) *The History of Sexuality,* Volume 2, *The Use of Pleasure* , Harmondsworth: Viking.

Foucault, M. (1988) *The History of Sexuality,* Volume 3, *Care of the Self,* New York: Vintage.

Foucault, M. (1989) *Madness and Civilization*, London: Routledge.

Freud, S. (1962) *Three Essays on the Theory of Sexuality*, New York: Avon Books.

Freud, S. (1995) *Psychological Writings and Letters*, New York: Continuum.

Freud, S. and Breuer, J. (1974) *Studies on Hysteria*, Harmondsworth: Pelican.

Friedland, R. and Boden, D. (1994) *NowHere, Space, Time and Modernity*, Berkeley, CA: University of California Press.

Friedman, M. (1991) *Monetarist Economics*, Oxford: Blackwell.

Friman, H. R. and Andreas, P. (1999) *The Illicit Global Economy and State Power*, Oxford: Rowman & Littlefield.

Fuss, D. (1990) *Essentially Speaking: Feminism, Nature and Difference*, London: Routledge.

Fuss, D. (1991) *Inside/Out*, London: Routledge.

Gallagher, C. and Laqueur, T. (1987) *The Making of the Modern Body*, Berkeley, CA: University of California Press.

Gamble, A. (1988) *The Free Economy and the Strong State. The Politics of Thatcherism*, Durham, NC: Duke University Press.

Gamson, J. (1998) 'Must identity movements self-destruct? A queer dilemma', in Nardi, P. M. and Schneider, B. E. (eds), *Social Perspectives in Lesbian and Gay Studies, a Reader*, London: Routledge.

Garber, M. (1992) *Vested Interests, Cross-dressing and Cultural Anxiety*, New York: Routledge.

Garver, E. (1987) *Machiavelli and the History of Prudence*, Madison, WI: University of Wisconsin Press.

Gay, P. (1984) *The Bourgeois Experience: Victoria to Freud*, New York: Oxford University Press.

Gerbner, G., Mowlana, H. and Schiller, H. (1996) *Invisible Crises. What Conglomerate Control of Media Means for America and the world*, Boulder, CO: Westview Press.

Gergen, K. J. (1999) *An Invitation to Social Construction*, London: Sage.

Gibson, P. C. (1993) *Dirty Looks*, London: BFI.

Giddens, A. (1992) *The Transformation of Intimacy, Sexuality, Love and Eroticism in Modern Societies*, Cambridge: Polity Press.

Giddens, A. (1994) *Beyond Left and Right. The future of Radical Politics*, Cambridge: Polity Press.

Giddens, A. (1998) *The Third Way: The Renewal of Social Democracy*, Cambridge: Polity Press.

Giddens, A. (2000) *The Third Way and its Critics*, Cambridge: Polity Press.

Gill, A. (1995) *Ruling Passions, Sex, Race and Empire*, London: BBC Books.

Gilroy, P. (1987) *There Ain't no Black in the Union Jack*, London: Hutchinson.

Gluckman, A. and Reed, B. (1997) *Homo Economics, Capitalism, Community and Lesbian and Gay Life*, London: Routledge.

Gorz, A. (1982) *Farewell to the Working Class*, London: Pluto.

Gramsci, A. (1971) *Selections from Prison Notebooks*, London: Lawrence and Wishart.

Grey, A. (1993) *Speaking of Sex. Limits of Language*, London: Cassell.

Griffin, C. (1993) 'Fear of a black (and working-class) planet: young women and the racialization of reproductive politics', in Wilkinson, S. and Kitzinger, C. (eds), *Heterosexuality, a Feminism and Psychology Reader*, London: Sage.

Haag, P. (1999) *Consent, Sexual Rights and the Transformation of American Liberalism*, Ithaca, NY: Cornell University Press.

Hage, G. (1998) *White Nation, Fantasies of White Supremacy in a Multicultural Society*, Annandale, NSW: Pluto.

Hall Carpenter Archives, Gay Men's Oral History Group (1989) *Walking after Midnight, Gay Men's Life Stories*, London: Routledge.

Hall, C. (1992) *White, Male and Middle-Class, Explorations in Feminism and History*, Cambridge: Polity Press.

Hall, C., McClelland, K. and Rendell, J. (2000) *Defining the Victorian Nation: Class, Race, Gender and the Reform Act of 1867*, Cambridge: Cambridge University Press.

Hall, S. (1988) *The Hard Road to Renewal: Thatcherism and the Crisis of the left*, London: Verso.

Hall, S. and Jacques, M. (1989) *New Times: The Changing Face of Politics in the 1990s*, London: Lawrence & Wishart.

Hallam, P. (1993) *The Book of Sodom*, London: Verso.

Halperin, D. M. (1990) *One Hundred Years of Homosexuality,* New York: Routledge.

Halsall, P. (2001) 'A history of heterosexuality?', *People with a History*, http://www.fordham.edu/halsall/pwh/hethist.html.

Haraway, D. J. (1989) *Primate Visions: Gender, Race and Nature in the World of Modern Science*, London: Routledge.

Haraway, D. J. (1997) *Modest_Witness@Second_Millennium.FemaleMan_Meets_OncoMouse*, New York: Routledge.

Harding, S. G. (1998) *Is Science Multicultural? Postcolonialisms, Feminisms and Epistemologies*, Bloomington, IN: Indiana University Press.

Hargreaves, I. and Christie, I. (1998) *Tomorrow's Politics: The Third Way and Beyond*, London: Demos.

Harris, L. and Crocker, E. (1997) *Femme*, London: Routledge.

Harris, P., Rees, P. and Lock, A. (2000) *Machiavelli, Marketing and Management*, London: Routledge.

Harrison, J. (1999) *Sex Education in Secondary Schools*, Buckingham: Open University Press.

Harvey, D. (1982) *Limits to Capital*, Oxford: Basil Blackwell.

Harvey, D. (1989) *The Condition of Postmodernity*, Oxford: Blackwell.

Haste, C. (1992) *Rules of Desire, Sex in Britain: World War I to the Present*, London: Chatto & Windus.

Hawkes, G. (1996) *A Sociology of Sex and Sexuality*, Buckingham: Open University Press.

Healy, M. (1996) *Gay Skins*, London: Cassell.

Hearn, J. and Morgan, D. (1990) *Men, Masculinities and Social Theory*, London: Unwin Hyman.

Hebdige, D. (1979) *Sub-culture, the Meaning of Style*, London: Methuen.

Hebert, R. and Link, A. (1982) *The Entrepreneur. Mainstream Views and Radical Critiques*, New York: Praeger.

Heller, T. C., Sosna, M. and Wellbury, D. E. (1986) *Reconstructing Individualism, Autonomy, Individuality, and the Self in Western Thought*, Stanford, CA: Stanford University Press.

Herman, E. S. and Chomsky, N. (1994) *Manufacturing Consent. The Political Economy of the Mass Media*, London: Vintage.

Higgs, D. (1999) *Queer Sites*, London: Routledge.

Hitchcock, T. (1997) *English Sexualities 1700–1800*, London: Macmillan.

Hobsbawm, E. H. and Ranger, T. (1983) *The Invention of Tradition*, Cambridge: Cambridge University Press.

Holland, J., Ramazanoglu, C., Sharpe, S. and Thomson, R. (1998) *The Male in the Head, Young People, Heterosexuality and Power*, London: Tufnell Press.

Home Office (2000) *Setting the Boundaries*, London: HMSO.

Howell, G. (1977) *The Penguin Book of Naughty Postcards*, Harmondsworth: Penguin.

Hunter, I., Saunders, D. and Williamson, D. (1993) *On Pornography*, London: Macmillan.

Hyam, R. (1991) *Empire and Sexuality*, Manchester: Manchester University Press.

Ingraham, C. (1999) *White Weddings: Romancing Heterosexuality in Popular Culture*, New York: Routledge.

Jackson, P. (1989) *Maps of Meaning*, London: Unwin Hyman.

Jackson, S. (1999) *Heterosexuality in Question*, London: Sage.

James, D. and Ley, D. (1993) *Place/Culture/Representation*, London: Routledge.

Jameson, F. (1991) *Postmodernism, or the Cultural Logic of Late Capitalism*, Durham, NC: Duke University Press.

Jameson, F. and Miyoshi, M. (1998) *The Cultures of Globalization*, Durham, NC: Duke University Press.

Jardine, L. (1999) *Ingenious Pursuits, Building the Scientific Revolution*, London: Little, Brown and Company.

Jay, A. (1987) *Management and Machiavelli: Discovering a New Science of Management in the Timeless Principles of Statecraft*, London: Hutchinson.

Jivani, A. (1997) *It's not Unusual. A History of Lesbian and Gay Britain in the Twentieth Century*, London: Michael O'Mara Books.

Johnson, A., Wadsworth, J., Welling, K., Field, J., with Bradshaw, S. (1994) *Sexual Attitudes and Lifestyles*, Oxford, Blackwell Scientific Publications.

Jordan, W. D. (1974) *The White Man's Burden: Historical Origins of Racism in the United States*, New York: Oxford University Press.

Kabbani, R. (1986) *Imperial Fictions*, London: Macmillan.

Kaplan, M. (1997*) Sexual Justice: Democratic Citzienship and the Politics of Desire*, London: Routledge.

Kapsalis, T. (1997) *Public Privates, Performing Gynecology from Both Ends of the Speculum*, Durham, NC: Duke University Press.

Katz, C. and Monk, J. (1993) *Full Circles, Geographies of Women over the Life Course*, London: Routledge.

Katz, J. (1983) *Gay/Lesbain Almanac: A New Documentary*, New York: Harper & Row.

Katz, J. (1990) 'The invention of heterosexuality', *Socialist Review*, **20**: 7–34.

Kavanagh, D. (1987) *Thatcherism and British Politics: The End of Consensus?*, Oxford: Oxford University Press.

Kempadoo, K. and Doezema, J. (1999) *Global Sex Workers, Rights, Resistance, and Redefinition*, London: Routledge.

Kennedy, P. (1994) *Preparing for the Twenty-first Century*, London: Fontana.

Kipnis, L. (1993) *Ecstasy Unlimited*, Minneapolis: University of Minnesota Press.

Kipnis, L. (1996) *Bound and Gagged*, New York: Grove Press.

Kirk, D. (1999) *Looted: The Philippines after the Bases*, New York: St Martin's Press.

Kirkup, G., Janes, L., Woodward, K. and Hovenden, F. (2000) *The Gendered Cyborg: A Reader*, London: Routledge.

Klein, N. (2000) *No Logo*, London: Flamingo.

Klug, F. (2000) *Values for a Godless Age. The story of the United Kingdoms's New Bill of Rights*, London: Penguin.

Kramer, L. (1997) *After the Lovedeath, Sexual Violence and the Making of Culture*, Berkeley, CA: University of California Press.

Kristeva, J. (1982) *Powers of Horror, an Essay on Abjection*, New York: Columbia University Press.

Kristeva, J. (1994) *Strangers to Ourselves*, New York: Columbia University Press.

Kroker, A. (1992) *The Possessed Individual*, New York: St Martin's Press.

Kroker, A. and Kroker, M. (1987) *Body Invaders: Panic Sex in America*, New York: St Martin's Press.

Kroker, A. and Kroker, M. (1996) *Hacking the Future*, Montreal: New World Perspectives.

Laclau, E. and Mouffe, C. (1985) *Hegemony and Socialist Strategy. Towards a Radical Democratic Politics*, London: Verso.

Laqueur, T. (1987) 'Orgasm, generation and the politics of reproductive biology', in Gallagher, C. and Laqueur, T. (eds), *The Making of the Modern Body*, Berkeley, CA: University of California Press.

Larrain, Jorge (1979) *The Concept of Ideology*, London: Hutchinson.

Lash, S. and Friedman, J. (1992) *Modernity and Identity*, Oxford: Blackwell.

Lash, S. and Urry, J. (1987) *The End of Organized Capitalism*, Cambridge: Polity Press.

Latouche, S. (1996) *The Westernization of the World*, Cambridge: Polity Press.

Lau, K. J. (2000) *New Age Capitalism, Making Money East of Eden*, Philadelphia: University of Pennsylvania Press.

Law, L. (2000) *Sex Work in Southeast Asia: The Place of Desire in a Time of HIV/AIDS*, New York: Routledge.

Leap, W. L. (1999) *Public Sex/Gay Space*, New York: Columbia University Press.

Levitas, R. (1986) *The Ideology of the New Right*, Cambridge, Polity Press.

Lister, R. (1997) *Citizenship, Feminist Perspectives*, London: Macmillan.

Loffreda, B. (2000) *Losing Matt Shepard*, New York: Columbia University Press.

Lovell, N. (1998) *Locality and Belonging*, London: Routledge.

A Lover's Guide (1991) Video, directed by S. Ludgate, London: Carlton Home Entertainment.

Lury, C. (1996) *Consumer Culture*, Cambridge: Polity Press.

Luttwak, E. (1998) *Turbo-Capitalism, Winners and Losers in the Global Economy*, London: Weidenfeld & Nicolson.

Lyotard, J.-F. (1979) *The Postmodern Condition: A Report on Knowledge*, Manchester: Manchester University Press.

McClintock, A. (1995) *Imperial Leather, Race, Gender and Sexuality in the Colonial Contest*, London: Routledge.

McGuigan, J. (1996) *Culture and the Public Sphere*, London: Routledge.

Machiavelli, N. (1961) *The Prince*, London: Penguin.

Machiavelli, N. (1979) 'The Mandrake Root', in Bondanella, P. and Musa, M. (eds), *The Portable Machiavelli*, London: Penguin.

MacKinnon, C. A. and Dworkin, A. (1997) *In Harm's Way, the Pornography Civil Rights Hearings*, Cambridge, MA: Harvard University Press.

Macpherson, C. B. (1962) *Political Theory of Possessive Individualism: Hobbes to Locke*, Oxford: Clarendon.

McRobbie, A. (1994) *Postmodernism and Popular Culture*, London, Routledge.

Madonna (1992) *Sex*, London: Secker and Warburg.

Mallet, V. (1999) *The Trouble with Tigers. The Rise and Fall of South-East Asia*, London: HarperCollins Business.

Malone, J. W. (2000) *Twenty-First Century Gay*, New York: M. Evans & Co.

Marcus, S. (1966) *The Other Victorians*, London: Weidenfeld & Nicolson.

Marcuse, H. (1966) *Eros and Civilization: a Philosophical Inquiry into Freud*, Boston: Beacon Press.

Martin, B. (1998) 'Sexualities without genders and other queer utopias', in Merck, M., Segal, N. and Wright, E. (eds), *Coming Out of Feminism?*, Oxford: Blackwell.

Massey, D. (1994) *Space, Place and Gender*, Cambridge: Polity Press.

Matthaei, J. (1997) 'The sexual division of labor, sexuality, and lesbian/gay liberation: toward a Marxist-Feminist analysis of sexuality in US capitalism', in Gluckman, A. and Reed, B. (eds), *Homo Economics, Capitalism, Community and Lesbian and Gay Life*, London: Routledge.

Mayhew, H. (1968) *London Labour and London Poor*, London: Constable.

Maynard, M. and Purvis, J. (1995) *(Hetero)Sexual Politics*, London: Taylor & Francis.

Mercer, D. (1998) *Future Revolutions, Unravelling the Uncertainties of Life and Work in the Twenty-first Century*, London: Orion Business Books.

Mercer, K. (1994) *Welcome to the Jungle, New Positions in Black Cultural Studies*, London: Routledge.

Merck, M., Segal, N. and Wright, E. (1998) *Coming Out of Feminism?*, Oxford: Blackwell.

Meredith, P. (1989) *Sex Education*, London: Routledge.

Miller, D. (1995) *Acknowledging Consumption, a Review of New Studies*, London: Routledge.

Mills, C. (1997) *The Racial Contract*, Ithaca, NY: Cornell University Press.

Minford, P. (1980) *Is Monetarism Enough?* London: Institute of Economic Affairs.

Mirza, H. S. (1997) *Black British Feminism, a Reader*, London, Routledge.

Mishan, E. J. (1980) *Pornography, Psychadelics and Technology, Essays on the Limits to Freedom*, London: George Allen and Unwin.

Modleski, T. (1982) *Loving with a Vengeance: Mass-produced Fantasies for Women*, Hamden, CT: Archon Books.

Mohanram, R. (1999) *Black Body, Women, Colonialism and Space*, St Leonards, NSW: Allen and Unwin.

Moon, K. H. S. (1997) *Sex Among Allies: Military Prostitution in US–Korea Relations*, New York: Columbia University Press.

Moran, L. J. 1996) *The Homosexual(ity) of Law*, London: Routledge.

Morrell, H. (1996) 'Women's safety', in Booth, C., Darke, J. and Yeandle, S. (eds), *Changing Places, Women's Lives in the City*, London: Paul Chapman Publishing.

Morton, D. (1996) *The Material Queer*, Boulder, CO: Westview Press.

Nagle, J. (1997) *Whores and other Feminists*, London: Routledge.

Nardi, P. M. and Schneider, B. E. (1998) *Social Perspectives in Lesbian and Gay Studies, a Reader*, London: Routledge.

Neret, G. (2001) *Erotica Universalis: Seventeenth and Eighteenth Century*, New York: Benedikt Taschen Verlag.

Nestle, J. (1988) *A Restricted Country*, London: Sheba.

Nevins, A. (1954) *Ford: The Times, the Man, the Company*, New York: Charles Scribner's Sons.

Nixon, S. (1996) *Hard Looks: Masculinities, Spectatorship and Contemporary Consumption*, London: UCL Press.

Norton, R. (1992) *Mother Clap's Molly House: the Gay Subculture in England 1700–1830*, London: Gay Men's Press.

Oborne, P. (1999) *Alastair Campbell. New Labour and the Rise of the Media Class*, London: Aurum.

O'Connell-Davidson, J. (1998) *Prostitution, Power and Freedom*, London: Polity Press.

O'Donnell, M. and Sharpe, S. (2000) *Uncertain Masculinities. Youth, Ethnicity and Class in Contemporary Britain*, London: Routledge.

Ohmae, K. (1990) *The Borderless World. Power and Strategy in the Global Marketplace*, London: HarperCollins.

Ohmae, K. (1995) *The End of the Nation State. The Rise of Regional Economies*, London: HarperCollins.

Ollman, B. (1979) *Social and Sexual Revolution, Essays on Marx and Reich*, London: Pluto.

Ong, A. (1999) *Flexible Citizenship, the Cultural Logics of Transnationality*, Durham, NC: Duke University Press.

Oppermann, M. (1998) *Sex Tourism and Prostitution. Aspects of Leisure, Recreation and Work*, Elmsford, NY: Cognizant Communication Corporation.

Orwell, G. (1954) *Nineteen Eighty-Four*, Harmondsworth: Penguin.

Parker, A., Russo, M., Sommer, D. and Yaeger, P. (1992) *Nationalisms and Sexualities*, London: Routledge.

Parker, R. and Aggleton, P. (1999) *Culture, Society and Sexuality, a Reader*, London: UCL Press.

Parker, R. and Gagnon, J. (1995) *Conceiving Sexuality*, London: Routledge.

Patton, C. (1990) *Inventing AIDS*, London: Routledge.

Pearce, F. and Woodiwiss, M. (1993) *Global Crime Connections*, Basingstoke: Macmillan.

Penelope, J. (1993) 'Heterosexual identity: out of the closets', in Wilkinson, S. and Kitzinger, C. (eds), *Heterosexuality, a Feminism and Psychology Reader*, London: Sage.

Penley, C. (1997) *NASA/TREK. Popular Science and Sex in America*, London: Verso.

Pfeil, F. (1995) *White Guys: Studies in Postmodern Domination and Difference*, London, Verso.

Phelan, S. (1997) *Playing with Fire, Queer Politics, Queer Theories*, London: Routledge.

Phillips, E. (1983) *The Left and the Erotic*, London: Lawrence & Wishart.

Pierson, R., Chaudhuri, N. and McAuley, B. (1998) *Nation, Empire, Colony. Historicizing Gender and Race*, Bloomington, IN: Indiana University Press.

Plissner, M. (1999) *The Control Room: How Television Calls the Shots in Presidential Elections*, New York: Free Press.

Plummer, K. (1995) *Telling Sexual Stories*, London: Routledge.

Preston, J. (1993) *My Life as a Pornographer*, New York: Richard Kasak Book Edition.

Prugl, E. (1999) *The Global Construction of Gender*, New York: Columbia University Press.

Queen, C. and Schimel, L. (1997) *PoMoSexuals, Challenging Assumptions about Gender and Sexuality*, San Francisco: Cleis Press.

Radway, J. (1987) *Reading the Romance: Women, Patriarchy and Popular Literature*, London: Verso.

Rand, E. (1995) *Barbie's Queer Accessories*, Durham, NC: Duke University Press.

Reich, W. (1970) *The Mass Psychology of Fascism*, London: Souvenir Press.

Reich, W. (1973) *The Function of the Orgasm*, London: Souvenir Press.

Rich, A. (1980) 'Compulsory heterosexuality and lesbian existence', *Signs*, 5: 631–60.

Richardson, D. (1996) *Theorising Heterosexuality: Telling it Straight*, Buckingham: Open University Press.

Richardson, D. (2000) *Rethinking Sexuality*, London: Sage.

Rifkin, J. (1995) *The End of Work: The Decline of the Global Labour Force and the Dawn of the Post-Market Era*, New York: Tarcher-Putnam.

Ritzer, G. (1996) *The McDonaldization of Society*, Thousand Oaks, CA: Pine Forge Press.

Rodgerson, G. and Wilson, E. (1991) *Pornography and Feminism: The Case Against Censorship*, London: Lawrence & Wishart.

Rogers, R. and Gumuchdjian, P. (1997) *Cities for a Small Planet*, London: Faber.

Rose, J. (1986) *Sexuality in the Field of Vision*, London: Verso.

Rose, J. (1998) *States of Fantasy*, London:Clarendon.

Rotenberg, M. and Mirsky, L. (2000) *The Rotenberg Collection: Forbidden Erotica*, New York: Benedikt Taschen Verlag.

Rousseau, G. S. (1991) *Perilous Enlightenment, Pre- and Post-modern Discourses, Sexual, Historical*, Manchester: Manchester University Press.

Rubin, G. (1993) 'Thinking sex: notes for a radical theory of the politics of sexuality', in Abelove, H., Barale, M. A. and Halperin, D. M. (eds), *The Lesbian and Gay Studies Reader*, London: Routledge.

Rubin, G. (1999) 'Thinking Sex: Notes for a Radical Theory of the Politics of Sexuality', in Parker, R. and Aggleton, P. (eds), *Culture, Society and Sexuality, a Reader*, London: UCL Press.

Rubin, H. (1998) *The Princessa, Machiavelli for Women*, London: Bloomsbury.

Russell, D. (1993) *Making Violence Sexy*, Buckingham: Open University Press.

Ryan, C. and Hall, M. (2001) *Sex Tourism*, London: Routledge.

Said, E. (1978) *Orientalism*, London: Penguin.

Santoro, M. (2000) *Profits and Principles. Global Capitalism and Human Rights in China*, Ithaca, NY, Cornell University Press.

Sarup, M. (1996) *Identity, Culture and the Postmodern World*, Edinburgh: Edinburgh University Press.

Sassen, S. (1998) *Globalization and its Discontents*, New York: The New Press.

Sawday, J. (1995) *The Body Emblazoned, Dissection and the Human Body in Renaissance Culture*, London: Routledge.

Sayer, D. (1987) *The Violence of Abstraction, the Analytic Foundations of Historical Materialism*, Oxford, Basil Blackwell.

Scambler, G. and Scambler, A. (1997) *Rethinking Prostitution*, London: Routledge.

Scott, J. W. (1993) 'The evidence of experience', in Abelove, H., Barale, M. A. and Halperin, D. M. (eds), *The Lesbian and Gay Studies Reader*, London: Routledge.

Scruton, R. (1986) *Sexual Desire*, London: Weidenfeld & Nicolson.

Seccombe, W. (1993) *Weathering the Storm. Working-class Families from the Industrial Revolution to the Fertility Decline*, London: Verso.

Sedgwick, E. K. (1991) *Epistemology of the Closet*, London: Penguin.

Segal, L. (1994) *Straight Sex*, London: Virago.

Segal, L. (1997) *New Sexual Agendas*, London: Macmillan.

Segal, L. and McIntosh, M. (1992) *Sex Exposed, Sexuality and the Pornography Debate*, London: Virago.

Seidler, V. (1997) *Man Enough: Embodying Masculinities*, London: Sage.

Seidman, S. (1990) *Romantic Longings*, London: Routledge.

Seidman, S. (1996) *Queer Theory/Sociology*, Oxford: Blackwell.

Seigel, J. (1999) 'Problematizing the self', in Bonnell, V. E. and Hunt, L. (eds), *Beyond the Cultural Turn*, Berkeley, CA: University of California Press.

Sennett, R. (1998) *The Corrosion of Character. The Personal Consequences of Work in the New Capitalism*, London: Norton.

Shanor, D. and Shanor, C. (1995) *China Today. How Population Control, Human Rights, Government Repression, Hong Kong, and Democratic Reform Affect Life in China and Will Shape World Events in the New Century*, New York: St Martin's Press.

Sheehy, S. (2000) *Connecting: the Enduring Power of Female Friendship*, New York: William Morrow & Co.

Sherman, S. (1992) *Lesbian and Gay Marriage: Private Commitments, Public Ceremonies*, Philadelphia: Temple University Press.

Showalter, E. (1991) *Sexual Anarchy: Gender and Culture at the Fin de Siècle*, London: Bloomsbury.

Sibley, D. (1995) *Geographies of Exclusion*, London: Routledge.

Simon, W. (1996) *Postmodern Sexualities*, London: Routledge.

Simpson, M. (1994) *Male Impersonators. Men Performing Masculinity*, London: Cassell.

Singer, L. (1993) *Erotic Welfare: Sexual Theory and Politics in the Age of Epidemic*, London: Routledge.

Skinner, Q. (1981) *Machiavelli*, Oxford: Oxford University Press.

Skrobanek, S. and Boonpakdee, N. (1997) *The Traffic in Women, Human Realities of the International Sex Trade*, London: Zed.

Smart, C. (1996) 'Collusion, collaboration and confession: on moving beyond the heterosexuality debate', in Richardson, D. (ed.), *Theorising Heterosexuality: Telling it Straight*, Buckingham: Open University Press.

Smith, A. M. (1994) *New Right Discourse on Race and Sexuality*, Cambridge: Cambridge University Press.

Smith, J. R. and Smith, L. G. (1974) *Beyond Monogamy; Recent Studies of Sexual Alternatives in Marriage*, Baltimore, MD: Johns Hopkins University Press.

Smyth, C. (1992) *Lesbians Talk Queer Notions*, London: Scarlet Press.

Soja, E. (1989) *Postmodern Geographies: The Reassertion of Space in Critical Social Theory*, London: Verso.

Soja, E. W. (2000) *Postmetropolis. Critical Studies of Cities and Regions*, Oxford: Blackwell.

Solinger, R. (1992) *Wake Up Little Susie. Single Pregnancy and Race before Roe v. Wade*, New York: Routledge.

Sollie, D. L. and Leslie, L. A. (1994) *Gender, Families and Close Relationships, Feminist Research Journeys*, London: Sage.

Soros, G. (1998) *The Crisis of Global Capitalism, Open Society Endangered*, London: Little, Brown & Co.

Squires, J. (1993) *Principled Positions: Postmodernism and the Rediscovery of Value*, London: Lawrence & Wishart.

Stannard, D. E. (1992) *American Holocaust: the Conquest of the New World*, New York: Oxford University Press.

Starr, K. (1998) *The Starr Report*, http://www.time/daily/scandal/starr_report/files.

Steedman, C. (1995) *Strange Dislocations: Childhood and the Idea of Human Interiority, 1780–1930*, Cambridge, MA: Harvard University Press.

Stein, A. (1993) *Sisters, Sexperts, Queers: Beyond the Lesbian Nation*, New York: Plume.

Stoler, A. L. (1995) *Race and the Education of Desire. Foucault's History of Sexuality and the Colonial Order of Things*, Durham, NC: Duke University Press.

Stoller, R. J. (1991) *Porn. Myths for the Twentieth Century*, New Haven, CT: Yale University Press.

Stone, A. R. (1996) *The War of Desire and Technology at the Close of the Mechanical Age*, London: MIT Press.

Stone, L. (1990) *The Family, Sex and Marriage in England, 1500–1800*, London: Penguin.

Storr, M. (1999) *Bisexuality: A Critical Reader*, London: Routledge.

Ten.8 (1992) *Critical Decade: Black British Photography in the 80s*, Birmingham: Ten.8.

Therborn, G. (1978) *What Does the Ruling Class Do When it Rules?*, London: New Left Books.

Thompson, B. (1994a) *Sadomasochism. Painful Pleasure or Pleasurable Play?*, London: Cassell.

Thompson, B. (1994b) *Soft Core*, London: Cassell.

Thompson, E. P. (1968) *The Making of the English Working Class*, Harmondsworth: Penguin.

Thompson, E. P. (1978) *The Poverty of Theory and Other Essays*, London: Merlin.

Thompson, E. P. (1998) *The Romantics: England in a Revolutionary Age*, London: Merlin.

Thornton, S. (1995) *Club Cultures. Music, Media and Subcultural Capital*, Cambridge: Polity Press.

Truong, T.-D. (1990) *Sex, Money and Morality: Prostitution ad Tourism in South East Asia*, London: Zed.

Ullman, S. R. (1997) *Sex Seen, The Emergence of Modern Sexuality in America*, Berkeley, CA: University of California Press.

United Nations (2000) *World Migration Report: 2000*, Geneva: United Nations.

Vance, C. S. (1998) 'Social construction theory: problems in the history of sexuality', in Nardi, P. M. and Schneider, B. E. (eds), *Social Perspectives in Lesbian and Gay Studies, a Reader*, London: Routledge.

Viano, E. C. (1999) *Global Organized Crime and International Security*, Aldershot: Ashgate.

Walby, S. (1997) *Gender Transformations*, London: Routledge.

Walkowitz, J. (1992) *City of Dreadful Delight*, London: Virago.

'Walter' (1995) *My Secret Life,* volume one, Ware: Wordsworth Editions.

Walvin, J. (1982) *A Child's World: A Social History of English childhood, 1800–1914*, Harmondsworth: Penguin.

Ware, V. (1992) *Beyond the Pale. White Women, Racism and History*, London: Verso.

Warner, M. (1993) *Fear of a Queer Planet*, Minneapolis: University of Minnesota Press.

Watney, S. (1987) *Policing Desire: Pornography, AIDS and the Media*, London: Methuen.

Weed, E. (1989) *Coming to Terms. Feminism, Theory, Politics*, London: Routledge.

Weeks, J. (1981) *Sex, Politics and Society: the regulation of sexuality*, London: Longman.

Weeks, J. (1985) *Sexuality and its Discontents, meanings, myths and modern sexualities*, London: Routledge.

Weeks, J. (1995) *Invented Moralities, Sexual Values in an Age of Uncertainty*, Cambridge: Polity Press.

Weeks, J. (1999) 'Discourse, desire and sexual deviance: some problems in a history of homosexuality', in Parker, R. and Aggleton, P. (eds), *Culture, Society and Sexuality, a Reader*, London: UCL Press.

Weeks, J. (2000) *Making Sexual History*, Cambridge: Polity Press.

Weeks, J. and Holland, J. (1996) *Sexual Cultures: Communities, Values, and Intimacy*, New York, St Martin's Press.

Weinstein, J. (1998) *Hate Speech, Pornography and Radical Attacks on Free Speech Doctrine*, Boulder, CO: Westview Press.

Weston, K. (1998) *LongSlowBurn, Sexuality and Social Science*, London: Routledge.

Whisman, V. (1996) *Queer by Choice*, London: Routledge.

White, K. (1993) *The First Sexual Revolution: The Emergence of Male Heterosexuality in Modern America*, New York: New York University Press.

Wiegman, R. (1995) *American Anatomies: Theorizing Race and Gender*, Durham, NC: Duke University Press.

Wilkinson, H. (2000) 'Family business', in Hargreaves, I. and Christie, I. (eds), *Tomorrow's Politics: the Third Way and Beyond*, London: Demos.

Wilkinson, S. and Kitzinger, C. (1993) *Heterosexuality, a Feminism and Psychology Reader*, London: Sage.

Williams, L. (1989) *Hard Core: Power, Pleasure, and the 'Frenzy of the Visible'*, Berkeley, CA: University of California Press.

Williams, P. (1997) *Directions in Housing Policy. Towards Sustainable Housing Policies for the UK*, London: Paul Chapman.

Wilson, E. (1991) *The Sphinx in the City*, London: Virago.

Winship, J. (1987) *Inside Women's Magazines*, London: Pandora.

Wittig, M. (1992) *The Straight Mind*, London: Harvester Wheatsheaf.

Wolmark, J. (1999) *Cybersexualities, a Reader on Feminist Theory, Cyborgs and Cyberspace*, Edinburgh: Edinburgh University Press.

Wolpe, A.-M. (1988) *Within School Walls*, London: Routledge.

'Wrong', *Marxism Today*, November/December 1998.

Young, I. M. (1990) *Justice and the Politics of Difference*, Princeton, NJ: Princeton University Press.

Young, R. (1995) *Colonial Desire*, London: Routledge.

Zeldin, T. (1995) *An Intimate History of Humanity*, London: Minerva.

Zizek, S. (1997) *The Plague of Fantasies*, London: Verso.

Index